on track ...

Killing Joke

every album, every song

Nic Ransome

SONICBOND

sonicbondpublishing.com

Sonicbond Publishing Limited
www.sonicbondpublishing.co.uk
Email: info@sonicbondpublishing.co.uk

First Published in the United Kingdom 2023
First Published in the United States 2023

British Library Cataloguing in Publication Data:
A Catalogue record for this book is available from the British Library

ISBN 978-1-78952-273-0

Typeset in ITC Garamond & ITC Avant Garde
Printed and bound in England

Graphic design and typesetting: Full Moon Media

Follow us on social media:

Twitter: https://twitter.com/SonicbondP

Instagram: https://www.instagram.com/sonicbondpublishing_/

Facebook: https://www.facebook.com/SonicbondPublishing/

Linktree QR code:

Dedication

For my brother, Mark (1969-2013): musician, bandmate, and resolute nonconformist. All the author's proceeds from this book will be donated to Friends of the Earth on Mark's behalf.

Thanks

In England and Wales: Rion, Lila, Alaska, Romani, Jordan, Bettina, Pamela, Robert, Mark P., Julian, and Jill Waller at the Cheltenham Local History Society; in Australia: Antony, Karin, Philippa, Simon, Melinda, Pete, Paul. Elsewhere: Darrin, Alexis. Special thanks to Christian – friend, sounding board and fellow Gatherer. Finally, many thanks to Stephen Lambe for commissioning this book.

Acknowledgments

Most of this book is the result of four decades of listening to Killing Joke and associated acts, but I am indebted to the comprehensive liner notes of Tony Raven, the Discogs community for discographic information, the music journalists from whose interviews and features I have quoted, Chris Bryans for the lavishly essential *A Prophecy Fulfilled*, which confirmed some facts about instruments and studios (and is where Geordie describes his guitar tone as 'cello-ey'), and Jaz Coleman for his magnificent, brain-boggling 'Ludibrium' *Letters from Cythera*.

Prologue

It's the beginning of 1986 in deepest, darkest winter. The UK has reached peak Thatcherism: the Westland affair, the Wapping dispute and unemployment at over 3 million. The City of London deregulation 'Big Bang' – a chaos capitalist's wet dream – is a few months away. On a freezing-cold Saturday night in a village hall nestled in a tiny Kent village in one of the safest Tory seats in England, my fledgling band is about to open the doors on our latest event. There being nowhere to play for 20 miles in any direction, for our first few months as a serious concern, we have had no choice but to book our own venues and promote our own gigs.

To circumvent licensing laws, we've got over 50 British pounds worth of lager and ale in the hall's kitchen (about £150 worth, allowing for inflation). Enough for the sold-out capacity crowd to have a free pint each. The painted backdrops and lighting, including a cool but probably insanely dangerous high-wattage UV bulb, are ready. Soundcheck done. Dream Clinic is in the settled five-piece line-up that would have ridiculous amounts of fun along with moderate success on the neo-psychedelic club and free-festival circuit over the next two years. Our material – eclectic but best described as space punk – is already mostly original, the rest comprising well-rehearsed covers by Gong, Here & Now and Hawkwind. Tonight, we're trying a new cover for the first time.

The doors open and the early crowd spills inside. Headbangers, goths, punks, hippies and casuals. Anything for a night out in the entertainment wasteland of the North Downs. Plus, a small hardcore of friends and fans. Things quickly get out of hand. The lone volunteer bouncer gives up trying to check tickets. The casuals raid the free bar and it's drained dry in 20 minutes. Fights break out. Tribe versus tribe. This is small-town England: alcohol, fighting and despair. If we can at least counter the despair, we'll be achieving something.

We take to the stage and launch into our first number, a Gordian-tight instrumental. Half the crowd want to listen, but the disrupters are intent on causing havoc. Not being PiL, we can't simply threaten to walk off if the crowd doesn't stop fighting. So, we keep on going. At least we're safe. There's enough of us to repel an attack. And we have weapons (aka instruments). Plus, we're in the zone. Looking at each other, it's clear that we all know this is a good one, probably our best yet. But the fighting is increasing in violence and footprint, fuelled by the growing complaints from late arrivals about the lack of free beer as promised on the ticket. You know, the free beer *they've paid for*. Maybe we're wrong. Maybe they're going to storm the stage after all. We all sense that this could go very bad very quickly. But still, none of us is about to run to the village phone box and call the plod. We probably don't even have the right change.

So, beer swigged, loins girded, guitars tuned (both me on bass and our guitarist Dave really attacked those strings), we launch into our next song.

It's that new cover. A scything guitar riff and queasy synth ostinato (courtesy of my brother Mark) are quickly joined by Mike's pounding drums and an insistent pulse from yours truly in G minor, with that sneaky sharpened fourth. Our singer Oli hits his on-the-up-beat cue dead centre and suddenly, we have *everyone's* attention. The hippies, the punks, the goths and the headbangers. Even the casuals. The fighting stops. All eyes are on the stage. All ears on the rented PA, which is miraculously working perfectly. On stage, we're living that fleeting feeling that all performers crave more and more: that *we are the focus of everything*. The song goes without a hitch (like I said, we took rehearsals seriously) and for that six-and-a-half minutes, peace breaks out.

The song was Killing Joke's 'Love Like Blood', first released just over a year earlier, demonstrating the seductive power of an ear-burrowing song by an iconic band performed with total commitment and plenty of attitude. We never played it again. Probably didn't want to jinx ourselves.

The peace didn't last, but we finished our set, and everyone survived the night (though the police did get involved afterwards, following more fighting outside after the gig ended). We were banned from the hall for life, even though we spent four hours obscenely early on Sunday morning cleaning up with pounding hangovers so that Sunday School could go ahead without pools of vomit, empty lager cans, discarded roaches and loveless blood stains. And so that we could recoup our deposit. Which we didn't. It wasn't quite U-Men setting fire to the moat at Bumbershoot, but it still felt like rock'n'roll, nonetheless. Despite our solid attempts at rebellion – both deliberate and accidental – somehow Thatcher was still in power on Monday morning, but we all knew that this would be a gig we'd remember however many we played after. And the thing we'd remember most was the multi-tribe power of Killing Joke.

on track ...

Killing Joke

Contents

Introduction

Fully formed in 1979 as Margaret Thatcher became Prime Minister of the United Kingdom, Killing Joke's output is the hidden soundtrack to 44-plus years of lethal capitalism and warmongering for profit, of coercive consumerism and a determined blunting of the intellect, of nuclear dread and accelerating civilisational entropy. And they're still going strong at the time of writing.

Even with their myriad and infamous splits and fallings-out (the band's motto is, after all: 'Out of conflict comes progress'), the Joke can boast one of the least-changing recording line-ups of any band that has lasted this long, combining almost-always-present co-founder, keyboard player, main lyricist and frontman Dr Jeremy 'Jaz' Coleman, sole abiding member Kevin 'Geordie' Walker (guitar), Martin 'Youth' Glover and Paul Raven (bass), and drummer 'Big Paul' Ferguson (co-founder of the Joke with Coleman). Among a roster of sometime members and guest musicians, most notable are drummers Martin Atkins, Geoff Dugmore and Benny Calvert – and, of course, Dave Grohl. As of 2008, the band's line-up is identical to the one that recorded their first EP in 1979.

There's a direct line from Killing Joke through Faith No More, Soundgarden, Nirvana, Nine Inch Nails and Tool. There are countless bands in whom you can hear them because of the direct influence they had on a succession of epoch-defining acts. Geordie is perhaps the most covertly influential guitarist of his generation. But KJ's extraordinary longevity has twisted this line into a feedback loop. One based on a refusal to regurgitate either sonic form or genre format.

Few bands have engaged with the world as consistently or as forcefully as the Joke. They have sustained a level of emotional and political engagement that is unique in its visceral power, intellectual rigour and musical eclecticism. The Joke have, if anything, become angrier as they've aged, though that anger is tempered with deep, hard-won wisdom.

You could argue that because the West has gone increasingly to hell since the 2008 crash, the Joke's existential angst and wry nihilism are suddenly on the zeitgeist, but the truth is that the past 44 years, since Reagan and Thatcher fronted a redefinition of the rules of economics based on neoconservative ideology – thereby triggering decades of neoliberalism – have been disastrous for many. Killing Joke have been one of the few bands to write and sing about how things really are, rather than how we have deluded ourselves into believing them to be.

The terrible dread of a New Cold War and increased threat of nuclear annihilation have rendered the 2020s depressingly similar to the 1980s. This has the sobering effect of making both 1986's *Brighter than a Thousand Suns* and 2015's *Pylon* as zeitgeist friendly as either were when they were first released. There is a deeper layer to the Joke's fascination with nuclear fission: the sense that it is the dark obverse of alchemy, science used to obliterate through literal illumination rather than as a process toward metaphorical enlightenment. Whether you understand it as neurobiologically primal, psychoanalytically Freudian or simply an aberrant consequence of capitalism, humankind appears to have a death drive that is both ineluctable and insatiable. The 'killing joke' is life itself – the literal punchline, annihilation. Rarely has a band's name so perfectly encapsulated their philosophical and aesthetic identity. And although I will treat the band as a plural noun throughout, there is a deep unity to the Joke's identity. Mythically the band are a *single integrated entity*.

> ...it's undeniable, isn't it? The chemistry of the four of us in the room. The presence of the four of us creates its own criteria...
> Youth, interviewed (with Jaz) by John Doran, *The Quietus*, 20 January 2010

The Joke as trickster embody what American philosopher, literary maverick and consciousness researcher Robert Anton Wilson called 'guerrilla ontology', which is a kind of covert existential provocation similar to Zen but expressed through Western rather than Eastern culture. These esoteric shock-and-awe tactics are not a million miles away from those performed by the KLF/JAMs, who are, as we will discover, closely associated with the Joke, if not musically, then by discombobulating Jungian synchronicity.

They say that 'a little knowledge is a dangerous thing', but in truth, there is nothing more dangerous to The Powers That Be than when a little knowledge becomes *too much* knowledge. For this is the path from naïve Fool to wise Jester, from neophyte to magus. 'Do your own research!' has become a joke at the expense of online 'conspiracy' addicts, but with the world ever more submerged by propaganda and disinformation, this edict can provide sanity rather than madness. But one needs a guide. A guide that is not beholden to vested interests, party-political ideology or personal grift. And there is none better than the Joke and their astounding combination of illuminating metaphor and primal stimulus. Killing Joke are the Atomic Priesthood of the neoliberal age, encoding the divine horror of nuclear dread in their music so generations to come can recoil at our abject terror and laugh sadly at the glimmers of hope we foolishly allowed ourselves.

Influences and Resonances

Killing Joke are one of the few bands who warrant the term *sui generis* (of their own genre). Hugely influential but apparently sprung from the aether fully formed like a belligerently goading god, which based on their genesis in a magickal ritual, may be closer to truth than simile, they still defy categorisation. Their core identity, irrespective of changing line-ups or branching genre paths, has remained utterly fixed, built around the ever-present core elements of Jaz Coleman's voice and Geordie Walker's guitar, both unique, and the visceral propulsion of the rhythm section, encapsulated at the band's commercial height by Big Paul and Raven but now re-conjured by Big Paul and Youth. It's no accident that KJ's career has traversed punk and metal, post-punk and alt-metal. Lyrically the band's concerns – and Coleman's expression of them – are perfectly aligned with the rage and rebellion of those closely-related genres. The Joke know when less is more and when more is more—and, crucially, how to combine the two.

Coleman brought a background in church, choral and classical music along with a satirical detachment, controlled hostility and uncanny dissonance that resonate with John Lydon. Big Paul combined the primal momentum of Ginger Baker, the foreboding tom-centric beats of Kenny Morris and the tribal style pioneered by David Barbarossa with the relentless metronomic march of Krautrock's robotised rhythms and a rolling disco-funk groove. Geordie brought the tonal pyrotechnics of Jeff Beck and Hendrix, the proto-punk of The Who, and post-punk's stripped-back angularity courtesy of John McKay and Keith Levene, alongside a fearsome musicality. Youth, the febrile, elastic rhythms of Jamaican dancehall, sound system and dub with a low-end link through Jah Wobble, and again that disco-funk groove, forging a rhythm section like no other. It's no accident that Public Image Ltd are referenced three times here as if any single act provided a template for KJ's uncompromising ethos, it was Lydon's post-Pistols mavericks. As Killing Joke, the four original members alchemically mixed these individual influences with outlier creative instincts and ineffable impetus into something utterly unique.

But there's still more to fold in. The gut-churning auricular doom of Black Sabbath. The untrammelled power and behemothic volume of Motörhead, with whom the nascent Joke shared rehearsal studios. The abrasive agitation of Gang of Four. The jagged oppression of Joy Division. The syncopated grooves of Chic, a Joke favourite. CAN, like PiL unyielding experimenters, who were formative for both Jaz and Youth. Led Zeppelin, whose instinctual, riff-centric take on rock seeps deeper into KJ's identity with every passing year. Plus, there's a profound strand of psychoactive-enhanced consciousness expansion centred on the mind-opening qualities of sound as vibration and performance as ritual (you could argue, with notable exceptions, that while the neo-psychedelic bands of the late 1970s and 1980s mimicked the surface culture and tropes of 1960s psychedelia without any of the deep countercultural transgression, the Joke grabbed hold of the original movement's social dissent and metaphysical incitement and propelled them inexorably forward).

But perhaps the key influence on the Joke, simply because they were an act upon whose qualities all the original members agreed, was the theatrically intense, lyrically potent, musically eclectic, sonically adventurous and primally raw, Sensational Alex Harvey Band. Ted McKenna's sublime balance between the primitive and the technical sounds like an outline for the Joke's approach to rhythm, while Geordie has namechecked guitarist Zal Cleminson (who appears alongside Syd Barrett and John Lydon on a page of the Mike Coles-designed booklet for *Democracy*). Coleman's strident, proselytising song intros are reminiscent of Harvey's (an example from 1974: 'I'll tell you something: it's your planet. Don't piss in the water supply'). Killing Joke have often taken the stage to 'Booids' from SAHB's final album, 1978's *Rock Drill*, an instrumental that thrums with KJ origin DNA.

Finally, there's the band to which the Joke are rarely compared, but to whom they are undoubtedly sonic and thematic cousins: full of uncannily synthesised atmosphere and dark Phrygian incantations while revelling in the absurdist paradox of the utopian and dystopian in continuous tension. They even hail from the same counterculture crucible of Ladbroke Grove. It is, of course, the mighty Hawkwind. Both bands bleed the long-submerged past and a prismatically imagined future into the immediate present.

There is, however, one genre with which the Joke perhaps have more affinity than any other and that is punk itself – specifically in terms of its confrontational goading and focused aggression. The original advert placed by Coleman and Ferguson in *Melody Maker* includes the line 'We Mean It Man'. Indeed, Youth's comment from the stage on *Live in Berlin* speaks more truth than the most astute analysis of artistic influences and stylistic associations: '…thanks for forty years of putting the boot in.' The almost 200 tracks covered here tell the story of the past 44 years and challenge us to be better than we are. And while we struggle to be better, Killing Joke continue to create the soundtrack to our slow apocalypse. So, whether you're a neophyte, a *Night Time* lurker or a Gatherer, I hope you find something to love, like blood. Go!

Author's Note

Music is one of the most subjective of all human experiences. Two people can share almost identical tastes but still diverge wildly on some genres and artists. While my brother Mark and I shared most of an aural cake, from Cardiacs to CAN, from Sabbath to Zappa, from Gentle Giant to Gong – his love of electronica, in particular trance and ambient, was pretty much exclusive to him, while my love of Pink Floyd and early Genesis, and obsession with neo-prog, were almost entirely mine. We both, of course, adored Killing Joke but had different favourite albums and our own favourite tracks. This is a roundabout way of saying that if you disagree with any of the views expressed in this book, then that is to be expected, though I at least hope you will agree with the spirit of celebration and engagement that drives the text. Please also note that rather than comment on the negatives of a particular album or song, I have always endeavoured to find something positive to say about even the most unloved material – partly because I cannot see the point in negativity in a book by a fan, and partly because I genuinely adore everything the Joke have recorded, albeit with different degrees of emphasis.

Killing Joke are unique in their sophisticated and disorientating use of keys and modes. There is myriad use of what are musicologically termed 'chromatic notes' or 'accidentals' – that is notes that sit outside a particular scale or mode – though there is nothing arbitrary about the way the Joke choose these discordant notes. I use sharpened or flattened to describe these often-dissonant accidentals. Geordie's penchant for sharpened fourths and dissonant clashes often makes it tough to discern an exact scale or mode, even though the root note of any musical section is usually immediately apparent. The tuned instruments regularly sit in alternate modes, in late Joke often the Phrygian.

Where I reference scales or modes, I am making an educated observation rather than implying that the band wrote in or used these exact keys or scales. My referencing of such (and rarely a specific key) is designed to elucidate the band's trademark dissonance, demonstrate their sonic richness, and track an outline of their musical development over 15 albums. While Jaz sings mostly in the minor key, the early albums feature extensive use of flattened and sharpened notes, usually at the end of a line. It's worth pointing out the extraordinary skill and pitch required by Coleman to hit these notes consistently, especially live.

Sometimes there are uncredited instruments in an arrangement. Where this is the case, I have listened closely and attempted an identification, though sometimes this was challenging, e.g. flute vs. ocarina. All four current members play multiple instruments, so I cannot be entirely sure who has contributed what, though have sometimes made an informed guess.

In terms of lyrics, the first two albums were released without accompanying words and Jaz has shared his amusement at the often erroneous takes on these. When I began listening to the Joke in September 1981, there was no web to trawl for lyrics, and few available interviews with the band against which to check a perceived meaning or emotional response. When I embarked on this project, I resolved to transcribe the lyrics to each song as I heard them, and then check these transcriptions against the album liners and booklets. Although a lyric book, *The Sacred and Profane Verse of Killing Joke 1979-2015*, was published in 2022, it is by no means exhaustive, and several key tracks are not included (also, I had finished the first draft of this book before I bought a copy). In addition to these 'missing' lyrics (including some from the first two albums), there are multiple Bonus and Related Tracks (officially released demos, session tracks, non-album songs and B-Sides) where there are still no lyrics available. In these cases, I have only referred to lines where I am as good as certain of the words; however, this still leaves a small margin of error. Jaz is infamous for writing lyrics – sometimes on his own but often in collaboration with Big Paul or the entire band – and then instinctively adapting, re-ordering, or finessing them at the microphone, so there is often a disparity between the printed lyrics on album liners/in booklets and the words as sung. In such cases, I have gone with the lyrics as recorded, rather than the words as made available with a release. For clarity, I have removed the brackets from all lines that include them on liners/in booklets, except where they are critical to comprehension.

I use the British terms 'bridge' and 'middle eight' throughout rather than the comparable American terms 'pre-chorus' and 'bridge'. I have defined verses throughout as those that are separated by a chorus or bridge, rather than following melody, chord structure or number of stanzas. This is simply for consistency and clarity. Remixes, of which there is a significant number across the band's career, are not exhaustively described, rather only mentioned here and there where directly relevant. Neither have I listed all released versions of a vinyl record or CD (there are places you can go for that). Cover versions of KJ songs – of which there are many – are not included. Nor are music videos or unreleased demos. Finally, I have not surveyed solo projects, collaborations, or work in other bands, except to mention such in passing where apt. To do so properly would mean another entire book.

Killing Joke (1980)

Personnel:
Jaz Coleman: lead vocals, synthesiser
Geordie Walker: guitar
Youth: bass guitar
Big Paul Ferguson: drums, backing vocals
Produced and mixed at: Marquee Studios, London by Killing Joke
Engineer: Phil Harding (uncredited)
Label: EG
Original release date: October 1980
Running time (original release): 35:00
Highest chart places: UK: 39, USA: Did not chart
Current edition: 2005 expanded remastered reissue on Virgin

As clear a statement of intent as any debut LP, Killing Joke's self-titled first album combines the uncompromising approach and rigour of execution that have been the band's hallmarks for well over 40 years. Self-produced and recorded at Marquee Studios over a couple of weeks in August 1980 with minimal overdubs, the group were assisted by fledgling engineer Phil Harding (Coleman has stated that Harding also assisted Killing Joke's mixing of the album).

The band had quickly developed beyond 1979's EP *Turn to Red* (see Non-Album Tracks) and moved to a heavier, more aggressive sound, though the love of dub evident at the outset is a strand of inspiration to which the band have returned throughout their career, most notably during Youth's involvement. Funk and dance grooves, also present as key elements on *Turn to Red*, would remain in the band's eclectic genre palette up till the first line-up change in 1982. Alongside that EP's nuclear dread, some other core KJ themes have their first run-out: social decay and the deadening effect of consumerism ('Requiem'), food insecurity and music as ritual ('Wardance'), the dystopian present ('The Wait', 'S.O.36'), the dystopian future ('Tomorrow's World'), humans as primal creatures ('Bloodsport', 'S.O.36', 'Primitive'). Many of the tracks were written while the band were on their first European tour early in 1980, and the experience of Cold War Berlin is prominent in the album's paranoia and dread.

The striking black-and-white gatefold cover initiated a long history of press baiting and controversy. Designed by Mike Coles, the art is based on a photograph taken by Don McCullin in Derry on 8 July 1971, less than seven months before Bloody Sunday. The original photo shows rioters fleeing CS gas canisters thrown by the British Army. Coles has added the words 'Killing Joke' in white, graffiti-style to the wall that is centre-shot. As raw as politics still are in Northern Ireland post-Brexit and with Stormont in perpetual crisis, it's worth imagining for a moment how provocative this cover would have been in October 1980, a mere nine years after Bloody Sunday and with 'The Troubles' still raging. The band's mascot, who had made his first appearance on Coles's cover art for the *Turn to Red* EP, appears inside the gatefold as a smarming Chaos MC with cigarette in mouth and what looks like a puppet's detachable-chin lines (this mascot will variously assume the guise of Joker, Harlequin, *Pulcinella*, Mr Punch, court jester and ventriloquist's dummy over the ensuing years). There is also a resurrected Jesus figure and an Easter cross on a hill in the deep background. Over the next 42-plus years, Coles would be as important to the Joke as Barney Bubbles was to Hawkwind in their 1970s heyday, going beyond cover art to create a visual aesthetic which is key to KJ's identity.

'Requiem' 3:45 (Killing Joke)
A flanging eighth-note synth sets the tone for the band's entire output. This is off-kilter propulsion. A future-shock dance with an unknown choreographer. The more we move the deeper we fall into a trance that could as easily illuminate secret wisdom as anaesthetise us to social control and state-sanctioned death. Geordie's distorted riff incorporates a sharpened fourth, setting a bar for the Joke's trademark dissonance. He's trailed by Big Paul's on-the-two bass drum, which adds to the solemn mood. The first verse of the first track on the first album describes the drone worker/soldier of a future-now urban hell who is 'cattle for slaughter.' In the first four lines, there is psychological anaesthesia, social dystopia, existential dilemma and meek acquiescence. This 'Requiem' is for us – a processional march to a mass funeral. Our lives have become devoid of meaning while we were busy complying with the military-industrial machine. We are but meat-sacks: organic automata. It's as prescient a statement of an oeuvre's thematic intent as you could find.

A Ferguson fill heralds Youth's walking-behind-the-hearse bass and the song's elegantly simple one-line chorus, full of fury at – and for – the exterminated herd. The final chorus, like life itself, is cut short after one of the most righteously disgusted declamations of the definite article in rock. It's all here and pretty much perfectly formed at birth: lyrics that are both allusive and direct (Jaz tending to specialise in the former and Big Paul the latter), Geordie's exquisite spine-jangling tone and rigorous riff-work, Ferguson's rhythmic restraint and dramatic lead-in fills, Youth's loose but propulsive bass, Coleman's uncanny synth atmosphere and dread-fuelled baritone, the ambiguous sixth-interval ending. Put simply: if you don't like this you probably don't like Killing Joke, but if you do, you have 44 years of recordings to (re)explore and will most likely enjoy the rest of this book.

The Joke's 'Requiem' resonates with that of Benjamin Britten, whose 1962 *War Requiem* includes Wilfred Owen's 1917 poem 'Anthem for Doomed Youth' in the libretto. Owen's poem and Stanza 76 of *Hávamál*, the Icelandic saga, define the twin poles of Killing Joke's worldview. The former describes First World War cannon fodder as cattle, while the latter, a quote beloved of Jaz and Geordie, honours the legacy of those who perform exceptional deeds: 'Cattle die/Kindred die/But I know of one thing that never dies/The glory of the great dead.' Much of the Joke's lyrics speak either to those who acquiesce to die as cattle, or those who resolve never to be cattle. Those who are forgotten and those who are remembered. Those who defer to external powers and those who determine their own destiny.

In September 1980, 'Requiem' was released as the second single from the album ('Wardance' was nominally the first) though in a different version with significantly less guitar in the mix. The single did not chart in the UK but did figure on the US *Billboard* Hot Dance Club Songs at 43.

'Wardance' 3:47 (Killing Joke)

> Our objective is to popularise our fanaticism... Our music is more than just a pleasure principle.
> Jaz Coleman, interviewed by Mark Everton, New Zealand TV, 1985

A brutally effective anti-anthem, 'Wardance' is pure post-punk in its three verses but straight-up punk in its chorus. It is presaged by the first recorded instance of Coleman's coughing (soon to become a Joke mainstay) and what sounds like the tape being eaten, then cuts to flanging guitar, a syncopated bassline and a chopped chord from Geordie, while a barely perceptible synth adds suspense. Falling bass harmonics suggest the pinging of our conditioning-triggered instincts. Big Paul pummels a 2/4 beat which is literally 'music to march to'. The verses are snarled with abject disgust – you can easily imagine the band's Joker mascot spitting these out. The voice effect, applied because the band didn't want to recreate the track's previous incarnation, was created by passing Jaz's voice through a fuzz box and a harmoniser.

As with many KJ songs, the allusion is to war seemingly being the natural state of humanity. It's a dance we all perform, however unwittingly, and resistance is futile. The chorus is a blunt-force chant over two punk-simple bar chords. In lieu of a middle eight, there's some bass flexing and tribal drumming; then we're straight into the third verse, where the second stanza nails the West's addiction to profitable conflict. The track breaks down and comes to a gear-grinding stop without the satisfaction of a resolution or the frisson of a fade-out.

Nominally the first single from the album, though in a version recorded at Gooseberry Sound Studios, London in January 1980, 'Wardance' was released in February 1980 with non-album track 'Pssyche' as the B-Side. It did not chart in the UK but reached 50 in the US *Billboard* Hot Dance Club Songs.

'Tomorrow's World' 5:30 (Killing Joke)

> What do you tell your children when they ask you about the future? How can you talk about ten years' time?
> Jaz Coleman, on stage, Brixton Academy, 4 November 2016

At one point a possible album title, this track cuts to the quick. A slow march that is both funereal and martial (evoking the weary trudging of soldiers returning from the front), and deliberately referencing and collating the previous two tracks, 'Tomorrow's World' is an anguished cry about the currency of war – specifically in a utopian future (the 'spangled new age' of the three-note synth motif) that quickly turns sour (a 'sci-fi lie' of grinding distortion). A dread-laced industrial intro gives way to Ferguson initiating the core riff with an insistent rhythm alongside Coleman's bell-like synth. Youth's riff aligns with the drums and Geordie plays a simple motif, first as single notes, then as chord calls with palm-muted response, which heralds the first verse.

Coleman accentuates every syllable with pointed venom, bitter irony and righteous fury at the world around him. A 'letter on your doorstep' – as easily a death notice as the conscription of the final line, 'call up – for your country'. The chorus is fraught with dissonance, while the second verse underscores the dual identity of conscript and fallen. Another chorus is followed by a subtly altered intro section, now with emphasis on the upbeat of each bar as Coleman screams. The first verse is repeated, underlining the horribly cyclical and nihilistically repetitive nature of war, while the music begins to break down with added reverb and dissonance into the final chorus. The intro riff comes back whole but immediately collapses, fading out on a single chord. A truly great anti-war song and a searing slice of fury aimed at those who perpetuate and acquiesce to mindless slaughter.

'Bloodsport' 4:47 (Killing Joke)

> We have canine teeth. We are animals that like blood.
> Jaz Coleman, on stage, Huxleys Neue Welt, Berlin, 19 November 2018

The only instrumental on the album, this is a great galloping slice of angular funk. Geordie kicks off the hunt while Jaz's synth adds immediate saboteur dissonance, but as if that's not enough blunt-force culture clash, Geordie adds yet more discord.

The groove jumps in with Big Paul's cantering drums and Youth's whipped bass while Coleman adds hounding Krautrock-disco sixteenth notes. A Ferguson fill takes us into a short breakdown with some stirrup-cup bass slides and on-the-two backward claps, then a return to the main trail and two more circuits. The third breakdown is extended with decaying dub and hoof-trampled industrial grind. There are shouts, cheers and whistling: a blooding of the crowd.

The track finishes with metallic howls and screeches, as though the sharp-jointed robot hounds that have been jerkily dancing in the automated hunt kennels have been suddenly unplugged – outfoxed by a red-furred interloper. The track is named for a short-lived band that featured associates and members of the Joke, with Alex Paterson on vocals.

'The Wait' 3:42 (Killing Joke)

> I don't know how, but detergent had gotten into the whole river where we were, and it was just foam. It destroyed everything and there were all these dead fish everywhere. It was the most depressing thing we've ever seen.
> Jaz Coleman, interviewed by Kory Grow, *Revolver*, 1 January 2013

An industrial synth sounds like clocking on time at a future abattoir. Inside the plant, our ears are battered by a thousand surplus citizens awaiting slaughter. 'The Wait' has a brutally efficient verse-chorus structure with a pared-down middle-eight breakdown featuring as much of a guitar solo as you'll hear from the staunchly minimalist Geordie. The two verses in Phrygian with an adrenal four-to-the-floor beat are based on a simple two-note riff from the guitar, with Youth doing some of his best work on the album, giving the song an urgent headlong momentum. The chorus, which is simply 'The wait' repeated four times, barrels up to the root mode's relative minor. Brutal efficiency in action.

The lyrics decry the moral degradation and social apathy of us compromised mortals. The poisoned body is as easily the drug addict's anaesthetised physiology as the body politic or the pagan idea of a poisoned water source symbolising a dying people. The second verse ramps up the existential despair with 'distortion' filling the silence after the screams 'subside'. Another showing from Coleman's synth-effect armoury of what sounds like foetal ultrasound noises underpin the breakdown, emphasising the hopelessness of waiting to be born into this maelstrom of violence and idiocy. A return to the intro riff, now with an ominous fifth-interval synth ostinato, leads into a final chorus and a fake, then a definitive ending. Life – not worth the wait.

'Complications' 3:08 (Killing Joke)

This is a masterclass in songwriting austerity, especially as it's the first track on the album to address the perennial Joke subject matter of nuclear Armageddon (which is also the theme of first official release, 'Turn to Red'). It's launched by Youth's looming bass riff, which is joined almost immediately by an ostinato synth and an incessant beat from Ferguson. A simple verse-chorus-middle-eight structure is twisted by the key progression. The verses are in Phrygian, creating a dark and dread-filled mood which fits the sharp irony of the lyrics perfectly. We're all part of a giant experiment, but we must enjoy being vivisected, even though we don't know who is the experimenter, or what is the product being tested.

The chorus, which is simply 'Complication' sung four times, steps down a semitone to the major key, which lifts the mood to a brighter more hopeful tone. This doubles the irony: the optimism of the major key is false, both in tandem with its lyrics and by association with the song's root mode. The second verse slices through our delusion, disorientates with dub reverb on 'alienation', then makes the apocalyptic theme more overt, which in turn gives the repeat of the word 'shelter' in the third verse deliberate nuclear associations. The middle eight is chillingly disconcerting with more reverb, a darker rising-falling bass riff and Geordie's angle-grinder guitar.

A subtle but telling word change in the last line of the first-verse reprise from 'the new age' to 'your new age' underscores the idea that we're all responsible for the world we live in, whether we acknowledge this fact or not. The end uses the lingering sixth interval, again creating a sense of foreboding. Also, please admire the wit in the song title, which in addition to being illustrative of the state of living in constant terror, is also a literal description of the chorus.

'S.O.36' 6:52 (Killing Joke)

This track is named for a legendary punk club, which in turn is named after the Kreuzberg postcode where the club is situated, Kreuzberg having been right beside the Berlin Wall when it was part of West Germany. 'S.O.36' is a bizarre combination of cannibalism and Cold War paranoia, the track being inspired by watching Germans in a beer hall eat pork, which the Joke's original firebreather Dave the Wizard had compared to the taste of human flesh. It's an astute thematic clash, as after the Second World War ended, the Allied powers carved Berlin into four sectors, one of which – the Soviet sector – eventually became East Berlin.

The song only has two short verses and a two-word chorus but creates a gruelling atmosphere that's resonant with the fractured pre-reunification city. The track begins with some found sound from German-language radio: a newscaster quoting East Germany's then leader Erich Honecker, saying there is no crisis in the relationship between the two German states, but also insisting there is no possibility of a relaxation in travel restrictions for citizens of East Germany. The band arrive after the half-minute mark in disconcerting slow motion, with reverbed gunshot snare and a guitar vamp, while the bass and vocal create morbid sonic friction. Coleman uses adjacent semitones at the end of the verse lines – a dissonant device that will become familiar over the next three albums. It's apt that club SO36 is still open at the time of writing, while the Berlin Wall has long since been torn down. As they say: punk will never die.

For an entertaining and historically authentic overview of the divided Germany and the Cold War paranoia and geopolitical instability of the 1980s – and featuring myriad original news broadcasts from the time like the one included in 'S.O.36' – watch the 2015 TV series *Deutschland 83* and its two sequels *86* (the release year of *Brighter than a Thousand Suns*) and *89* (which covers the fall of the Berlin Wall).

'Primitive' 3:39 (Killing Joke)

Another compact track, with two verses and a bridge but no chorus, 'Primitive' appears to do exactly what it says on the clay pot when Coleman sings that we're moving toward 'the primitive day', though there is implicit opacity about whether this is a good thing. A tribal drum pattern launches a syncopated tonic bass pulse on the off-beats of another slow march, this time in Lydian Dominant: a regressive procession towards endarkenment and the end of civilisation, or maybe a striving towards something better driven by 'intuition'. Geordie adds an ostinato to a rising-falling guitar riff and Jaz magnifies the tension. A shift into minor gives us a punk-chord bridge, which drops out before it can resolve to the tonic, instead going back to the Lydian Dominant. Our destination is unclear.

The second verse magnifies the ambiguity: the primitive feeling might lead us somewhere other than where we expect. Or maybe we need to go backwards before we can move forward to something better. A bridge reprise with tribal fills and primal vocalising leads to the foreshadowed minor drop-out on the sixth interval, leaving us in limbo but suggesting that the choice of direction is ultimately ours. Primitive in theme but sophisticated in terms of composition – a paradox that will be central to the Joke's career.

'Change' 4:01 (Killing Joke)

Although 'Change' does not appear on the original UK album release, it sits on the 1980 US version between 'Complications' and 'S.O.36' and was the B-Side to 'Requiem'. It was remastered in 2005, along with the rest of the album. The track's origins are a session that the Joke did for Honey Bane with John Lydon producing.

With a funk groove that has been compared to the syncopated rhythm which drives War's 'Me and Baby Brother', a similarity acknowledged by Killing Joke, 'Change' is the post-punk death-disco sibling to 'Bloodsport'. Against a unison guitar-and-bass riff in Dorian (the funk mode), on-the-upbeat stings alternate between synth, reverbed drum hits and guitar slashes. Also drenched in reverb, the blunt, minimalist lyrics elucidate the tension between waiting and reacting that defines all change – or lack of it. The chorus in Mixolydian heightens the sense of ambiguity, as underpinned by a low-slung two-note guitar riff, Coleman completes the sparse lyric with the single word 'Change'.

A repeat of the intro adds metallic shearing from Geordie, which in turn takes us into a glorious wall of noise that still sounds uncompromisingly spartan. A double fill heralds the final chorus, with Coleman's vocal becoming increasingly aggravated, snarling for everyone who needs change but sees nothing but constant apathy – or loves to do nothing and fears change. Even darker, the surprisingly definitive ending and final cymbal hit seem to suggest termination before change can happen.

In 1992, Youth oversaw two CD singles featuring remixes of 'Change' and 'Requiem' by him, Spiral Tribe, and Greg Hunter & Kris Weston. Along with curation of the same year's *Laugh? I Nearly Bought One!* compilation, this proved to be an essential bridge to Youth's reunion with the band for 1994's *Pandemonium*.

Bonus Tracks

A dub version of 'Change' really digs into the track's already reverb-rich mix, highlighting Geordie's wailing guitar and Ferguson's metronomic style, especially on the cymbals, while tamping down the overt aggression of the original. A remastered single version of 'Requiem' is interesting only in comparison to the album version: the sole discernible difference being the lack of guitar in the verses on the single version (and in the four bars of intro before the vocal starts). This creates a wider dynamic and sonic differential between verse and chorus, presumably rendering it more impactful for radio broadcast. It's obvious which version the band prefer, as on every compilation, they choose the album version. Rough Mixes of 'Primitive' and 'Bloodsport' are for the fanatical completist only.

What's THIS For...! (1981)

Personnel:
Jaz Coleman: lead vocals, synthesiser
Geordie Walker: guitar
Youth: bass guitar
Big Paul Ferguson: drums, backing vocals
Produced and mixed at: Townhouse Studios, London by Killing Joke and Nick Launay (uncredited)
Engineer: Nick Launay (uncredited), Hugh Padgham (uncredited; two tracks only)
Label: EG
Release date: June 1981
Running time (original release): 41:39
Highest chart places: UK: 42, USA: Did not chart
Current edition: 2005 expanded remastered reissue on Virgin

> At the Reading Hexagon on 1 February 1981, we played a gig with a fire-eater doing a fire ritual. It was sold out and the place was going crazy. All of a sudden, everything went into slow motion and absolute silence, like everyone in the audience was moving underwater. Then, like a wave, everything just crashed back into reality and the place was pogoing again. It was collective – the whole band experienced it. We've talked about it for 30 years, and I've written about it in-depth. Basically, we were on a magnetic field and it produced this very strange effect. I've studied it with people like Uri Geller and Jimmy Page, who had similar experiences.
> Jaz Coleman, interviewed by Tristan Parker, *Time Out*, 19 October 2015

Appearing a mere nine months after their debut, *What's THIS for...!* (or, as I call it, 'WTF?' in honour of the lack of lyrics) solidified the band's cult status but also delivered a brutally lean iteration of Killing Joke's visceral sound and antagonistic stance. The tribal elements are amplified here, with Big Paul contributing some of his most rhythmically intricate drum patterns and fills, while the synth is mostly absent, heightening the militantly minimalist arrangements. Engineer and producer Nick Launay had engineered, produced and mixed PiL's *The Flowers of Romance* and that album's extreme sonic dissociation is a clear benchmark for KJ's second album, which was recorded at Townhouse Studios between December 1980 and February 1981. It's worth mentioning here that Jaz and Geordie made their first visit to Iceland in April 1981 and travelled there again in the summer of the same year – trips that led inexorably to Jaz's legendary departure for the same country in February 1982.

The album's title – rendered as *what's THIS for...!* – is one of those intentionally goading bits of typography that holds the implicit challenge not to mess with it, especially in terms of capitalising the first letters of the uncapitalised words. This provocation is heightened by the fact you'd expect a question mark, not an exclamation mark after the ellipsis (which itself is deliberately pedantic). The title is both statement *and* question, capturing the paradoxically blunt nature of the Joke's identity and subject matter.

The eye-catching cover art, again by an uncredited Mike Coles, features a reappearance of the KJ mascot, though here he's in clown face. He is peering out from multiple vantage points, creating a disconcertingly uncanny effect. The left side of the street is on Colegate in Norwich, England, which is opposite St. Michael Coslany Church – now, appropriately enough, home to The Oak Circus Centre. My late brother Mark – a Gatherer and a highly proficient juggler – lived in Norwich for many years and always got a kick out of knowing that the album cover was partly shot in his home city (see the illustrations for a contemporary photograph of Colegate, side-by-side with the album cover). On the right, in place of where the church would be, is empty space other than a lone figure, dressed for a holiday (the figure has been cut out from a black-and-white photo of a couple at the seaside). The figure watches what is both a sunset and the first bloom of a mushroom cloud in a stylised blood-red sky. The overall effect is one of dissonance and unease, so is apt for the music and lyrics within. This iconic artwork – and that of the 'Follow the Leaders' single – would be re-used countless times by Coles and the band over the next 41-plus years. *What's THIS For…!* reached 42 in the UK Albums Chart.

This is the first Killing Joke album I heard, aged 14, on the A-Side of a taped-from-vinyl C90 cassette in September 1981 (I'm pretty sure this came from the older brother of my younger brother Mark's school friend). The B-Side was *KJ 1980*, so I listened to that second. This is probably one of the reasons why *What's THIS For…!* remains my favourite KJ album. That and because it's a cathartic, paradoxical masterpiece of focused dissent and chaotic rage.

'The Fall of Because' 5:12 (Killing Joke)

> 27. There is great danger in me; for who doth not understand these runes shall make a great miss. He shall fall down into the pit called Because, and there he shall perish with the dogs of Reason.
> *Liber AL vel Legis*, Aiwass/Kelly/Crowley

And so, we come to the first direct reference to Aleister Crowley, beloved of too many bands to mention, though relevant here are Led Zeppelin (with whom KJ have both musical and social links) and Throbbing Gristle and related acts, whose uncompromising approach is something akin to the Joke's. To use a term coined by the late American philosopher Robert Anton Wilson, Crowley was, like Wilson himself, a 'guerrilla ontologist': a trickster of a human being (double pun intended). So, it's no surprise that Killing Joke, the most tricksterish of all bands, draw inspiration from Crowley and his work. The association of 'because' and falling first appears in Crowley's *The Book of The Law* (*Liber AL* II), and then in its subsequent commentary (*Liber AL* III), where the phrase 'the fall of because' first appears. Crowley himself spent a lifetime interpreting and re-interpreting the words of the spiritual entity Aiwass, who dictated *The Book* to him in 1904 via his then-wife Rose Edith Kelly. The 'fall' of 'because' is both multifarious and ambiguous. An obsession with 'because' – with logic and reason at the expense of instinct and spirit – might lead to a second 'fall' e.g. apocalypse. But 'the fall of because' – an end to Aristotelian dualism, and a recognition of the interconnectedness of all things – might lead to a New Age, in Crowley's Thelema the Aeon of Horus, in which humans are as gods.

Layers build across the intro: two bars of lone four-to-the-floor bass drum, a signature Geordie riff in Lydian, root-note bass and drums like a neophyte incessantly knocking on the Lodge door in threes, hypnotically tribal drum patterns, and finally, the vocal. The tone is nihilistic: there is no meaning, so we may as well be six feet under. Each line ends with a stretched-out ostinato final syllable, accentuating Lydian's brightness, which only the Joke can make sound as dark as this. Again, the elegantly simple musical sophistication is all about implicit irony and deliberate ambiguity. Listen out for Youth's fretless-bass slides on the verses and Geordie's right-side sixteenth-note staccato during the chorus, which presages one of the cornerstones of alternative metal.

'Tension' 4:33 (Killing Joke)

Another tribal drum pattern heralds this skin-taut exercise in rhythmic and melodic momentum as a delivery system for a song about mental stasis. Along with handclaps on the two and four, Geordie joins with palm-muted chops and chords on the three and four, establishing the major key, but this is immediately undermined by the bass and vocal which add flattened third and seventh to create dissonant tension (you could even argue that the verses are in both E major and E minor simultaneously). Youth's fretless bass is the star here, constantly in motion, weaving in and out of the inexorably rhythmic pulse (Youth himself memorably describes his playing on the album as 'voodoo funk'). The first three lines of verse one are in the first person, with the lyric delineating a vicious circle of existence, but the fourth line jumps to the second person. This relates back to 'The Fall of Because', in which no explanation could be found. Now we're sure there must be one, the human impulse to seek meaning seemingly indestructible.

The major-key chorus is cut to the marrow. The change suggests a faint promise of resolution as the previous dissonance is absent, but the lyrics insist that the tension can only grow, especially when Coleman sings 'builds' on the minor's flattened third. Verse three locks us into a downward spiral: 'there's nothing left to say'. The track ends with a repeated chorus, now a call-and-response, which cycles till it fades out. There's no relief or resolution here, except maybe the physical release of dancing yourself oblivious to the primal drums and throbbing bass, replacing cold sweat with hot perspiration. For a band who loathe sports so totally, especially football (soccer), the resonance with terrace chants is wonderfully perverse.

'Unspeakable' 5:19 (Killing Joke)

A song that makes you feel as though you're trapped in the dystopian rut it's designed to conjure, 'Unspeakable' is another primal exercise in sophisticated dissonance. The clearest way to describe its sonic complexity is to say that it is in both the major and minor keys at once. It's also a proper earworm and will be crawling around your cochlea for days after you've listened to it. Some heartbeat stick-clicks are followed by a synth drone, a deceptive bar of four-to-the-floor, then a trademark Big Paul tribal drum pattern. Youth joins with a funky bass riff, complete with jazz-style fret slides. Geordie follows in his wake. Coleman intones the first verse, and there are some intriguing ideas here: 'facts and figures turn anticlockwise' could be a metaphorical definition of fake news, 'many signposts leading to the same place' perfectly describes political propaganda, while the Middle England curtain-twitching of 'I wonder who chose the colour scheme, it's very nice' always makes me think of Cardiacs. Coleman sings a sharpened fourth as the last note of alternate lines, ramping up the discord, especially on the last line of each verse where he holds the note for longer.

A whiplash effect announces the chorus, with 'Unspeakable!' sung over a dissonance-free major-to-major vamp (though the major-minor tension remains, amplifying that queasy feeling you get when a song's notes refuse to resolve into a recognisable shape). The second and final verse summons those dread-filled dreams in which you can't escape from whatever horror you fear most: 'keep running because it's nightmare time.' Another chorus, a sci-fi synth middle eight, a last herd-corralling whiplash and the chorus is repeated to fade, though now as call – 'Unspeakable!' – and response – 'Wow, wow, wow, wow…' As if we're constantly amazed by our ceaseless ability to run only to stand still, to act in ways that are literally unspeakable then tell ourselves outright lies or deny what we're doing entirely.

'Butcher' 6:13 (Killing Joke)

> Three-and-a-half thousand nuclear tests on this planet. Remembering that the Earth is not just alive but intelligent. It's a fucking abomination.
> Jaz Coleman, on stage, the Roundhouse, 17 November 2018

Another personal favourite, 'Butcher' is supremely prescient about the havoc that humans wreak on the planet with their greed and the deadening anaesthetic that capitalism pumps into our minds with propaganda and consumerism. Lyrically it could have been written last week. Musically and rhythmically, the song is subtly complex, with ceaseless tweaks to the arrangement that create a subliminal sense of disorientation even though the song appears to be of conventional structure.

The drums are immediately deceptive, first with a non-repeating pattern of stick-clicks, then with a single bar that omits the four, and then a four-to-the-floor with reverb on the four, later with the four again omitted. Geordie creates one of his most dissonant motifs with a flattened seventh and sharpened fourth. Verse one observes our mindless distraction, condemns politicians and business executives while recognising their victims, and pulls no punches about what we continue to do to Mother Earth. The chorus moves through an unsettling chord progression with a subtle shift on the second cycle and ends with the pointed single line 'You should know why'.

Verse two highlights media brainwashing, presages Coleman's notorious retreat to Iceland in February 1982 and ends with the prophetically ambiguous line 'Out of the virus, immunity comes'. The middle eight is a minimalist reprise of the intro's synth motif. The drums are soon tape-reversed: we are literally going backwards. This is early Joke at their best, disrupting both conscience and consciousness. Asking the difficult questions but providing no easy answers. Marrying thematic discord with harmonic dissonance. Plus, if all that wasn't disorienting enough, there's stereo panning at the top and random organ notes on the playout.

'Follow the Leaders' 5:37 (Killing Joke)

From one of the most discordant tracks on the album to one of the least. Released in May 1981 as the sole single from *What's THIS For…!* with 'Tension' as the B-Side, 'Follow the Leaders' reached 55 in the UK Singles Chart and 25 in the US *Billboard* Hot Dance Club Songs, the band's highest position on that chart so far. The 10" version includes 'Follow the Leaders (Dub)', the first official remix released by the Joke, though the 1979 Island Records EP *Turn to Red* includes dub and disco mixes of the title track, initiating a tradition of remixes that has continued to the present.

A disco beat, a sixteenth-note synth and a funk bass groove are joined by a guitar chord with a sharpened fourth (even the catchy dance tracks are notable for their dissonance early in the Joke's career). Each line of Coleman's vocal, which also incorporates the sharpened fourth, is followed by a burst of tribal drumming from Big Paul. The chorus – a faux call-and-response – is a simple punk-style chord progression, while there are some ear-pricking breaks with different elements accentuated. The lyrics across the three verses have a tricksterish quality, drawing you in with a song that's ostensibly about youth culture's seductive qualities but quickly darkens, till verse three: 'Man killed man and blood was shed'. The final line heaves with exasperated irony. The fade-out is deliberately interminable as we follow the leaders to our certain doom.

'Madness' 7:43 (Killing Joke)

Built on a hypnotically repetitive semi-syncopation with perception-twisting rubato, 'Madness' does a good job of evoking a feeling of extreme alienation, even though the track is the least musically dissonant on the album (subsequent live versions increase the discord). Intense feelings of disorientation are conjured by the lyrics and anguished vocal delivery, especially Youth's backing refrains, rendered horribly apt by him having suffered an LSD-triggered mental collapse towards the end of 1980, immediately before the recording sessions for the album began (a collapse he ultimately had to leave the band fully to recover from).

After the stuttering march beat is established, someone conjures what sounds like a psychotic wasp trapped in the studio before the root is firmly established with the guitar vamping off it, while Youth's fretless bass imbues the whole thing with woozy instability. The lyrics are deliberately non-linear, evocative rather than didactic, though no less compelling or intense. Images summon relationships with a significant other, society, culture, and God – relationships that become skewed or irreversibly altered once you've seen through the 'madness'. The final repeats of the chorus add layers of guitar plus fresh asymmetric drum patterns (some of Big Paul's best work on an album which brilliantly showcases his distinctive style) as the track is dragged off to its padded cell.

'Who Told You How?' 3:37 (Killing Joke)

The only (as good as) instrumental on the album is a short, sharp jab of industrial unease, with an intricate arrangement, intriguing sonics and a Middle Eastern vibe. Following a loose verse-chorus form, the track establishes the minor key but also features a by-now-familiar sharpened fourth in the verse and a sharpened seventh in the chorus. A rolling drum pattern is layered with two cycles of 6/8, creating immediate rhythmic tension. Ferguson also incorporates what sounds like metal pipes and oil drums into the syncopated landscape. A synth adds a simple but insistent riff which gives the whole thing a film-music feel, perhaps suggesting the chase sequence from a dystopian conspiracy thriller. Youth's fretless bass creates restless cycles of expansion-contraction. The chorus has Coleman intoning the song's title – ambiguous enough to pull on countless possible threads, all of them asking us to question our ingrained assumptions and knee-jerk responses. The track ends with distorted/backward metallic voices, suggesting we're automata, run on pre-programmed machine code rather than free will.

'Exit' 3:44 (Killing Joke)

The album ends with another aptly named short track, this one in ultra-dark A-flat Phrygian, whose theoretical key has six flats and one double-flat. A dog barks while a noodling bedsit guitar finds the root chord. Pounding toms beat out a syncopated stomp. Bass and guitar forge counterpoint motifs as

Coleman swaps a disappointed 'Aw' to a challenging 'Oh!'. A new riff bridges into a murky breakdown with a future-factory drone added to the thundering drums. The dread is tangible.

Verse two goes darker with the wonderfully self-descriptive 'discord dances, discord Earth' and the bluntly agitational: 'Harvest thanks didn't go quite right!' As though we've collectively lost our pagan mojo, a state of affairs that will be directly addressed on *Fire Dances*. The bridge riff returns with added layers of guitar featuring a sharpened seventh, until everything is zeroed except the drums, before a long fade to oblivion – suggesting that everything eventually ends and all we can do is sigh and say 'Aw'.

Bonus Tracks

First up is an instrumental dub remix of 'Follow the Leaders', which provides a showcase for Youth's probing bass against a stripped-down version of the track's mechanised-disco backdrop. A second dub remix, this time of 'Madness' is only slightly different from the original. The final track is 'Brilliant', the non-album B-Side of the single 'Empire Song', which was released in March 1982, four months before *Revelations* from which it comes. So, although it might not feel like it, this remastered edition is in chronological order.

'Brilliant' 3:58 (Killing Joke)

A primal instrumental in both feel and arrangement, this track builds layers of found sound, vocalisation, and studio tape effects over a tribal shuffle and a simple bass riff. There are bestial roars, wolf howls, pig squeals, monkey calls, road drills and an alarm clock, all of which eventually collapse into a wall of noise before the track finally drops down to drums and bass – and then stops dead. Two-thirds of the way in, Geordie adds some Hawaiian lounge chords, which are about as far as you could travel from the rest of the track both sonically and in terms of mood, proving yet again that even when you think you know where the Joke are taking you, there'll always be a surprise punchline lurking just around the corner.

Brilliant would also be the name of Youth's post-Joke band with Jimmy Cauty, later of The Orb and the KLF (Bill Drummond, the other founding half of the KLF, was Brilliant's A&R and signed them to WEA). The other founding half of The Orb was, of course, Alex Paterson who is the Joke's long-time friend, plus sometime roommate and roadie. You could plausibly argue – as Coleman suggests in *Letters from Cythera* – that without Killing Joke, neither the KLF nor The Orb would exist in the form they do. You could even go so far as to suggest that Jaz and Big Paul's inadvertent fire ritual led indirectly to the K Foundation burning a million pounds and inadvertently 'immanentising the eschaton', thereby re-vivifying KJ's apocalyptic fury. As Robert Anton Wilson says: engage with magick, and synchronicities will proliferate. (Read *Letters from Cythera* for the full Coleman/Drummond interstellar ley-lines intersection.)

Revelations (1982)

Personnel:
Jaz Coleman: lead vocals, synthesiser
Geordie Walker: guitar
Youth: bass guitar
Big Paul Ferguson: drums, backing vocals
Produced and mixed at: Mountain Studios, Wales and Konrad Plank's studio, Cologne, West Germany by Konrad ('Conny') Plank
Engineer: Conny Plank
Label: EG
Release date: July 1982
Running time (original release): 37:05
Highest chart places: UK: 12, USA: Did not chart, New Zealand: 33
Current edition: 2005 expanded remastered reissue on Virgin

Recorded between the tail end of 1981 and the beginning of 1982, this is the first KJ album neither nominally produced by the band nor recorded on the band's London home turf. Konrad 'Conny' Plank had produced Kraftwerk, Neu! and CAN, as well as Devo and Ultravox, so appeared to be a good fit for a band with obvious Krautrock influences and a key synthesiser element, but the experience was not a happy one for the band. Youth had still not recovered from his LSD-induced breakdown. Coleman was increasingly focused on his occult studies and pilgrimages, and his intensely personal and sometimes deliberately obtuse lyrics reflect this. Much of the writing for the album took place at Mountain Studios in Wales, which is close to several stone circles and prehistoric sites. This sacred landscape clearly fed into the album's occult and ritual elements (and there's a nice synchronicity here too: Mountain Studios was run by Thomas Crimble, Hawkwind's sometime bass player).

The tracks are noticeably shorter, focusing the sawtooth edges of the Joke's punk attitude, uncompromising worldview, and grindingly dissonant music. Considering the record's arcane and often impenetrable lyrical content along with its extreme atonal dissonance, it's still somewhat ironic that *Revelations* gave the band their highest UK Albums Chart placement up to that point of 12, along with an overall career second-best six weeks on the chart.

Around the release of *What's THIS For...!* in June 1981, Geordie began to favour his SG Junior over the Les Paul, which gave his sound an even harsher, colder edge (the Junior has markedly treble-forward sonics compared to the SG Standard). At the same time, Youth dropped the customised fretless and returned to his signature Rickenbacker (though the fretless would continue to make appearances, notably when the band appeared on *Top of the Pops* to perform 'Empire Song'). Another key element of the Joke's aural landscape is first introduced on *Revelations*. This is the down-tunings used by guitar and bass which, combined with heavier strings, contribute to the band's proto-grunge and alt-metal sonics. Geordie down-tuned by a semitone while recording *Revelations* (presumably Youth followed suit). These lower tunings create a thickness of tone and timbral weight, which perfectly suit the Joke's primal intensity.

The album's title resonates with one of the band's key paradoxes, the Joke's lyrics calling for both 'revelations' (individual enlightenment and freedom from the tyranny of ego) and 'revolutions' (social enlightenment and freedom from the tyranny of dictators) – and sometimes for one instead of the other. Keep us guessing. Keep us thinking. *Revelations* proved to be Youth's last recording with the band till 1994's *Pandemonium*. The front cover artwork, the first not by Mike Coles, was devised by the band. An occult talisman is pinned underneath the blue cloth (you can just see the indentations of the pins holding it in place). The liner/booklet artwork utilises Illuminati (eye in the triangle) and Masonic (square and compasses) symbolism, adding to the esoteric vibe (Robert Calvert's The Hawkwind Log from 1971's *In Search of Space* also features Masonic imagery on its cover).

'The Hum' 4:58 (Killing Joke)

> Jaz wrote the lyrics… predominantly from something that had influenced us both. It was a piece written in an occult magazine called *The Feast of the Hive*, and it was a particularly vivid account of people living in a hive-mind mentality, and that sort of spawned the lyrics to 'The Hum'. That track still has the ponderous groove that I really liked.
> Big Paul, interviewed by Alex in NYC, *Flaming Pablum*, 4 September 2004

'The Hum' is a flight towards fight and death by acolytes who are by turns apathetic, oblivious or brainwashed: part of a hive mind. We start in what is now our dissonant, synth-drone comfort zone, but then the drums enter, and we can tell something has changed. This is a motorik-adjacent beat which sounds unlike anything the band have done rhythmically to date, but perfectly underpins the familiar unease, harmonic arrangement, and song structure. The other big change is the bass, which has shed its funk groove and dub rubato and is now pinned directly to the drums, presaging Youth's imminent departure and his replacement by one of the greatest exponents of brutally rhythmic low-end minimalism ever to wield a four-string.

There's a clever piece of thematic sonics at the end of each chorus, where the riff appears to become stuck as what sounds like both an old-fashioned bell fire alarm and a pneumatic drill are added to the mix, echoing the fate of the drones. A descending drum fill finally drags the key back down a semitone for the next verse, the half-tone shift emphasising the feeling of inevitability and creeping dread. The second verse offers a direct connection to the song's occult source material, in which the hive's rite adherents are either sacrifice or killer. Perpetrator and victim appear equally complicit and equally fooled (echoing a similar idea in 'Pssyche').

The line 'A hive don't hold no humble bee!' has been referenced by Coleman as delineating the tension between conformity and the radical action required to provoke self-discovery – a tension that was obviously present throughout the recording of the album. Following a familiar shift from third person to first at the end of verse three, the third chorus does exactly what it's been threatening to do and becomes stuck, repeating to fade as the mesmerised drone fodder walks directly into the ritualised cannons, mouths smeared with an inane grin.

'Empire Song' 3:19 (Killing Joke)

This is a short, sharp diatribe about the British Empire with private-school associations. Coleman, his vocals more prominent in the mix than on the previous two albums, launches straight into the first verse with a line that perfectly describes what Irish journalist Fintan O'Toole describes as 'heroic failure': the incompetent English exceptionalism that encapsulates everything from the Charge of the Light Brigade to Brexit. The song conjures the moral decrepitude of the British establishment, from boarding schools to the colonial military. The verses mark one of the earliest appearances by the Phrygian mode in the KJ discography, albeit with an added sharpened seventh.

The chorus is in the root key of C-sharp major (seven sharps!), making the whole thing as unforgiving as a cavalry officer's sabre. Our own complicity as British subjects is called out in the final chorus lyrics, which are sung over the verse motif as we switch between 'my turn' and 'your turn'. 'Empire Song' was the first of two singles from *Revelations*. Released in March 1982, it reached 43 in the UK Singles Chart.

'We Have Joy' 2:56 (Killing Joke)

A furnace of violence and lust, summoning Christianity, Empire and social decay – and all wrapped in the most acute satirical irony – 'We Have Joy' is a phosphorous burn of a track that predicts the Joke's musical direction post-2003 with a blistering assault of metal-adjacent thrash, and flesh-shredding proto-grunge guitarwork, but here in service of maximal dissonance. It's also a masterclass in the use of key changes to create disorientation.

In double waltz time, Geordie initiates a simple first/fourth/octave riff in Lydian (though the guitar sounds detuned somewhat, creating amplified discord) with Big Paul shadowing the rhythm on a muted cymbal. Jaz sings the first verse over this motif, his vocal again cleaner and more melodic than on the previous two albums but still incorporating dissonant notes, here a flattened third. Before we become settled, the first chorus key-shift crunches down for the first 'We have Joy!' then grinds back up for the second incantation.

The second verse has the entire band in full flow and includes some theologically needling lines. Another chorus, now with a satisfying twang on Youth's bass, leads to a rhythmically taut but harmonically chaotic waltz-time middle eight, Coleman manically laughing and whooping while he saws his violin like a demon. There are also a couple of perception-puncturing stop-starts leaving only drums and the sound of struck glass, which foreshadow the extensive use of dropouts by technical and math metal. It's a slow dance of decadence and death. The song ends with an extended vamp, the chorus lyric cycling to a hard stop, leaving both the song and our understanding of it unresolved.

'Chop-Chop' 4:19 (Killing Joke)

Like 'Requiem', this is a lament for the herd mentality that keeps its cattle politically and spiritually asleep, an observation that 'all but the few' notice anything. The title is an allusive pun: hurrying up and decapitation (or literally getting 'out of' or 'off' your head). The edict to hurry has two meanings here: the addiction of the masses to self-anaesthetise through lifestyle consumption, and the fact that those who 'notice', aka the outsiders, need to hurry up with the work of becoming self-aware because both time and the system are against them.

Structurally, the song is another masterclass in concision, with a verse-bridge-chorus architecture spanning the two cycles of lyrics. A Geordie chord strum and a particularly un-Joke-like major descending arpeggio lead into tinkling glass, followed by a tribal drumbeat and a driving bass riff. Jaz sings the first verse, lamenting the drab boxes of an English suburban new town, watching the residents who are 'barely half awake'. Then before we get comfortable in our interest-free three-piece suite, the chorus lurches to Phrygian with Jaz observing the anaesthetised cattle accompanied by a disappointedly deflating synth effect. 'Chop-Chop' was released as a single in June 1982 and did not chart.

'The Pandys are Coming' 4:27 (Killing Joke)

> My great, great, great grandfather was Mangal Pandey, who led the insurrection against the British [in 1857] and is revered in Mother India as one of the great nationalists. Then there's B. N. Pandey, who wrote *The Break Up of British India* and was very close to Gandhi. My grandfather was in the 1962 war with China; he executed two of his own men for not going forward, and he believed in global revolution.
> Jaz Coleman, interviewed by Ian Fortnam, *Metal Hammer*, 15 September 2015

Another track about the long sunset of the British Empire, this time from Coleman's unique perspective. On his mother Gloria's side, he is Anglo-Indian with the family name 'Pandy', a form of 'Pandit', which is originally the name of a group of Hindu Brahmins. The lyrics are again poetic, a collage of traditions, oppression, revolt and finding home.

The track starts with what sounds like Indian double-reed pipes playing a descending motif in what Western music would describe as Lydian, though the actual notes stray from the diatonic (Jaz achieved the extraordinary pipe sound using his OB-X synthesiser's ring modulator). This motif conjures images of Eastern exoticism from British movies of the 1950s and 1960s, especially the run of Hammer films using subcontinental elements, later echoed in *Indiana Jones and the Temple of Doom*. In all these narratives, the threat to the Anglosphere protagonists equates to an indigenous culture of some type, more specifically to its religious and occult practices.

Coleman uses a deliberately atonal delivery, which resolves somewhat at the end of each line (Coleman has mentioned his fascination with quartertones in relation to this track). The 'pipes' come back, now with a kinetic drum pattern, galloping bass and louder guitar strum, before the 'pipes' again drop out and Jaz sings the second verse. Then we hit a discordant bridge with Youth climbing semitones, leading to a middle eight in which Geordie spins a new riff. The ensemble restates the main motif to fade, now with chattering human voices deep in the mix, creating a hypnotic vibe that conjures Coleman's yearning for a 'place that wasn't a place' and a 'race that wasn't a race': a tribal gathering outside both blood and time.

'Chapter Three' 3:13 (Killing Joke)

A furious ditty with dual meanings, 'Chapter Three' (stylised 'Chapter III' on the original release) appears on the surface to be a diatribe about the stupidity and horror of war and nationalism but holds a hidden meaning relating to Coleman's outsider status: both within the band and in general. 'Wise thoughts to broad horizons' refers to Coleman's plans to widen his vanishing point in order to establish at least a nation – meaning to self-determine both his geographical and spiritual independence.

With nursery rhyme style simplicity, the track runs in a deceptively complex 8/8 with syncopated emphasis on beats one, three and six. The bass starts in a detuned/slowed-down Lydian as Jaz sings the first verse. The first bridge is in Mixolydian and revolves around the idea of 'simplicity', which seems deliberately ironic in terms of both content and form. A second bridge in Lydian, this one instrumental, has a joltingly discordant key change. An elongated 'Hey!' is followed by a step down to Mixolydian for a kind of chorus, in which Jaz observes the monomaniacal focus required by those who follow an occult path. Then a progression resolves back in the Lydian for a final line of the chorus, Coleman's self-rallying cry for his imminent departure for Iceland. But as ever, the Joke create deliberate satirical tension between the lyric (which commands change) and the key (which literally resolves back to 'the same'). The whole thing then repeats, but this time with a triple go at that last line and a wonderfully succinct hard ending. It's hard not to admire the track's deliberately paradoxical complex simplicity.

'Have a Nice Day' 3:13 (Killing Joke)
Opening with a radioactive-fallout synth effect that foreshadows the similar one at the start of 'Darkness Before Dawn', 'Have a Nice Day' is, depending on your ears, either unbearably dissonant or just plain unbearable. It's another song about the band's core subject matter of nuclear holocaust, encapsulated in the evocative words 'four minutes still turns my insides out', a reference to the Cold War's four-minute warning, but perhaps also to the length of an idealised KJ track.

The title and lyric are an obvious comment on the supreme cognitive dissonance within the American tradition of wishing everyone a 'nice day' while bombing the hell out of them. British Gen Xer telly-heads will know that in a similarly satirical vein, 'HAVE A NICE DAY' is painted on the bomb that falls towards the English tithing of Tollard Farnham, Dorset in the original opening titles of *The Comic Strip Presents...*, which debuted 2 November 1982 on the first night of Channel 4. Verse one is split between D-sharp Phrygian (with an added sharpened second) and D major, with the verse ending on a nursery-rhyme style vocal motif which drops down to a plain D. This is why it's so harsh on your ears. Jaz exclaims the brutally bitter 'So sad!' before the D-sharp Phrygian motif returns to fade. A song intended to be as discordant as its subject matter.

'Land of Milk and Honey' 2:38 (Killing Joke)
A dual assault on the consumerist paradise and commercial merry-go-round that are held up as the pinnacle of society and art, where product and money rule, 'Land of Milk and Honey' is another brutally lean song. An inescapably propulsive eight-to-the-floor creates the perfect mood for another chant-style call-and-response chorus, here in a pitch-degraded C major – the populist key literally undermined – with Coleman taking the final syllable down from natural second ('milk and ho-') to flattened second ('-ney'). The blindly optimistic call part of each line is interrupted by a response that first berates then pacifies the caller, till both parties agree on the final line. It's a typical Killing Joke punchline. No questioning or rebellion will be tolerated.

Key-shift gears grind and we drop down to almost B-flat major for the first verse, which revisits the perennial Joke subject matter of self-anaesthetisation and apathy. Verse three skewers the aspic-trapped loop in which all musicians find themselves if they taste even fleeting success: 'Change the tune now, sales go dwindle.'

The final chorus, now bludgeoned into submission, restates the song title, but there's dissent buried in the music: this time, Jaz takes the final syllable down from flattened third ('milk and ho-') to natural second ('-ney'), emphasising the implicit discord of the song's theme and further disorientating the listener. Geordie plays us out with a nerve-scraping motif, which quickly becomes a hard clash before the song is cut off.

'Good Samaritan' 3:28 (Killing Joke)

The closest the Joke have come to a ballad so far, 'Good Samaritan' is a handbrake-turn change in mood, pace and sonics, with a bare-bones arrangement. The two main guitar motifs centre on rising arpeggios, but each takes a detour into a note clash. Although in each case, the dissonance is of a far milder flavour than anywhere else on the album, there is still a deliberate lack of resolution, and this is echoed in the lyrics: everything feels like it's in limbo, disjointed, ambiguous. The title seems ironically to suggest someone who simply is not capable of helping themselves, far less of helping someone else.

The lyrics appear to be stream-of-consciousness but still couched in Joke irony. Verse two evokes Empire, religion, Masonic ritual, dystopia and apocalypse. Crowley's Aeon of Horus is covertly summoned by 'a Hawk-headed man' in a Marvel comic. The last stanza seems to be a statement of serene acceptance, but the final two lines puncture this. 'So happy' is accompanied by a less-dissonant, maybe even hopeful, motif, but Jaz drags the line down atonally, prompting the guitar to revert to the first motif, which now sounds deeply mournful rather than contemplative: 'Lah, la-la-lah, la-la la-lah la-lah, aah…' It's hard to escape the feeling that our protagonist could be in the cell of a psychiatric facility, heavily medicated or even lobotomised, rocking gently forward and back, forward and back, forward and back.

'Dregs' 4:57 (Killing Joke)

'Dregs' is both a return to Youth's loping, dub-infused bass, but also his first swansong with the band. Across the album, you can hear his dub and dance tendencies being pushed to the edges, as a more rhythmically metronomic, sonically heavy, and densely mixed style takes over. It's perhaps easy to lay responsibility for this at the desk of Conny Plank, but the band are clearly evolving here – and the fruits of that evolution can be tasted on the next two studio albums.

In a quasi-motorik 4/4 and with a single counterpointed motif repeated for the entire duration, this is the closest the Joke come to out-and-out Krautrock, with a track that has strong resonances with CAN and Neu!. Youth plays a dub-style first-to-fifth riff (this being a particular favourite of CAN bassist Holger Czukay), while Geordie provides extreme dissonance with an Augmented Hexatonic scale (if you were wondering). After that four-to-the-floor intro, Big Paul locks into an insistently mesmerising tribal pattern. The words feel like an in-studio improvisation from Coleman, such being another hallmark of the experimental end of Krautrock. Other than some puncturing of the pretensions of the prevailing culture from the Joke's outsider perspective, many of the words are playground nonsense that provide suitable consonance and alliteration, which is all enhanced by some heroic coughing. If you're minded there's also an implicit joke that these lyrics are the literal 'dregs'.

Bonus Tracks

'We Have Joy' 4:21 (Killing Joke)

This leaves an entirely different taste in the mouth: bitter lime and salt rather than the flame-thrower chilli of the album version. Using the basic architecture of the original, the alternate has an entirely different mood. While the shorter version is defined by aggression and attack, this longer version is ironically more contained, like a coiled snake rather than a striking one. It's a rare example of an alt being, not only as good as the original but also as good as any track on the album. There are tuned timpani and tendon-shredding layers of industrial shearing and drilling, while Jaz wields his devil's violin throughout. The end sounds like an invasion by insectoid aliens akin to those in Hammer's *Quatermass and the Pit* (1967).

Fire Dances (1983)

Personnel:
Jaz Coleman: lead vocals, synthesiser
Geordie Walker: guitar
Raven: bass guitar
Big Paul Ferguson: drums, backing vocals
Produced and mixed at: Basing Street Studios, London by Killing Joke
Co-producer: John Porter, 'Let's All Go' only
Engineer: Nigel Mills
Label: EG
Release date: July 1983
Running time (original release): 40:06
Highest chart places: UK: 29, USA: Did not chart
Current edition: 2008 expanded remastered reissue on Virgin

> [We] wanted to "create a musical renaissance via a strict musical form". That's what I wrote in my diary in 1979. No guitar solos, no blues except in parody, no Americanisms. We talked endlessly about things like, what is an English rhythm? We didn't have a folk tradition to draw from. Killing Joke was rediscovering the tradition.
> Jaz Coleman, interviewed by Peter Watts, *UNCUT*, 16 November 2018

With the departure of Youth and the arrival of Raven, the Joke continued their association with Conny Plank, recording a set for live EP *Ha* (stylised *"HA"*) in August 1982, followed by the non-album 'Birds of a Feather' tracks along with the original version of 'The Gathering' in September 1982 at Strawberry Studios. Around the time of these sessions, Geordie switched to his now-famous Gibson ES-295 hollow-body guitar (he subsequently purchased a second). This has been his guitar ever since and Geordie's golden sonic-legion resonator has become an instantly recognisable part of the Killing Joke story. Apart from the guitar's warm tone (Geordie calls it 'cello-ey') it also has a trapeze bridge which Geordie uses in lieu of a whammy bar to bend the strings. At the same time, Geordie dropped down a further half-step to D Standard tuning (with Raven doing the same). This tuning subsequently became the default for the band, though Geordie also uses open tuning. The ES-295 and down-tuning (plus Geordie's idiosyncratic use of effects and amplification, which I won't cover here) immediately became the core facet of the Joke's unique soundscape.

The 'Birds of a Feather' single was to be the last collaboration between the band and Plank, and on *Fire Dances* you can immediately hear how the band diverge from the musical and rhythmic idioms established on *Revelations*. Recorded between February and March 1983, the production is stripped right back with the synth almost entirely omitted, the drums foregrounded and the rhythms more feral: all of which make sense when creating an album that revels in the primitive. Compare and contrast the Plank and Joke-produced versions of 'The Gathering' to hear the full impact of the change of approach. The band have expressed some displeasure with the final album, but there's something about the set's manic energy that is utterly enthralling if you're prepared to surrender to it.

Fire Dances is Killing Joke's most melodically harmonious set of songs up to this point, while in terms of ideas and themes, it is both joyful and unashamedly upbeat about our potential for change if we can learn to surrender to our basic instincts within rituals both pagan and occult. If we can rediscover the 'basic man' and submit to the occult idea of 'will'. The bulk of the writing for the album took place at Mountain Studios in Wales. Again, the remote location and Neolithic history clearly inspired the album's ancestor worship and honouring of nature's cycles. You could even argue that *Fire Dances* is, in spirit, a concept album, with every song addressing the same broad subject matter: the spiritual evolution of the human being through gatherings, rites, and a conscious reactivation of the old ways. It's exactly this primal nature, melodic frisson and unvarnished optimism that make *Fire Dances* one of my favourite Joke albums. Raven created the striking rune-resonant font used on the cover and liner/booklet. The 2008 reissue, along with all the other KJ album remasters released that year, are dedicated to 'Our brother Paul Vincent Raven 1961-2007'.

'The Gathering' 3:12 (Killing Joke)
Following on directly from 'Birds of a Feather', the album's opening track takes the 'gather, gather, gather' idea from that single and thrusts it centre stage. As though, rhythmically at least, we've run into this track straight from 'Flock the B Side', we start with a similar rolling groove, like a mob of 'obby 'osses trotting lopsidedly to a Beltane pyre. There's also the first appearance of a cowbell as part of Big Paul's kit. Raven lays down an urgent get-down-the-front bass riff while Geordie jostles in counterpoint. The first verse welcomes back to the venue our old friend call-and-response as it pegs itself to the positive elements of spending time with your tribe, deliberately referencing the primal at the core of the tribal. The 'basic man' is the primal man, a human free of psychological and social conditioning.

The bridge sways from key to key before a root-stomped chorus affirms the invitation. It's no accident that 'gatherer' has connotations with our hunter-gatherer ancestors. Then we stage dive into another cycle. The middle eight is four bars of Geordie keeping us on tenterhooks for an encore before the band retake the stage for a reprise of the chorus lyrics over the verse motif. There's a final instrumental take of the chorus section, which fades out as the assembled Gatherers leave the venue feeling disorientated but elated.

'Fun and Games' 4:06 (Killing Joke)
An upbeat march to the pagan festivities, 'Fun and Games' continues the album's theme of old-ways congregations with a hymn to letting loose the

shackles of conformity and civilisation, 'domestication – lost overnight' as the second verse has it. A familiar tribal beat follows a crackling fire and the striking of an old-fashioned mantel clock: juxtaposing the pagan calendar of death and rebirth with the human-made concept of time, but also telling us that it's time to let go of time completely. The lyrics also relate this path to being childlike with references to 'playmates', 'playpens falling' and the surety that 'the child will conquer'.

Unlike earlier Joke tracks which emphasise the dark side of human instinct, such as 'Primitive', here the feeling is festive and liberating, as though we're being accompanied by the band to the same Beltane rite conjured by the previous track. Although there's now no dissonance in the backing, Jaz takes the vocal line down to a flattened sixth, to instil a sense of danger and tension. The lyrics set the scene with a shining moon and voices in your head calling you to 'play wild – volatile'. Sunset is when the rational gives way to the primitive. Night-time is when the primal emerges – if one is prepared to follow one's instinct and slip loose from one's social conditioning. The chorus couplet contrasts 'way' (as in path) with 'ways' (as in pagan traditions), while 'unknown days' underlines the idea of enjoying time outside time. The outro creates a vibe that's unsettling but inviting: a fire which warms our pagan hearts but could as easily consume a human sacrifice.

'Rejuvenation' 4:01 (Killing Joke)

> If you're looking for a saviour god who is going to intervene on this earthly level, I don't think it works like that. Human existence on this earth is pretty amoral. But in the greater scheme of things, you have to study the ideas of parallel universes by Everett [American physicist Hugh Everett III]. There's no such thing as death. We're only just discovering multiple timelines. We'll be able to go into the past, and future. In the distant future, Paul Raven is not dead yet. We're just starting to access this world. Which is one of the great things about living in the 21st century. Our conception of time as we know it will eventually dissolve.
>
> Jaz Coleman, interviewed by Ian Fortnam, *Classic Rock*, 21 October 2016

This is arguably the pinnacle of early-career Joke's compositional architecture and I always enjoy how much it resonates with *Heaven Born*-era Cardiacs. The lyrics here are the first that hint at the occult and drugs as possible portals to the awakened state of the 'new man', which the primal state can allow one to access – going backwards in order to move forward. The title is possibly an allusion to the 'Great Work' of the hermetic tradition and the 'Philosopher's Stone' of alchemy: 'rejuvenation' as a metaphor for spiritual illumination.

Big Paul launches into a tub-thumping beat with everyone else in D major Phrygian (which is D Phrygian with a sharpened third: a perfect balance between dark and light; or darkness with potential). The lyrics commence with nothing but positivity for the dual processes of awakening and finding one's tribe. In the chorus, Jaz asks us to take his hand, 'Because it's taking shape – new man come along.'

Verse two introduces a note of warning: primal tribes are as likely to commit genocide as dance naked around a bonfire invoking pagan gods and goddesses. Anyone who's studied the occult or mysticism will know that the membrane between self-revelation as a human good and the occult as an excuse for fascism is often gossamer-thin. The brilliant lyric 'eliminate the obstacle' is as applicable to the esoteric path of enlightenment as it is to bloody murder.

'Frenzy' 3:47 (Killing Joke)

Structured like a Sufi ritual, 'Frenzy' continues the theme of awakening to the spiritual journey with a headlong chorus-free 'tumble-tumble here we go'. A frantic beat and almost-unison guitar, bass and vocal rip through the verses using the Middle Eastern-infused Double Harmonic scale, while a minimalist bridge setting major against minor keys allows us to take a disorientated breath. Jaz is our guide, starting the journey from a personal perspective, 'sun in my blood now'. It's as though we've emerged from the night-time of the first three tracks and identify again with solar rather than lunar energies.

The final verse opens out our perspective as we see the cities 'come and go' and then see 'beyond'. Entire civilisations rise and fall, but the truth of enlightenment that dwells beyond the veil endures. The track ends with a unison reprise of the main verse motif, which gradually speeds up as we dance ourselves into a transcendent frenzy till we collapse. But again, there is ambiguity. Leaving your conscience 'way behind' cuts both ways: sloughing-off conditioning to reach enlightenment or hardening one's heart to others and focusing only on one's 'self'. This is echoed in the music after the second bridge with a lingering dissonant note from Raven after the main motif has already restarted.

'Harlequin' 3:57 (Killing Joke)

A change of pace from the frenetic dervish-style spiritual ecstasy of 'Frenzy', this is a more contemplative track, which focuses on the two-edged sword of the trickster archetype at the core of the court jester and the French-suited Joker: both referenced by the band and their designers over Killing Joke's long career. The historical source for these troublemaking characters is the Italian commedia dell'arte *Arlecchino* from the late sixteenth century, who in turn is descended from a devil or demon character. Although Mr Punch, inspiration for the original Joke mascot, shares many characteristics with the Joker/jester (for example, both carry sticks) he is, in fact, descended from another commedia dell'arte character, *Pulcinella*, who dates from the early seventeenth century. *Pulcinella* became a key character of Neapolitan puppet theatre and made his first recorded appearance in England in 1662 with the anglicised name 'Punchinello'.

The trickster archetype can be as destructive as it is illuminating, partly because the truth is usually painful, and partly because being deliberately disruptive can easily become an end in itself rather than a means to an end, as proven by myriad cults. A slow-strum vamp, as though a court jester is about to sing an entitlement-puncturing song about the King's haemorrhoids, leads into a groove that's subtly infused with flamenco-style syncopation, perhaps referencing the deep Moorish influences on that musical tradition. Against this incessant beat, a tiny, high-pitched voice cries what sounds like 'Can anybody hear me?' – the trickster spirit animating the mix.

In the first verse, there's a childlike sense to the provocation of not knowing 'good or bad' but the key line relates how laughter can so easily turn dark, as humour becomes 'out of hand la-la'. The idea that the diamonds of the traditional Harlequin's costume are 'sharp you know' is a telling piece of wordplay. The verses are divided by a discordant bridge, in which you can imagine the trickster Harlequin letting loose his demons – anarchic provocation becoming sheer bloody malice. It's not for nothing that the DC Comics Joker and his partner in chaos, Harley Quinn are two of the most seductive and intriguing villains in Western culture – or that Heath Ledger drew inspiration from Coleman when crafting his psychotic iteration of the cracked-smile trickster.

The third and final verse, which follows an attention-focusing stop and decay to almost-silence, confirms that the Harlequin is 'a child of folly' like his antecedent, the Tarot's Fool, who is even older than *Arlecchino*, dating from the mid-fifteenth century. The Harlequin now understands 'good' and 'bad' but dismisses them both. He wants to play his games outside of accepted moral parameters. Again, the tension is between the trickster who wants to provoke self-reflection and positive change, and the deliberately offensive narcissist for whom nothing is off limits. The Harlequin's spirit – and that of the trickster within – will endure even after this song has come to a dead stop, just as Ledger's tragic genius endures through his extraordinary performance.

'Feast of Blaze' 3:33 (Killing Joke)

> I knew Maxine Sanders [co-founder of Alexandrian Wicca]. In the village I was brought up in, there was a hereditarian witch. I had a good experience with this… When it comes to religion, I revere the feminine. The feminine is our Mother Earth, that gives us food and nourishes us. I think this has been fundamental of Killing Joke from the beginning. This is what we have always venerated. Seeing god in the female.
> Jaz Coleman, interviewed by *Wortraub*, 1 April 2006

As optimistic as Killing Joke have ever been, 'Feast of Blaze' continues the album's pre-Christian themes, with a paean to pagan feast days and celebrating with a like-minded tribe. Anyone who's been to Lewes, Sussex on Bonfire Night, or felt that pagan pull at any English 5 November Guy Fawkes celebration will recognise the mood. The rhythms, especially on the bass, are similar to those on the earlier 'Pssyche', but here the mood is upbeat and festive rather than paranoid and aggressive, though Geordie's woozy note-bend in the chorus is like a magic-mushroom trip constantly threatening to go bad. Jaz finds room for his signature barks of 'Oh!' and 'Hey!', though here they sound at their most inviting. This feast is one of 'wine' and 'plenty', 'where the "wilful" man shall go', referencing the 'man of will' in both Nietzschean philosophy and the occult, specifically in Crowley's Thelema. Another reference to the self-analysis and self-discovery of the 'Great Work'.

'Song and Dance' 5:11 (Killing Joke)
This is one of those tracks that takes you a few weeks to realise you like, rather than the kind that you move in with straight away. It's also a key track in the band's musical evolution as the key changes here are more complex than we've come to expect, creating the tension that was previously provided by dissonance. The subject matter is, again, 'the basic man' aka the primal man of pagan rites, of ancestor worship, of wine and fire, of song and dance, but here with a slant that is towards the personal. The idea of going backwards to move forward is reiterated – a potent metaphor for the importance of invoking and honouring the spirits of our antecedents. The importance of music and rhythm to our lives, and to the expansion and deepening of our experience, is emphasised and the track uses melodic and harmonic devices to tell a story in a way that is new for the Joke. By this stage in proceedings, you'd be forgiven for imagining that this is a full-blown concept album.

The pun on assembly is particularly smart: a meeting of primal people is also where the primal human is 'assembled' as in 'put together'. A drum fill takes us into the first verse, which steps up a key, then as 'the song became alive' the key steps back down, reminding us of the prologue. Then, before we've settled into that key, and as the lyric goes from 'song' to 'dance', the key dips down again, with the bass echoing the deeper vibrations of rhythm over melody.

The middle eight's lyrics are the crux of the story. Ancestors awake and 'in our joy they take their joy'. Through ritual, which allows us to step outside time, to lose ourselves, the contemporary human has become the ancient human. They are us and we are them. The final line again has 'way' as both literal path and tradition. We end with some insistent sticks from Big Paul, like a tapping on your shoulder, reminding you to look both behind and beyond.

'Dominator' 4:28 (Killing Joke)
A throwback to early Joke, this track is driven by a twisted dance groove from Raven and Big Paul, with Geordie adding minimalist angular dissonance.

There's even a jerky synth line that's reminiscent of the band's earliest studio recordings. The rhythm, featuring some insistent cowbell, suggests the gradual encroaching of a limber wolfpack upon its victim, which resonates with the menacing one-line chorus 'Move in on them'. In the verses, Coleman's vocal is of a piece with the rest of the album: more melodic and with a cleaner vocal style. There's deliberate frisson between the upbeat music and the lyrics, which state in no uncertain terms the idea that a 'basic man' who knows what he wants must not let anyone else stand in his way or pull him down. He must become a 'dominator soul'. The third verse restates the idea that ritual – here a ritual of domination over physical matter and social conditioning – is a dance. The whole thing cycles back to the intro motif and ends with a boom.

'Let's All Go' 3:19 (Killing Joke)

> Well, I work with ancient sculptures, and I'd like to say I have a Celtic soul. I'm very attracted to remote places, and I'm very attracted to places of power. I still can't say what that power is, but yeah, I'm very, very attracted to the Neolithic sites.
> Big Paul, interviewed by Alex in NYC, *Flaming Pablum*, 4 September 2004

'Let's All Go' was the only single from *Fire Dances*, released as 'Let's All Go (to the Fire Dances)' in June 1983, before the album. It reached 51 in the UK Singles Chart. Starting with a snare-drum roll, the track announces its ecstatic credentials with a descending and almost-complete Mixolydian scale. The verses juxtapose childlike play and nursery rhymes with pagan rites, further deepening the album's overall theme. Returning to childhood with its stories and fables can send us back to our primal past. To be human, we need ritual. We are all 'basic'. Instead of the flattened end-of-line note of earlier tracks, Jaz uses a three-semitone ladder at the close of each verse, maintaining tension but signalling a new, more optimistic mood. The chorus, in what at this point sounds like a revolutionary major key, is Jaz's incitement: 'Let's all go to the fire dances.'

'Lust Almighty' 3:57 (Killing Joke)

The pagan festivities end, appropriately enough, with a track about sex, to complete the primitive set along with physical ferocity, dance and mind-altering substances. The title tips its hat to the centrality of sex to pagan religions and the occult: one's sexual partner is worshipped as though they are a god or goddess. As the lyrics across the album relate: we can't, as humans, possibly hope to repress these primal instincts. They are all things that non-human animals do (though the mind-altering substances part is less common). The track starts with some reverbed breathing before a cantering drum pattern and writhing bass riff get things going. There is only one short verse, which is repeated twice, with the album's final entreaty: to remember the 'sex between your legs' and 'twist in the dance'. Suspended between two bridges is a breakdown of pounding drums and a Geordie two-note siren, tenterhooks of arousal before the dance resumes. The song ends with a hard stop, dousing the fire till night falls and we do the whole thing again.

Bonus Tracks

'Me or You?' 3:13 (Killing Joke)

This is a genuinely heretical track for the band and it's no surprise it's a non-album track. A gauzy, innocent ditty, it's the closest the Joke come to a traditional love song (the band are on record as not liking this track *at all*). It's also particularly reminiscent of The Damned at their most accessible, especially in terms of the ability to create more conventional hooks. It's interesting to conjecture where the Joke would have gone if they'd followed this path rather than the one that leads from the band's subsequent single, 'Eighties', as on this evidence they were as capable of writing delicate pop earworms as they were apocalyptic marches to oblivion. 'Me or You?' was released in October 1983 with 'Wilful Days' as B-Side and reached 57 in the UK Singles Chart.

'Wilful Days' 5:03 (Killing Joke)

This is a stonking track – indeed, it's so good the band named their 1995 compilation after it. Recorded with 'Me or You?' at Basing Street Studios, London in August 1983, with John Porter co-producing, this is thematically linked to the pagan/occult subject matter of *Fire Dances*, but musically it's a darker proposition. It's also a fabulous example of the Joke's evolving use of dissonance, with the band pulling in three different musical directions at once but still creating an organic, cohesive whole.

Raven establishes a simple Phrygian riff (which will again have Hawkwind resonances for fans of that band), while Big Paul creates a marching groove that sounds like an army of trickster demons descending on an unsuspecting village. Geordie adds a Double Harmonic riff and Jaz intones some of his favourite edicts: 'Go!', 'Move!'. The key shifts up as the demons wait for the stragglers to catch up, then back down for the first two verses, which Jaz sings in Mixolydian. But listen to how immensely pleasing are the sonics created by these three theoretically clashing musical layers. This is the very essence of Killing Joke and something they do here with both extraordinary sophistication and primitive minimalism. It's their unique essence – an essence that many have tried to copy but none have managed to clone. It's the perfect track to bridge from the optimism and potential for change of *Fire Dances* to the familiar darkness and fury of *Night Time*.

In addition to the 'Me or You?' single, there are six additional bonus tracks. First up is a longer version of 'Dominator' with a more pronounced synth line, extra cowbell and a fourth verse not on the shorter album version. The Strawberry Studios/Plank version of 'The Gathering' (recorded during the 'Birds of a Feather' sessions) features a funkier bass part with some popping from Raven. As with 'We Have Joy', this alternate is fully the equal of the album version and some might even prefer its spiky, lumbering groove. The final four tracks are from a 4 July 1983 Peel Session (broadcast on 12 July) that is not on the 2008 *Peel Sessions* compilation. As expected from BBC Maida Vale studios, the engineering (Martin Colley) and production (John Porter) are superb, with Geordie higher in the mix than on the studio albums. For anyone wanting to study the Joke's guitar lines, the Peel Sessions are the place to start.

Night Time (1985)

Personnel:
Jaz Coleman: lead vocals, keyboards
Geordie Walker: guitar
Raven: bass guitar
Big Paul Ferguson: drums, backing vocals
Produced and mixed at: Hansa Tonstudio, West Berlin, West Germany by Chris Kimsey
Engineer: Thomas Stiehler
Label: EG
Release date: March 1985
Running time (original release): 39:34
Highest chart places: UK: 11, USA: Did not chart, New Zealand: 8
Current edition: 2008 expanded remastered reissue on Virgin

Night Time continued the trajectory of the band from *Fire Dances*, moving ever closer to pop accessibility, though in terms of subject matter and themes, this is a far darker proposition than its predecessor, which perhaps explains why it wasn't as internationally successful as hoped. If any Killing Joke album was going to break the US it really should have been this one, but such resolutely refused to occur, leaving the group's influence on an entire generation of American bands a cult obsession rather than a commercial inevitability. In the UK, at least, the record provided both KJ's career-high placement of 11 and most weeks on the chart at nine (though set against 12 and six, respectively, for the far more challenging *Revelations*, you can see how this was a disappointment to management and label). The album reached eight on the New Zealand Albums Chart, accelerating Coleman's long-time fascination with Aotearoa (the Māori name for New Zealand, literally 'island of the long white cloud').

The album was written over four weeks at Nomis Studios in Olympia, London, and recorded in August and September 1984 at the legendary Hansa Tonstudio in what was then West Berlin. *Night Time* was produced and mixed by Chris Kimsey, who harnessed KJ's primal energy, incandescent fury and existential angst into an engaging and accessible package without blunting the edges. This is the album where the Joke appear to settle into a style: riff-heavy songs, dissonant guitar, propulsive bass, pounding drums, atmospheric synth lines – plus less overtly aggressive, though still rage-laced vocals. It's also the album that captures the band finding the sweet spot between punk dissent, industrial dread, goth torment and pop pleasure. Though not a concept album, there is a definite through-line, focusing on the terror of global conflagration and the underbelly of human experience. The band's exploits during the recording of *Night Time* are the stuff of legend, with Berlin providing a perfectly poetic location for over-indulgence in the pleasures of the flesh. While *Fire Dances* foregrounds a uniquely British paganism, *Night Time*'s tracks have an innately international point of view, having been inspired by the band's experiences across multiple countries, including West Germany and Switzerland. If *Revelations* is the sun setting on Empire and *Fire Dances* is the glow of a pagan bonfire in the chill of a winter evening, *Night Time* is the city through to the darkest hour. You could take the analogy even further and peg *Brighter than a Thousand Suns* as a civilisation's false dawn, making the four albums an informal cycle.

Night Time nominally provided three singles. 'Eighties' was released in April 1984, almost a year before the album proper, reaching a UK Singles Chart position of 60. 'Love Like Blood' was released in January 1985, a few weeks before the album, as a lead-in, reaching 16 in the UK Singles Chart and staying on the chart for nine weeks (the band's highest ever UK placing and number of weeks for a single). 'Love Like Blood' also charted in multiple other countries, including Top 10 placings in Belgium, the Netherlands and New Zealand, and Top 30 positions in West Germany and Ireland. 'Kings and Queens' was released soon after the album in March 1985 but only reached 58 in the UK (43 in New Zealand), demonstrating how much 'Love Like Blood' is an outlier in the band's history but also how songs ostensibly about love, however dark, seem to do better commercially than all others.

'Night Time' 4:55 (Killing Joke)

Though it is directly inspired by the band's time in Berlin, this is an evocation of night-time anywhere that humans congregate to indulge. It is dark music for dark times: temporally, politically, and philosophically. The lyrical collaboration of Jaz and Big Paul again demonstrates a poetic telepathy, with the writing process defined by the two finishing each other's thoughts and ideas in a shared lyric book. Here the combination of Ferguson's more emotive images and Coleman's more astringent allusions attains a sophistication and impact that's a high watermark for the band.

Musically, the Joke are now writing mostly in simple minor keys and Jaz is no longer adding dissonant accidentals to the end of his vocal lines, but Geordie still provides subtle discord – a single clown at a wake rather than twin clowns at a funeral. Rhythmically, we're again in march time, which gives the track its momentum and heralds the darkly oppressive tone of the album. A Geordie screech and descending rapid-fire guitar notes throw us headlong into the dead of night. Raven and Geordie launch into counterpoint riffs that diverge rhythmically in the second half of the motif – a Killing Joke speciality when Raven's on bass duties. There are industrial effects that evoke sirens, air raids and whistling bombs. The wonderfully disconcerting idea of 'turning out the sun' (the sun is simultaneously turning off and turning inside out) sets the scene. The end of the second line is a great example of how the Joke often deliberately create lyrics that don't scan so Jaz can bend, stretch and emphasise particular words and syllables, in this case, 'machine'.

A drum fill propels us into the second verse, where there's some sublime wordplay and foreshadowing. 'Bloodstains' is an echo sent back from track three, 'daytime' is still dark, showing the 'face behind the mask', given ominous gloss here. Night is a 'drunken time where all can lie', the double meaning crystal clear even in the pitch black. The bridge and a fill take us into the short chorus. The first half of each line lifts us into the Mixolydian with optimism about the delights in store, but the second half drops down to the minor, the second line's second half emphasising the 'mad' of 'sweet madness of night', one of Coleman's deliberate syllable-scanning distortions.

Verse three has the subtly dystopian 'party troops and governments' and a call not to embrace your fears as one would expect, but to run from them. When the intro motif returns, there are dissonant guitar swoops and ostinatos evoking search lights scything through the night. The bridge and a final drum fill lead us not into a chorus reprise but ominously back into the intro section, again evoking gunfire, sirens and helicopter blades.

'Darkness Before Dawn' 5:18 (Killing Joke)

As with 'Night Time', this track seamlessly balances Coleman and Ferguson lyrics, while driven by music that encapsulates the tightly wound tension between Coleman and Geordie in terms of musical composition. Wordless voices cry out, and then an apocalyptic synth effect heralds the start of the song proper as Raven's driving bass riff provides the substrate for Geordie's insistent sixteenth notes and a haunting keyboard melody, the arrangement already creating spine-tingling tension. Raven's riff creates both forward propulsion and dangling suspense as Coleman intones the first verse of an evocative take on enduring a dark night of the soul – a perennial metaphor for spiritual rebirth. The song's title refers to the proverb that the darkest hour is the one before the dawn, an idea apparently first noted by English historian Thomas Fuller, who in 1650 wrote: 'It is always darkest just before the day dawneth.'

In lieu of a chorus, there's an instrumental section with two clearly delineated halves, increasing the unresolved tension. The first section has cymbal splashes on the third and fourth beats, plus martial voices, while the second section, with its TV sci-fi keyboard riff, has cymbal shots on the third and fourth off-beats. These off-beats seem to be the protagonist resisting his fate, while the downbeats are fate establishing and re-establishing its dominance. This rhythmic tension is also supported by melodic suspense. In the first half, the downbeats stay resolutely in G minor, but in the second half, the off-beats strain towards G major, from darkness to light, but don't make it – instead falling back down again to the minor.

The eerie bridge comprises reverbed guitar and a synth line which sounds like it's come straight out of a horror soundtrack. It's as though we're literally suspended between giving in to fate and forging ahead towards the promised glimmer of a life-affirming dawn. Again, there's the downbeats-only section of the chorus instrumental, making it clear that fate has the upper hand, followed by the final intro section and verse four, which Coleman has referenced as encapsulating the band's synchronicity-fuelled foundation, the meeting of these four souls being karmic.

Although the lyrics end with optimism, what follows suggests that darkness will always have the winning hand, creating evocative ambiguity between the potential in the lyrics and the haunting fatalism of the music. An urgent drum fill takes us into both halves of the chorus, the major key making a last-ditch stand before being overwhelmed by fill-heralded repetitions of the literally downbeat section, now with screaming souls buried deep in the mix: we may survive till dawn, but the darkness will always return. This fades into an unsettlingly ambiguous triad from Geordie. Perfection – and one of my favourite tracks by the band.

'Love Like Blood' 6:48 (Killing Joke)

> ['Love Like Blood'] was inspired by the author Yukio Mishima, who wrote *The Samurai Ethic and Modern Japan*. He was a great author. It was his views on writing with your blood as an artist that really inspired me. It's a metaphor for the commitment an artist must take to his art form. And I loved the warrior principle, to freedom with blood, if you like. The song itself was a distillation of everything that we hold dear, and one must aspire to walk and talk what you write about in your songs – actually live it. That's the other part of art, isn't it? You can't just be conceptual, writing songs. It's the way you live your life, as well. It's as important as the way you play your instruments or the music you create.
> Jaz Coleman, interviewed by Greg Prato, *Songfacts*, 29 October 2015

A hymn to the evanescence of life and the tension between a short life going out in glory and a long life decaying into oblivion, 'Love Like Blood' relates back to the 'glory of the great dead' from the *Hávamál*. And all analogous to the fleeting ecstasy of passion and the inevitability of love's own 'death'.

Geordie's upwards-arcing guitar riff is full of yearning, immediately in counterpoint to a disorienting keyboard line. A hi-hat ride and fill take us into the main riff, a driving chug on bass and guitar, which moves upwards, then drops, then moves up again, evoking the Sisyphean endurance event of being alive (or, if you're lucky, in love). The main riff's additional sharpened fourth is a testament to the Joke's unswerving adherence to dissonance. Verse one ends with 'so cut the rose in full bloom', which is resonant with everything from Shakespeare's sonnets to The Who's incantation 'Hope I die before I get old!'. A drum fill takes us to an eerie, purgatory-evoking bridge, and then we're into the chorus, centred on the lovely suspense-inducing counterpoint of the bass line moving down while the vocal line moves up. The message of being courageous and seizing the moment is tempered with the idea that we must all live as though we are immortal, dreaming of 'promised lands and fields'. And we must all 'learn to die' without fear. Love and life, like blood, race the heart but can (or in the case of life, will, however many billions of dollars you have) bleed you dry, though it's the 'red tears' 'shed on grey' that give life colour and meaning.

A retracted bridge with more eerie synth takes us to a chorus reprise, then on into an extended bridge, a grand piano hammering like death himself knocking on the door with his scythe, first on the one of every other bar, and then, with doubled insistence, at the top of each bar. Another chorus and we're full circle back to the main motif, which repeats, but now with some reverbed off-beat drum fills and bass drop-outs till fading away completely, even this choice seeming to suggest that this is how most of us will go: not with a unison root chord, but a fade-out.

'Kings and Queens' 4:38 (Killing Joke)

In one of the most personal tracks on the album, the Joke express their resolve to live like kings and queens even though they have nothing. The brutally efficient, yet stunningly effective music is machine-tooled to perfection. The track starts with industrial noises – monstrous boots of dread clomping about in your unconscious, echoing in your nightmares. Although engineered for accessibility, this harking back to the Joke's roots is magnificently evocative. The song proper, in a bouncy, almost jaunty syncopation, is built atop another propulsive bass line from Raven. Full disclosure: in my humble opinion, this bass part is one of the greatest on any track by anyone. It's the absolute epitome of less being more. One note across two octaves with two grace notes: elegant simplicity. Of course, it's what Raven does with these notes that's the key, the rhythm that gives the line its majestic potency.

The song's most pointed statement is 'rejoice and kill your heart'. It's an enjoinder to suppress your conscience and live for the moment, something that all of us have done, and many of us must do daily to make ends meet. The definitive ending is a reverbed drum pattern, which could be heard either as self-satisfied royals being beheaded or revolting peasants being shot: or maybe both. In its final bar, the track encapsulates the irony of living like kings and queens when others have nothing, and the dissonance created by doing such willingly.

'Tabazan' 4:34 (Killing Joke)

A writhing, squirming, fluid-soaked mass of tantric delay, burgeoning ecstasy and triumphant release, 'Tabazan' opens with effects that emulate fuck-and-birth breathing, culminating in the whoosh of orgasm, ultrasound heartbeats and waters breaking. An Eastern-sounding guitar riff, a throbbing bass pulse and off-beat cymbal splashes take us into the first verse, which questions whether we have our priorities straight regarding meaning and value, Jaz resolving to search for a 'new gold' (with the implicit 'new god').

A short chorus accelerates the erotic pace, while the second verse warns of the repression of desire. An instrumental double-reprise of the chorus leads into an almost-celebratory major-key middle eight with vocal, again highlighting the Joke's deliberately disconcerting approach to song structure. The deep irony of these lines, evoking how we worship the fruits of sublimation rather than sexuality itself, are underpinned by the tension generated by Raven's dissonant step-ups.

The third verse accepts that we humans will always be slaves to our biology, so we might as well revel in it. Another chorus raises the blood flow and a climactic fourth verse has Coleman intoning an orgasmic mantra (the first 'forth' rendered woozy with a slowed-down effect), which repeats to fade. The song's deep-tissue message is two-fold: the Reichian (as in Wilhelm Reich) idea that to repress primal urges is self-destructive to both the individual and society and the Thelemite idea that sex magick is an effective (and pleasurable) route to transcendence and god-hood. The track's title comes from the address of Raven's Geneva pad at the time, on Rue Tabazan in the city's heart.

'Multitudes' 4:56 (Killing Joke)

In a prescient track about flag-waving nationalism, right-wing populism, conforming and nonconformity, the Joke state the position of pretty much every outsider who can't relate to the multitude, tries to fit in and then realises that not only can't they conform, but doing so would mean denying the essence of who they are – they would be 'playing rhythms out of time'. Dissonance in the major-key chorus suggests that the existential crisis of the rebel can never be resolved. The last clause is ambiguous, as it could as easily be outsiders calling for more rebels to join them as it could be the multitudes telling the rebels to get back in line.

The third and final verse suggests that maybe one day enough 'restless souls' will 'begin to wake' and swell the numbers of the nonconformists, before a queasy middle eight has Geordie alternating between major keys and Raven laying down a stilted rhythm with a Tina Weymouth feel. Over this vertiginous meltdown, Jaz proclaims there is always 'perfection within decades of dissatisfaction and disillusion' if only we can find and recognise it as such. The final line, sung over a haunting repeat of the intro section with Big Paul throwing off a series of syncopated fills, makes it clear that trying to make ends meet 'the best I can' is pointless when the means has 'no end' that makes sense. The track terminates with an ominous synth effect, confirming that the outsider can never be at home among the multitudes.

'Europe' 4:35 (Killing Joke)

For their live performances in the mid-1980s, the Joke performed in front of two huge flags: the Stars and Stripes of the USA on one side and the Hammer and Sickle of the USSR on the other. This visual representation of being stuck between the immovable object of Soviet Russia and the unstoppable force of America encapsulates the central theme of this song, which takes us from the first-person intimacy of 'Multitudes' to a narrator's eye view of the Cold War as seen from Europe.

The most goth-resonant track on the album, with the Joke sounding akin to their post-punk cousins The Cure and Siouxsie and The Banshees, uses simple song structure as a weapon-delivery system for the lyrics and their meaning. Based on elegantly simple riffs plus an eerie keyboard atmosphere for the intro, verses and outro, with an almost-melody for the choruses, the song's heart is an ominous middle-eight-and-bridge combo that states the musical DNA of the whole album in microcosm, Geordie's sixteenth-note machine-gun again embedding the subject matter.

The poetically ambiguous lyrics appear to be deeply ironic, veering from a yearning for the 'gods of Europe' to awaken to the nihilistic/primal incantation: 'Reason dead forever – god let it be soon.' In terms of subject matter, these ideas are similarly contradictory: Classical Europe must rise again or be annihilated by the 'black sun' of nuclear holocaust, paired with: imperial Europe must never rise again because whenever it does, there's genocide. It's a lose-lose game. You either kill others with your empire or get killed by someone else's – and the Joke want done with this absurdity. Writing this as Europe is yet again torn apart, this time by war in Ukraine and renewed threats of nuclear holocaust, the prescience of this message cuts deep.

'Eighties' 3:50 (Killing Joke)

The album closer is best known for the controversy surrounding its similarity to Nirvana's 'Come as You Are' from 1991's *Nevermind,* but more than enough has been written about this, so let's discuss why the anthemic 'Eighties' is still such a powerful song – why it could as easily have been written last week as in 1983. A magnificent summation of the dread of the entire album, the song packs an awful lot into its four short minutes: Cold War paranoia, the greed and selfishness of the me-first, take-all-you-can ethos, the death cult of consumerism. For all the overt sentiment, the most compelling subtext of the lyrics is that the word 'living' appears 12 times, yet the message seems clear: 'living' isn't what most of us were doing in the 1980s, rather running just to stay still and dancing to dull the pain of the running. If we were lucky.

A glimmer of hope is provided by the line 'Eighties, I'm in love with the coming race', which is a reference to Edward Bulwer-Lytton's 1871 science-fiction novel *The Coming Race,* which Coleman uses here as a metaphor for a tribe of initiates who will survive the imminent nuclear apocalypse by sheltering deep underground. Finally, it's worth noting that the version of

'Eighties' on the album appears to have been sped up (or slowed down), so isn't in any identifiable key. The single version, released 11 months before the album, was recorded at Olympic Studios in February 1984.

Bonus Tracks

These start with a Kid Jensen session from 1984 (recorded on 5 April and transmitted on 17 April), including a shortened, faster, punchier version of 'Eighties', 'Love Like Blood' instrumental B-Side 'Blue Feather' with vocal, and two tracks not available elsewhere: 'New Culture' and 'All Play Rebel'. 'New Culture' has a new wave/pop vibe on the unusually melodic verse but reverts to dissonance on the bridge and is also notable for a surprising pub-piano outro. 'Blue Feather' has some of Coleman's most poetic lyrics, including references to the iron curtain and a 'quill pen', and was apparently inspired by him coincidentally finding blue feathers at key moments. 'All Play Rebel' is built around a call-and-response chant, an unmistakably Raven bass riff and a properly catchy chorus, with an outro that reminds you that the Joke and Public Image Ltd were contemporaries.

'A New Day' 4:08 (Coleman/Ferguson/Kimsey/Raven/Walker)

This non-album single was recorded at The Hit Factory in NYC in May 1984 and co-written and produced by Chris Kimsey. Thematically it connects to 'Eighties' with references to running by day and dancing by night, but here these ideas are shown in a more positive light. The lyrics – an invitation to carve out your own life on your own terms with like-minded outsiders – are surprisingly optimistic for this point in the band's trajectory. The song has a pop bounciness and melodic quality with uplifting major-key verses, but counterpoint is provided by Geordie's dizzying guitar motif and an ambiguous minor-key chorus. The track ends with a marching-band-style drum pattern, leaving us with that archetypal Joke ambiguity between order and chaos: of our bodies, of our routines, of our individual identities, and of the societies we choose to create. 'A New Day' reached 56 in the UK Singles Chart in July 1984. The B-Side 'Dance Day', a remix of the A-Side, appears on the *RMXD* compilation.

The reissue's bonus tracks are rounded out by remixes of 'Blue Feather' (essentially the original Kimsey session recording of the track with Coleman's vocal restored), 'Multitudes' (a mostly instrumental mix confusingly titled 'The Madding Crowd', originally the B-Side of 'Kings and Queens'), 'Love Like Blood' (the 'Gestalt Mix') and 'Kings and Queens' ('Geordie's Dub Mix').

Brighter than a Thousand Suns (1986)

Personnel:
Jaz Coleman: voice, keyboards
Geordie: guitar
Paul Raven: bass guitar
Big Paul Ferguson: drums, percussion
Produced and mixed at: Hansa Tonstudio, Berlin by Chris Kimsey (restored original mixes of 'Adorations', 'Sanity', 'Chessboards', 'Twilight of the Mortal', 'Love of the Masses', 'Wintergardens', 'Rubicon', 'Goodbye to the Village', 'Exile')
Produced at: Battery Studios, London by Chris Tsangarides ('A Southern Sky' original mix)
Mixed by: Bob Kraushaar ('A Southern Sky' original mix)
Produced at: RAK Studios, London by Stewart Levine (restored original mixes of 'Victory', 'Ecstasy')
Engineer: Thomas Stiehler (Chris Kimsey restored original mixes), Glen Skinner (restored original mixes of 'Victory', 'Ecstasy')
Label: EG
Release date: November 1986
Running time (original CD release): 60:32
Highest chart places: UK: 54, USA: 194
Current edition: 2008 expanded remastered reissue on Virgin

Released only a few months after the Chernobyl disaster, and the first Killing Joke album to appear on CD in the UK, *Brighter than a Thousand Suns* reached 54 in the UK Albums Chart, disappointing for the record company in the context of *Night Time*'s UK high of 11, but an ironic vindication of Killing Joke's eventual antagonism towards the album as released. It crept onto the US *Billboard* 200 at 194. As with *Night Time*, *Brighter* was mostly written at Nomis Studios in London, with the main sessions taking place at Hansa Tonstudio, Berlin in October 1985. Vocals were recorded at the Wisseloord Studio in Hilversum, Netherlands.

The title refers to a verse of the *Bhagavad Gita* that Robert Oppenheimer called to mind on 16 July 1945 upon seeing the world's first nuclear bomb detonate above the New Mexico desert, which in English translates as: 'If the radiance of a thousand suns were to burst at once in the sky, that would be the splendour of the mighty one' (Chapter 11, Verse 12; the original verse describes Krishna revealing his divine form to Arjuna). Coleman's grandfather was a Sanskrit scholar and Coleman had already noted how there are verses in the *Mahabharata* which could be interpreted as describing a nuclear detonation.

While earlier albums have a viscerally pessimistic attitude to the end of all life on Earth, here the approach is more nuanced, with the band delivering a set of songs that interrogates the paradox of the human condition, in all its beautiful insanity.

Reproduced on the liner/booklet, 'Onion Peelings', the fourteenth chapter of Aleister Crowley's *The Book of Lies* is the epitome of Western Zen, describing an endless fractal pattern of laughter within sadness, within laughter, within sadness and so on. It ends with the master, Brother Perdurabo, insisting that even this paradox is nonsense, as true occult wisdom cannot be communicated with words. So, it's the perfect verse to epitomise the contradictions of Killing Joke's sixth studio album. The paradox of the band's most harmonically sophisticated group of songs failing to be commercially successful. Of its uplifting melodies conveying dark themes. Of the suite's core subject matter: the absurdist nature of humankind's dual obsession with creation and destruction. Where previously our Mr Punch had cajoled, raged and harangued, here our spirit-animal court jester is a crying-on-the-outside clown masking a laughing-on-the-inside trickster.

Bar the Tsangarides-produced 'A Southern Sky', the album was remixed by Julian Mendelsohn in a bid for commercial appeal (the band's last conscious attempt at such). These mixes added excess reverb, especially to the vocals, extended some tracks to 12" length and generally sanded down the still-jagged edges of Geordie's guitar. The version that was released in 1986 with these mixes is vastly inferior to the restored Chris Kimsey mixes and it was a revelation finally to hear the album as the band and Kimsey originally intended when the remaster was released in 2008. It is that restored version that is discussed here.

'Adorations' 4:28 (Killing Joke)

After a 1950s-style sci-fi sound effect that throws us right back to the first two albums (and which has a far greater impact than the damp squib that starts the Mendelsohn mix), Big Paul and Raven lay down a locked pulse that is at once irregular and mechanical. Geordie slices through the air with his six-string reaper's scythe, then adds a simple three-note descending Dorian motif while Jaz holds the line in the minor key, his voice clear and clean (it's always a revelation after listening to early Joke with its primal snarling, that Coleman has a genuinely emotive and affecting singing voice – and that voice is at its most sonorous on this album). The first verse introduces the paradoxical theme of the song, distilled in that prey/pray pun: 'Prey to the predator, love as we're falling down.'

The chorus, spun from Geordie's plaintive descending motif, takes this paradox and breaks it open with a simple truth, a decoding of the 'patterns': our worst and best experiences are inextricably conjoined. We cannot fight this truth; all we can do is venerate it. A short middle eight steps down a semitone, creating disorientation and unease. In keeping with the song's tensions, the major key is rendered mournful through counterpoint, with Raven stepping through key changes on the way back to the root, which takes us into the final verse: 'From apes or sons of god, let every act be sacred.' As primal beasts rutting in caves or alchemists reaching for the heavens, everything we do worships *The All* that is both us and not us. Never has paradox sounded so harmonious.

Released in August 1986 before the album, 'Adorations' was the first single from *Brighter* and reached 42 in the UK Singles Chart, disappointing considering the UK Top 20 placing and international chart success of 'Love Like Blood'. It also peaked at 34 in New Zealand.

'Sanity' 4:15 (Killing Joke)

> The pressure to have a hit came from the industry well before 'Love Like Blood'. After that, it only strengthened more, which led to the band breaking up and me leaving. But I think we did a great job during this time and wrote some great songs. It may not have been what we initially intended or ultimately wanted, but that's how you grow and evolve. It's a classic trial-and-error process.
> Big Paul Ferguson, interviewed by *Ox-Fanzine*, issue 157 August/September 2021

This is a beautifully structured, melancholic minor-key hymn to humankind: its deficits and glories, its rise and fall. A short, ominous synth effect leads into a keyboard and gated-drum intro that sounds especially progressive both in terms of chords and sonics. The one concession to the band's trademark harmonic tension is a sixth-interval synth bass line. Raven and Geordie join the arrangement as we hit a short chorus, an implicit injunction for humans to recover/find their moral compass 'for sanity's sake'. The second verse adds bass and additional dissonance in Geordie's haunting descending motif. The lyrics highlight the importance of memory, of our history to our future – for humanity, and for each of us personally.

A short bridge takes us into the third verse, which describes the best that awaits us according to the song's evocative poetry. As Coleman has said, 'the only optimism is realism'; we can only affect what we can control. Then we step up a tone for the song's final two lines, which contain its philosophical essence: the past and the future are a timeless dance expressed in the present by how we live now.

'Sanity' was released as the second and final single from the album in October 1986, a few weeks before the album release. It only reached 70 in the UK and didn't make an impact internationally (one can only conjecture what would have been the fate of the infinitely superior Kimsey mix). This signalled the beginning of the end for this incarnation of the band, even if they didn't know it yet.

'Chessboards' 5:47 (Killing Joke)

This track follows on from 'Sanity' and 'Adorations' with further development of the album's subject matter: the paradox of life and death in a godless universe. The first verse here references Crowley's 'Onion Peelings' directly: 'we've been crying, crying'. The chorus, each line ending in '…tears run down', continues the idea that when faced with the brutality of existence, all one can do is weep. In the second verse, we're described as passive pieces played by the hand of fate.

The core truth of a song is often found near its temporal centre, whether poetic, musical, or both. The middle eight is traditionally in a different key to the verses and chorus and that convention is adhered to here with lyrics that pin the crux of the track: 'compassion in us cries'. All we have is our mind's ability to comprehend and our heart's capacity for empathy. And these two attributes are as powerful as any civilisation or the hand of an aloof god. We can learn to move ourselves.

Musically, the song is a good example of the band's growing harmonic complexity, partly down to Coleman's increasing interest in classical composition (the shift from C Lydian bridge to C minor chorus is particularly elegant). There are more modes/keys used here than in previous songs, and although the dissonance is almost entirely gone – though there's no way Geordie would ever relinquish his trademark sharpened fourths – there's tension in the multiple key changes. Some familiar vocalised whoops from Jaz take us full circle, moving from the Mixolydian of the verses back to the Lydian of the intro/bridge and ending on that mode's bright fourth: a musical metaphor for the glimmering of our inherent capacity for positive change.

'Twilight of the Mortal' 4:13 (Killing Joke)

The Joke's deepening musical sophistication continues with another track featuring multiple chord progressions and clever use of relative keys (a pair of major and minor), which taken together, evoke and undermine the hubristic, 'heroic' pomposity of humans and their ephemeral civilisations – the subject matter of the lyrics. The title is a play on Nietzsche's *Twilight of the Idols*, with the Joke suggesting it is man as Earth-bound god that needs to be smashed with a hammer. The first two verses distil the essence of humankind's overreach: aware that life is short but resolving to vanquish reality with illusory immortality, while simultaneously waging wars so we can triumph over life with death. As hubris is to civilisation, so egotism is to the individual. Both are a form of narcissism. This is why the annihilation of a civilisation – a core lyrical theme of *Brighter* – can be a potent metaphor for the destruction of the ego that is essential to enlightenment. Civilisational collapse is here analogous to ego death.

Verse three echoes this analogy by finding resolution in the alchemical 'Great Work', Crowley's 'Law' ('Love under Will') and Jung's individuation, paths that are focused on acceptance – of our own dark shadow and physical mortality – and the eternal life of the spirit rather than the body. Living well and striving for illumination while you're alive is what matters, as the dipping sun of death comes to us all. This is echoed in the music's endpoint, which rather than cycle back to the intro motif, as has been the Joke's preferred song structure for five albums, ends with a reprise of the middle eight's ascending chord progression and a reset to major: life is always cut short and then it's someone else's turn.

'Love of the Masses' 6:07 (Killing Joke)

Infinitely preferable to the Mendelsohn mix, on which the lead vocal is so drenched in reverb that it's pretty much unlistenable, this restored version is also longer by a minute and a half, reinstating the third verse, which was cut on the original 1986 release. This omission detracts from our understanding of the song, as the last verse carries the track's core meaning: we can be heroes as part of a 'common destiny', in which all are 'affected without prejudice' and self is forfeited 'amongst the masses'. This verse also clarifies the double meaning of the chorus, which alludes to the love of the masses for a 'hero', but also love for the masses by each individual part of that mass. In answer to the question 'Why do we love them?' the answer suggested here is because we are them and they are us. None of us is special, or rather: all of us are special.

The music deftly uses harmonic counterpoint to create momentum and tension, and there are some deeply satisfying prog-style chord progressions, with the instrumental middle eight being somewhat reminiscent of *Drama*-era Yes. There's also an effective use of a double-triplet rhythm, used intermittently to punctuate the pivot between sections. The track uses Joke's signature symmetrical song structure to good effect, echoing the first verse idea of flowing 'backwards to our source' as we fade out on a reprise of the verse motif.

'A Southern Sky' 4:38 (Killing Joke)

Recorded in August 1986, ten months after the Kimsey sessions, this is Coleman's first paean to New Zealand. He first visited Aotearoa before the band recorded *Brighter* and has been based there since the early 1990s, becoming a citizen in 1995. He's understandably reticent to share the exact location and name of the small island on which he has put down roots, referring to it only as 'Cythera', a name with mythical associations (see the track 'In Cythera' on *MMXII*).

'A Southern Sky' also foreshadows the splintering of the band during the recording of the next album, as this track is, both musically and in terms of subject matter, pretty much all Coleman, though Big Paul gets to do his version of 1980s power-ballad drumming in the choruses. Raven's pulsing root notes are texture only, while Geordie is so low in the mix, he's barely there at all. But none of that matters in the moment, as melodically and harmonically, this is supremely elegant songwriting, again making use of relative keys. Coleman's voice has never sounded better in its clean form, with all those years as a church chorister paying off.

The Romantic-style lyrics are self-explanatory, though the first two lines of verse two pin a key idea: 'man is finding wealth' in nature rather than in material things. This is an idea to which the Joke often return, most bluntly on the track 'Money is Not Our God' from *Extremities*. Again, the middle eight contains the song's core sentiment: Coleman can see his long-term future in this place, 'continuity when all's said and done'. In *Letters from Cythera*, Coleman recounts how a trip to New Zealand in November 1986 – the month *Brighter* was released – sealed his intent to find the ideal location for his Southern Hemisphere redoubt and eventually settle there.

'Victory' 3:57 (Killing Joke)

'Victory' uses a 1980s-style arrangement and sonics to revisit the funk grooves of the first two albums, creating a body twitch that's anchored by Raven's perfectly weighted bass. This is also the track on which the difference between the original (now-restored) mix and Mendelsohn's is most marked, with the first-release version running to 7:11. It's not so utterly hideous as to require erasure from KJ's history, but it should really have been a 12" B-Side. By contrast, Kimsey's original mix is lean and evocative, showcasing the song's strengths without excessive knob-twiddling.

The track uses counterpoint to create tension, encapsulating the paradox of what we humans consider to be a triumph versus what we perhaps should. The verses combine a bass riff in the minor, a guitar motif in Phrygian, and synth and vocal lines in Mixolydian, but woven together in such a way as never to crossover from tension into outright dissonance. The first verse evokes the Iran-Iraq War, which ran from 1980 to 1988 and, specifically in the US's support for Iraq, planted the seeds for both Iraq wars. The regional instability had wider reach (Russia supported Iran) and contributed to the Cold War nuclear threat, so central to Killing Joke's oeuvre. The end of the third verse and the chorus reprise firmly plant the band's flag: 'fools are bent on making history'; is this 'some kind of victory', especially for those who do not wish to live in perpetual bloody conflict? 'Where is the sanity?' implores Jaz, a call-back to the album's second track.

'Wintergardens' 5:32 (Killing Joke)

A plaintive guitar figure from Geordie sets the minor-key mood for this meditation on humankind's status as 'god-children', able to create weapons of annihilation like gods, but, like children, unable to apply the wisdom and foresight with which to control their use or proliferation. The song title is poignantly tragic, calling to mind the brittle, crystalline beauty of nature in the deepest cold, while simultaneously summoning the idea of perpetual nuclear winter: 'one season always.' Coleman's voice is particularly affecting, reminding us once again what a unique vocalist he is, as proficient at gut-churning growl as a soul-piercing lament. The march rhythm in the drums conjures our accelerating descent into self-destruction while the chiming guitar heralds its imminence. In contrast, Raven's slap-and-pop bass fizzes with childlike exuberance. The chorus highlights this contrast: we run and play 'like children' in winter gardens, then we run and cry as we behold the lethal chaos that we've wrought.

'Rubicon' 6:35 (Killing Joke)

This is an absolute barnstormer and, taken entirely on its own merits rather than in comparison with earlier Joke, it's one of their standout tracks. Lyrically, it is one of the most holistic encapsulations of the Killing Joke worldview, commenting on religion, science, politics and spirituality. Everything here is centred around the album's core theme of humankind's extraordinary capacity for self-destruction – and that within that death drive is always the glimmer of hope that humans can be, and achieve, more than their basest instincts dictate.

Everything here is a paradox: an 'age of miracles' culminating in an atomic bomb, the 'ascent of man' circling the planet in destructive 'speed and steel', god is 'on every side – and in every legion', because everyone imbues their delusion with the certainty of religion, whether their ideology is theocratic or totalitarian (no surprise that the band loathe ideological fanaticism as much as they loathe religious dogma). The chorus is where we find that glimmer of hope: 'revolution' is a point of no return, for good or ill; similarly, 'evolution' is a metaphorical crossing of the Rubicon. This trajectory is humankind either traversing the self-annihilation tipping point or irreversibly ascending to a more self-aware state. The second bridge is bitterly evocative: bells toll and 'holy banners fly', and 'all will talk of freedom'. Big Paul's incessant double-time marking in the middle eight provides a timely reminder of our accelerating Doomsday Clock. Tick-tock.

It's ironic that the Mendelsohn mix, which is stretched out to 7:06, features a manic Coleman laugh in the middle eight and ends with an extended atomic boom, both of which perhaps Kimsey and the band thought were too on the nose, considering this is the album's de facto title track.

'Goodbye to the Village' 5:17 (Killing Joke)

This is a bitter farewell to the England of the early 1960s (the band were all born between 1958 and 1961, tail-end post-war children), which despite its feudal flaws and Empire apologism, contained a warmth of community and tribal belonging which has since been all but obliterated by 'progress'. The first verse paints an encroaching dystopia. The title of the Joke's 2015 album is foreshadowed by 'forests of pylons', albeit without the glorious pun implicit in the singular. Verse two reminds us that a land is only as healthy as its watercourses, and England's waterways have been 'running ill' for most of the past 60 years (this also resonates with the toxic river foam of 'The Wait'). The third verse adds contaminated earth to poisoned water, adding a mythic Arthurian element: 'Where soil will not provide, no king and land are one.'

The final lines, repeated to fade, are a disconsolate return of the first-person to second-person shift, similarly and potently used on earlier albums.

'Exile' 6:27 (Killing Joke)
Brighter, by now feeling every bit as much a concept album as the previous three LPs, ends with a metronomic lament for everything lost to conformity, industry and 'civilisation'. The almost-repeat of the bass chime and propulsive rhythm that open the previous track pins the final two songs together in a way that gives the whole album a suite-like feel. The lyrics suggest that everything we invest in the march of progress is ultimately lost: we lose what we had to give up, and we lose what we so desperately wanted to build. Rather than the raging pessimism of the earlier albums, here, the sense is a deep sadness for the futility of our hubris, a hubris that exiles us from ourselves to the extent that we find it easier to accept annihilation than to change our trajectory.

Coleman expresses the deep irony of us humans only realising the magnitude of what we've done once we've done it, as Oppenheimer did in the New Mexico desert when he recalled an additional verse of the *Bhagavad Gita*: 'Now I am become Death, the destroyer of worlds' (Chapter 11, Verse 32). The band even question their own oft-stated intent of using music to foment change through dissent: 'No revolutions in four-four time'. The final image is one of despair – of nature stagnated and life dammed (and damned) at the source.

Bonus Tracks

'Ecstasy' 4:10 (Killing Joke)
Produced by Stewart Levine during the same sessions as 'Victory' in March-April 1986, 'Ecstasy' combines multiple modes and keys, all rooted in C, and one has to wonder whether it being on Side 'C' of the 'Adorations' double-pack 7" is an elaborate musicological in-joke. The bright Lydian intro gives way to a minor-key motif underneath Mixolydian vocals, an uncanny musical dissonance encapsulating the paradox in 'the cruelty of rapture'. The lyrics engage with the elusive feminine archetypal/occult energy, describing how she 'plays in games with me'.

The funky chorus is Coleman's one-line cry of 'I've reached ecstasy!' suggesting he's in the trance of an ecstatic mystic. A short, angular breakdown with some prime Jaz vocalising underpins the feeling that this dance is shared by a trickster goddess and her holy fool. I recommend listening to this track between 'A Southern Sky' and 'Victory' if playing it with the rest of the album, as 'Exile' ideally needs to be the last song you hear in one sitting.

The other two bonus tracks are 12" remixes of 'Adorations' (The Supernatural Mix) and 'Sanity' (The Insane Mix) by Zeus B. Held. The latter is far superior to the former.

Outside the Gate (1988)

Personnel:
Jaz Coleman: voice, keyboards
Geordie Walker: guitar, bass guitar
Raven: bass guitar (uncredited)
Jimmy Copley: drums
Jeff Scantlebury: percussion
Additional rap on 'Stay One Jump Ahead': JC 001 aka Jonathan Chandra Pandy
Produced at: The Whitehouse by Coleman/Walker
Recorded by: Martin Rex
Mixed at: RAK Studios by Glenn Skinner
Label: EG
Release date: July 1988
Running time (original CD release): 50:11
Highest chart places: UK: 92, US: not released
Current edition: 2008 expanded remastered reissue on Virgin

Thirty-five years after the event, it's hard to imagine just how much of a wrench – even a betrayal – this album felt when it was first released in 1988 (it had been recorded almost a year earlier in late summer 1987). In hindsight, it can be listened to without knee-jerk prejudice or unreasonable expectations and under these circumstances, it's a set with multiple delights and surprises: sonically intriguing, compositionally sophisticated, lyrically complex and with no less rage or provocation than any of the previous KJ albums, even if presented in a radically different package. The early sessions for the album were fraught, compounded by Big Paul leaving the band. This opened the door for drummer Jimmy Copley and percussionist Jeff Scantlebury, who bring rock-solid rhythms and jazz-funk grooves, respectively. Raven removed his name from the project before its release.

Centred on Coleman's Arabic-idiom inspiration and classical-music exploration, *Outside the Gate* has a mosaic-like quality, combining 1980s electronic pop, Art of Noise-style faux-orchestral soundscapes and progressive rock. The other key facet is Geordie's guitar, showcasing his absolute mastery of the instrument: throwing off majestic prog riffs, soaring mini-solos and delicately picked motifs like all this has been his day job for the past nine years. The absence of Big Paul, who often collaborated on lyrics for the previous albums, means that songs become more personal, with the esoteric elements moving from subtext to centre stage. Though it's easy to be frustrated with this change, it reflects a key moment in Coleman's creative evolution through a laying bare of his unique worldview: by turns possessing the social critique of a hair-trigger anarchist and the deep thinking of a philosopher-adept, the proselytising of a firebrand preacher and the introspection of a bohemian poet, the fury of a lump hammer and the wistfulness of a willow branch.

None of these tracks are ever played live (even 'America', which personally I'd love to hear in an industrial metal arrangement by the current line-up) and the album bore nothing but negative associations for Big Paul and Raven, while Geordie has now all but disowned it. Even Jaz himself later admitted that, as some already suspected, *Outside the Gate* isn't really a Killing Joke album in any meaningful sense (though there is so much Geordie on the record that it would have been bizarre for the album to land as a Coleman solo work). It's inarguable that without half the band going their separate ways at this point, Killing Joke's history would not ultimately have followed the trajectory it did, so whether you revel in this album's experimental eclecticism and multi-layered occult references, as I do, or simply loathe it with a passion, it's a fact that this bizarre, uneven set is a critical part of a necessary history that would lead to eight more albums and counting.

The cover art design by Andrzej Klimowski is a collage of Coleman's and Geordie's faces, giving the impression that Geordie has been torn open to reveal Coleman within, a neat metaphor for the way the album hides occult wisdom inside popular music idioms. The original release was dedicated to Conny Plank, who had died in December 1987, aged only 47. *Outside the Gate* was not released in the US and wasn't toured at all. It reached an uninspiring 92 in the UK Albums Chart. Indeed, it underperformed to such an extent that EG and their distributor Virgin cut the band loose, with the hard-won silver lining that Killing Joke would never again have to compromise with the demands of a major label.

'America' 3:48 (Coleman/Walker)

Prominently featuring Coleman's synth and vocal, this track is both a wholesale departure from the Killing Joke sound up to this point and a natural evolutionary step from *Brighter*. Coleman's classical influences and compositional craft are at once apparent, with a song structure that has multiple repeats of the bridge and chorus around two verses with several key changes. The classical tropes, especially the chord sequences, give the track an inescapably progressive sound, while the lack of foregrounded guitar drives the sonics far from what we've come to expect. Apart from the bridge, where he provides a full-on prog-style picked ascending motif, Geordie is pretty much drowned out by waves of synth.

The lyrics drip with irony as Jaz decries the USA. The bridge extends and deepens the perversity while the verses mercilessly puncture the American worldview: 'West is best and might is right'. Everyone must compromise to fit in, but this causes one's 'moral code' to be 'on overload'. All this is simply the price of riches and freedom. No one wants to be a 'loser' wasting away in a bar, even though America still seems to be full of those. The track's most inflammatory lines ooze bitter sarcasm as 'fireworks in the Gulf' are juxtaposed with 'champagne at home'.

'America' was the first of two singles from *Outside the Gate*. Released in April 1988, it reached 77 in the UK Singles Chart. The cover art, again by Andrzej Klimowski, is notable as it features a collage including the Empire State Building, a mosque and Islamic crescent moon, a fashionable NYC Soho socialite, and Batman, the Joker's nemesis (one could read Batman as the USA to the band's Killing Joker).

'My Love of This Land' 4:12 (Coleman/Walker)

In direct contrast to the previous track and following on from *Brighter*'s 'Goodbye to the Village', here's a gentler take on the end of England as it was until the huge upheavals that began in the 1960s – changes which Coleman witnessed growing up in Cheltenham, Gloucestershire in the English West Country. The arrangement is nicely balanced, Geordie's guitar prominent throughout, with keyboards leading the verses while bass and drums give the chorus momentum. Coleman may not write traditional love songs, but he certainly knows how to write affectionate love letters to places with which he has bonded.

A plaintive minor-key motif from Geordie that wouldn't be out of place on a Fish-era Marillion track lays the scene for the sun setting on 'England's green and pleasant land', the first of two quotes from William Blake's poem 'And did those feet in ancient time' which was set to music by Parry as 'Jerusalem'. Jaz wants to rip down the fences that are scarring the landscape, ignoring the 'voice of education' in his head that wants to rationalise and dissuade. Lyrically, the chorus is a rather lovely encapsulation of the feelings experienced by anyone who's lived in and appreciated the pastoral beauty of the English countryside.

The middle eight is deceptively clever, using its chord progression to move quickly from pensive lull through lush abandon to ominous tension, and Geordie's warm wash of vibrato guitar is critical to this effect. The second (here adapted) quote from the Blake poem closes the third verse: 'And did those feet in ancient times, or was it just our imaginations?' The further we move from rural life the harder it is to imagine that Jesus, or other far older mystical beings, set foot in Albion. It's a perfectly formed and evocative song that rewards listening with open ears. The second and final single from *Outside the Gate*, 'My Love of This Land' was released in July 1988. It reached 89 in the UK Singles Chart.

'Stay One Jump Ahead' 3:11 (Coleman/Walker)

This is where we lurch from the sublime to the utterly bonkers, with Coleman's only attempt at rap (though there are a couple of post-2003 tracks that have something of a nu-metal vibe to their vocal delivery). Taken on its own merits, this is a wonderfully nutty combination of vital hooks, visceral rhythms and vituperative sentiment, again attacking the lethal hypocrisy of the American dream. Copley and Scantlebury stand out on this track, plus

Above: Killing Joke in 1982. L-R: Jaz Coleman, Paul Raven, Big Paul Ferguson, Geordie Walker. (*David Corio; Michael Ochs Archive/Getty Images*)

Below: The reformed original line-up in 2015. L-R: Youth, Jaz, Geordie, Big Paul. (*Tom Barnes*)

Left: 'The fire increases, masks decay.' 'The Wait', *Killing Joke* 1980. (*Virgin Records*)

Right: 'Discord dances, discord Earth.' 'Exit', *What's THIS For...!* 1981. (*Virgin Records*)

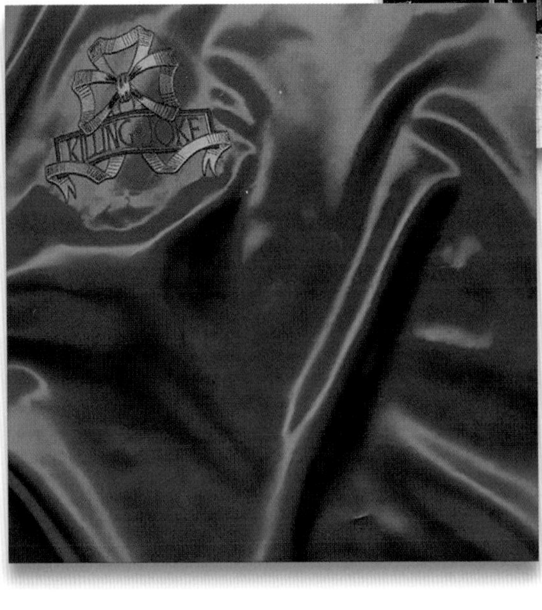

Left: 'Back to square one and the old school backfire.' 'Empire Song', *Revelations* 1982. (*Virgin Records*)

Right: 'Banner and festival where the wine and plenty flow.' 'Feast of Blaze', *Fire Dances* 1983. (*Virgin Records*)

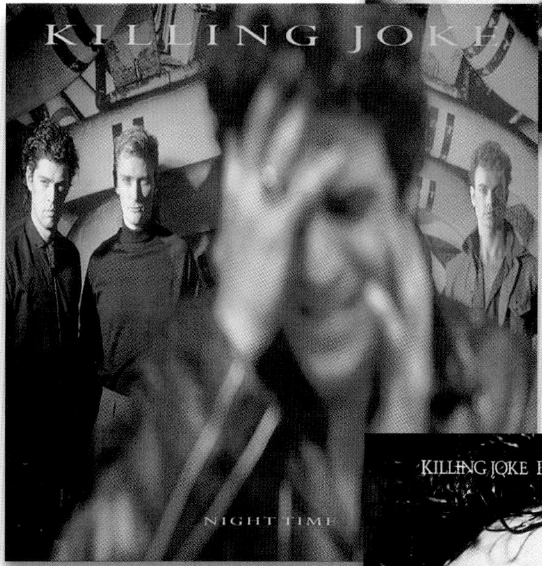

Left: 'And through the madness through the terror we must pass.' 'Darkness Before Dawn', *Night Time* 1985. (*Virgin Records*)

Right: 'Liberty in new dimensions ruthless and spectacular.' 'Rubicon', *Brighter than a Thousand Suns* 1986. (*Virgin Records*)

Above: St. Mary's Church, Charlton Kings where Coleman absorbed the English choral tradition. (*Nic Ransome*)

Left: 11 Portland Road, Notting Hill in 2023. Location of Big Paul's flat where he and Jaz first met in 1978. (*Nic Ransome*)

Right: 3 Berkeley Place, Cheltenham in 2023. In 1979, this was 3 High Street, where the four original members first played together. (*Gillian Skeffington*)

Below: Junction of Elgin Crescent and Ladbroke Grove in 2023; location of 'Malicious Mansions', a squat where the band lived in the early days. (*Nic Ransome*)

Left: 'So I ascend to the blinding light. Then plummet to the thickest darkness.' 'The Calling', *Outside the Gate* 1988. (*Virgin Records*)

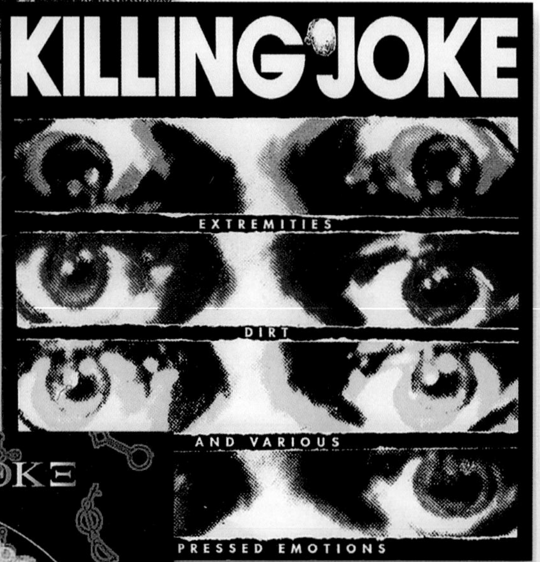

Right: 'Money property assets before lives. Green gestures of a dying planet.' 'Age of Greed', *Extremities, Dirt and Various Repressed Emotions* 1990. (*Candlelight Records*)

Left: 'Leave my body, lose myself. Leave this planet, leave this hell.' 'Whiteout', *Pandemonium* 1994. (*Cooking Vinyl*)

Right: 'When we awake to the whisper of the voice.' 'Aeon', *Democracy* 1996. (*Cooking Vinyl*)

Left: 'This sense of emptiness. As we create this mess.' 'Seeing Red', *Killing Joke* 2003. (*Spinefarm Records*)

Right: 'Led to the slaughter, led by false hope.' 'Judas Goat', *Hosannas from the Basements of Hell* 2006. (*Cooking Vinyl*)

Left: 'And the fire that drives us overcomes all pain.' 'Honour the Fire', *Absolute Dissent* 2010. (*Spinefarm Records*)

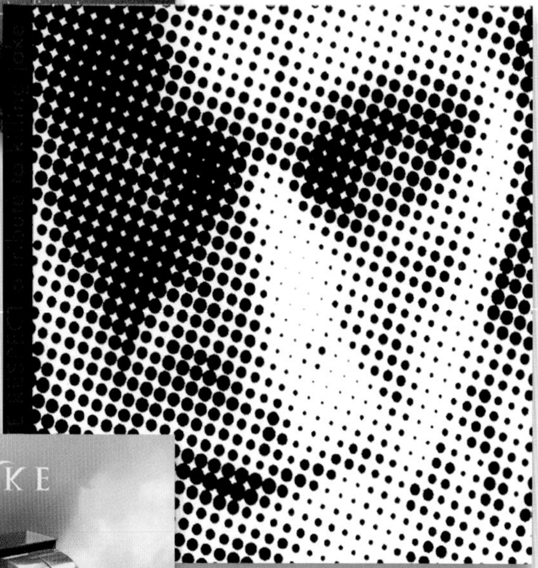

Right: Never cloned, often honoured. *Absolute Respect* 2010. (*Spinefarm Records*)

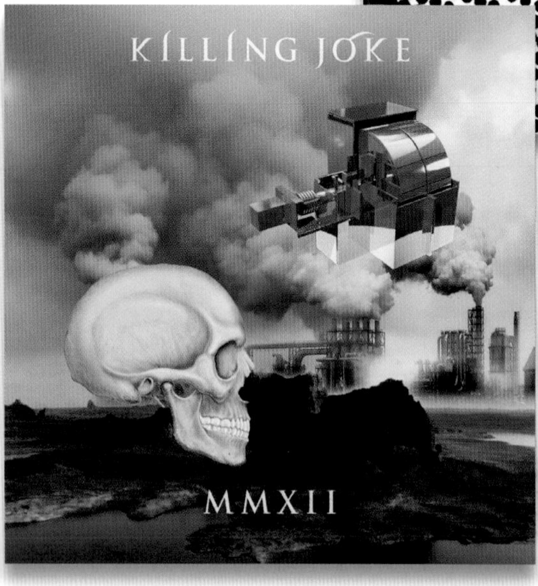

Left: 'There's a list going round and it's likely you're on it.' 'FEMA Camp', *MMXII* 2012. (*Spinefarm Records*)

Right: 'To every man a hope above. To every child a tale of love.' 'Into the Unknown', *Pylon* 2015. (*Spinefarm Records*)

Left: The 2020 version of *Turn to Red*. Cover art by Mike Coles including detail of Centre Point, London. (*Killing Joke Records*)

Right: The gloriously apocalyptic cacophony of Mike Coles's cover art for the 2022 *Lord of Chaos* EP. (*Spinefarm Records*)

Left: The Mike Coles cover art for 1979's *Turn to Red* EP, featuring the first appearance of Joke mascot Mr Punch. (*Killing Joke Records*)

Right: London's Centre Point in 2023, used by Mike Coles for the cover art of the *Turn to Red* EP. (*Nic Ransome*)

Right: Colegate, Norwich in 2022. Background to the Mike Coles cover art for *What's THIS For...!* (*Jordan/Alaska*)

Below: Colegate, Norwich showing St. Michael Coslany Church, now The Oak Circus Centre. (*Jordan/Alaska*)

Left: 1996's psytrance-heavy *Alchemy – The Remixes* features Juno Reactor, Total Eclipse and Hallucinogen. (*Butterfly Recordings*)

Right: The first recording by the reformed original line-up since 1982, *Duende – The Spanish Sessions*, 2008. (*Killing Joke Records*)

Right: Re-released multiple times, *The Unperverted Pantomime* (here in 2006 guise) centres on a landmark live recording from 1979. (*Killing Joke Records*)

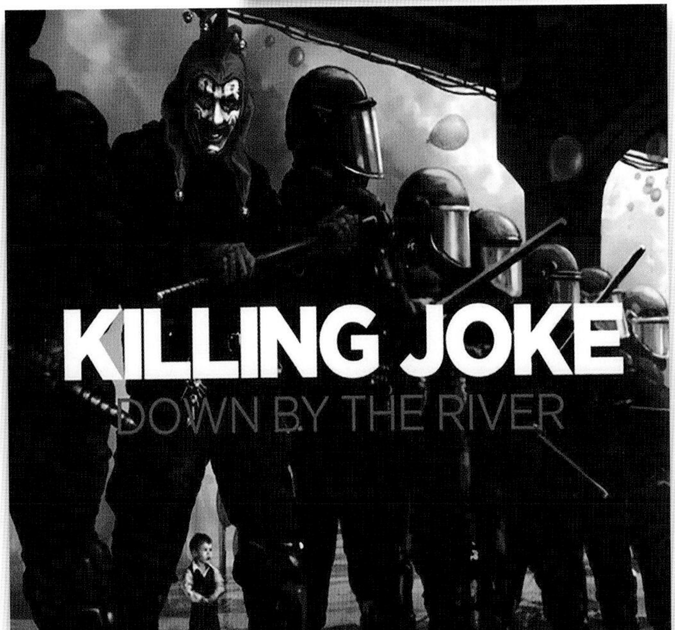

Left: Designed by Big Paul, a suitably dissonant cover for the 2011 recording from London's Royal Festival Hall. (*Killing Joke Records*)

Left: The bill for Reading Rocks 1986. Killing Joke headlined the Friday night.

Below: The author (under pink balloon) wrecking to Cardiacs at Reading 1986. (*Chris Crawford*)

Right: The Mike Coles programme cover for Follow the Leaders at the Royal Albert Hall. (*Nic Ransome*)

Below: 'How do you get to the Albert Hall?' 'Magick!' Follow the Leaders, 12 March 2023.

Above: Cheltenham mural by Andy 'Dice' Davies of Jaz with *Ordre des Arts et des Lettres* medallion. (*Nic Ransome*)

Below: *Fortissimo di saldatura!* aka Welding volume! (*Ester Segarra*)

there's some lovely growling bass. There's also a tweet-and-you'll-miss-it guest spot for Anglo-Indian-Irish rapper JC 001, aka Jonathan Chandra Pandy, who goes head-to-head with Jaz. It's probably not a coincidence that the band this track most resembles is the KLF/JAMs.

A superior 'Extended Mix' on the original album release features three additional no-punches-pulled verses (references to Iran-Contra, the White House as Great Satan, the sinking of the Rainbow Warrior, the City of London Big Bang and the Great Storm of 1987) as well as an extended flow from JC 001, which is a big-up to Geordie. Plus, the title of the Joke's 1994 album is foreshadowed. This 'Extended Mix' does not feature on the reissue but does appear on the 2008 Virgin compilation *RMXD*. The remaster features a 'Dub' remix not included in 1988.

'Unto the Ends of the Earth' 6:08 (Coleman/Walker)

Another song about Coleman's New Zealand escape, this time from the perspective of yearning to be there with, we assume, a significant other. This track was written during a time of escalating Cold War tension, heightened by the Iran-Iraq war (which finally ended in August 1988 after the album was originally released).

Musically the track is somewhat disjointed with multiple motifs and idioms competing for space, including early musical evocations of Oceania and more synthesised orchestral sonics, but the vocal carries the song with its obvious passion for Coleman's Pacific hideaway and inescapable paranoia of the coming nuclear 'long winter'. The ending is particularly affecting, with Jaz imploring his audience of one to '…listen! I hear the Pied Piper!', but this time the Pied Piper wants to lead them to a Southern Hemisphere escape rather than the pagan rituals of rural England as on *Fire Dances*. Or is this Pied Piper a trickster, who wants to lead them back to the chaos of the city? In October 1987, Coleman was all but ready to emigrate to New Zealand when a clairvoyant told him that this was not the time (recounted in *Letters from Cythera*). It's arguable that if Coleman had left the UK for good at this juncture, it would have been the end of Killing Joke – or at least their history would have been entirely different.

'The Calling' 4:45 (Coleman/Walker)

This is the first of two tracks on the album that deal overtly with the occult and magickal practices, here specifically rituals designed to release and integrate the so-called 'forgotten ones' as described in *The Courtauld Talks* (see below). 'The Calling' is the tradition and practice of magick, challenging 'the faithful to find themselves'. This quote from *The Courtauld Talks* is pertinent:

> Margaret Crosby, the author of the writing I have previously read, who goes under the name of Soror Andahadna, explains further the implications of

polarity. The forgotten ones are your sources of personal magickal power. The higher you reach to the gods of light, the lower you must plunge to the gods of darkness. And, furthermore, to ignore their presence, is to guarantee their eventual dominion over your will. Kenneth Grant, the author of *Outside the Circles of Time* adds: the forgotten ones are the forces which the Christians declared Satanic and which by suppression have now grown to formidable dimensions threatening imminent disaster for humanity.
Jaz Coleman, The Courtauld Institute, London, 19 September 1987

Coleman's aim, as described in the lyrics, is to 'ascend to the blinding light' and then 'plummet to the thickest darkness'. This is an encapsulation of the occult maxim 'As above, so below', which in practice means experiencing both extremes so that balance may be found. It means one must 'worship polarity'. The other key idea in the lyrics is that every person must take control of their own magickal path: 'Follow yourselves as leaders'. This is a deliberate antithesis to the idea ironically described in the song 'Follow the Leaders' in which we are painted as alienated automata with no will or individuality. The song's last line references the 'Great Work'.

'Obsession' 3:35 (Coleman/Walker)
It's hard not to think about 9/11 when listening to this track, with its references to multi-national monopolies, disputes between Abrahamic religions, adrenalin, suspense, and release, along with the line, 'we build the tower, tower falls down' (though there's a Tarot reference here also). As with 'Empire Song' and the Falklands War, it seems that Killing Joke have a kind of magickal precognition – or at least an ability to tap directly into the bleeding edge of the zeitgeist. Coleman often explains this by stating that the 'objective was to predict the future by writing it'. The chorus lyrics are the apotheosis of Coleman's imagery on this album, contrasting the fall of civilisation (a recurrent theme here and on *Brighter*) with the sex-magick orgasm. Sex and dying. Humans as horny death cult.

'Tiahuanaco' 3:27 (Coleman/Walker)
A change of pace and tone heralded by some reflective Geordie picking, this musical travelogue tells the story of Coleman's experiences in South America, in particular a visit to Tiahuanaco in what is now Bolivia. The juxtaposition of the sacred and the profane is deeply evocative: Coleman wants to see gods, but instead, all he can see is a girl 'begging for food'. Then an epiphany: the 'weeping god' is in that girl's face. Again, the fall-of-civilisation theme, but here Jaz is in the ruins of the Tiwanaku culture, which includes the Akapana pyramid, the Gate of the Sun arch and the Kalasasaya complex. The subtext is clear: one day there'll be beggars in the ruins of the West. Every civilisation believes it will last forever, but every civilisation falls. As the song ends with some full-flight prog, Coleman finds 'determination' rather than despair.

'Outside the Gate' 8:57 (Coleman/Walker)

The epic title track combines the microcosm of magickal practice with the macrocosm of a world gone mad using the lens of Coleman's own travels as a seeker of knowledge and wisdom. The chorus holds the song's essence as Jaz dons his mask and passes through the arch, 'outside the gate'. The 'gate' is nominally the Gate of the Sun from the previous track but is archetypally the arch through which every neophyte must pass to become an initiate. Through which every initiate must pass to become an adept. Through which every adept must pass to become a magus. We're always outside the gate because once we're through the arch, another gate awaits, the last gate being death.

Flowing water and gossamer keyboards set the ethereal scene. A Middle Eastern riff interjects, and the song segues into a minor-key verse which finds Coleman reflecting in both senses. He sees his shadow in the pain and hate of the world, rendering it 'underworld' and, recognising this, resolves to acknowledge and confront the evil within himself. The Middle Eastern riff returns, heralding the chorus, which is followed by a bridge with some Fripp-style guitar and orchestral stabs. A soaring Geordie figure spins into the second verse. The middle eight further showcases Geordie in melodic mode (and, of course, he's as adept at yearning melody as he is at eviscerating dissonance) before the Arabic riff returns, now dervish-manic and in an irregular 13/12 as Coleman intones: 'He invokes entities vast and mindless!' In *The Courtauld Talks*, Coleman gives detailed background to this choice of time signature, including how the number 13 signifies 'Pluto, or plutonium, symbolising regeneration as the basis of the rhythm'.

Having survived this ritual, the third verse is a hymn to everything that the true freedom of initiation can bring. The final chorus provides both closure and promise as Jaz again dons his mask and passes through the arch, but this time he closes the gate. There is a potent double meaning here: to enter the domain of the 'Great Work', you must symbolically wear a spiritual mask, go through an arch, and close the gate on the mundane world behind you, but to re-enter the material world, you must do the same thing in reverse, lest you go mad. The final three minutes suggest this journey, from synth-effect stone-scrape openings and closings, to an evocative section featuring some gorgeous interplay between keyboards and guitar.

Bonus Tracks

'May Day' 3:53 (Coleman/Walker)

Recorded during the same sessions as demos for songs that ended up on the album proper (three of these demos are included as Bonus Tracks) this is a delicate ballad of yearning, with thematic links to *Fire Dances*. The lyrics are again dangerously close to a genuine love song, though the subtextual sex magick and pagan references suggest that the female in question is more than human, perhaps symbolically a goddess in human form.

In the bardic chorus, Coleman waits for 'May Day to come'. May Day is Celtic Beltane, a fire festival, but Coleman has no fire left because his passion has burnt through it. The verses, as now should be recognised as an ongoing theme, lament the industrialisation and corruption of the land, but however bad it gets, Jaz can still take solace in 'the earth and the stars'. There is also a first appearance of lines re-used in 'Tiahuanaco'.

'Jihad' 6:04 (Coleman/Walker)
The B-Side to 'America' is an instrumental in which Coleman explores his fascination with Arabic music, a passion which led to the 1990 collaboration with Anne Dudley, *Songs from the Victorious City*. The title literally means 'struggle' or 'striving' in Arabic, both an armed or nonviolent struggle of resistance against an occupying force, and an internal striving for wisdom: the quest for self-knowledge, which is a key part of both Islam and Islamic mysticism such as Sufism and often referred to as the 'Greater' jihad. Whereas here, the music is almost entirely created using keyboards and synths emulating Middle Eastern instruments and arrangements (though Jeff Scantlebury's percussion adds a semi-authentic gloss) 1994's *Pandemonium* would utilise Arabic musicians and instruments.

There are also early versions of 'My Love of This Land' and 'Obsession', plus an instrumental version of 'Unto the Ends of the Earth', the 12" extended mix of 'America' (worth a listen, especially if you want to open a direct portal to the 1980s) and a funk-maximised 'dub' mix of 'Stay One Jump Ahead' driven by Jeff Scantlebury's groove-deep percussion.

The Courtauld Talks (1989)
This is an hour-long public lecture by Coleman, given on 19 September 1987 at The Courtauld Institute in London, within weeks of completion of the *Outside the Gate* sessions but well before the album's release. Geordie, Jeff Scantlebury and Coleman provide an accompaniment on acoustic guitar, percussion and synthesiser, respectively. The sonics provide a hypnotic soundscape that focuses the mind on Coleman's words, which range across the essence of Killing Joke, the occult, psychology, the nuclear age, the recording of *Outside the Gate*'s title track and geopolitical instability. It's a fascinating time capsule of Coleman's worldview at the time and demonstrates the by-turns Mercurial and Plutonian nature of a ceaselessly catalysing mind that is never more aflame than when confronting the darkest corners of human experience. It's also a revealing companion piece to *Brighter*, due to Coleman's focus on thermonuclear apocalypse and civilisational collapse. The cover art features the original version of the triple-headed serpent logo as drawn by Geordie (originally as a symbol for the Gathering). If you find the lecture suitably intriguing (it's available to stream), your next stop should be Coleman's book *Letters from Cythera*. Though nominally a Killing Joke release, this is not usually counted as a KJ album.

Extremities, Dirt and Various Repressed Emotions (1990)

Personnel:
Jaz Coleman: vocals, keyboards
Geordie: guitar
Raven: bass
Martin Atkins: drums, vocals
Sounds and Technical Support: John Bechdel
Produced at: Townhouse Studios and Terminal 24 by Killing Joke and Martin Rex
Engineered by: Martin Rex
Mixed at: Marcus Studios by Martin Rex
Label: Aggressive Rock Produktionen (AGR)/Noise
Release date: November 1990
Running time (original CD release): 65:03
Highest chart places: UK: Did not chart
Current edition: 2007 expanded remastered reissue on Candlelight Records

The late 1980s and early 1990s were a period of intense and labyrinthine churn for Killing Joke. Following the commercial disaster of *Outside the Gate*, Coleman and Geordie entered a protracted legal dispute with EG. When the situation seemed dire, the Joke found a catalyst for momentum in ex-PiL drummer Martin Atkins who had a post-punk attitude, business acumen and a nimble, but suitably aggressive playing style. Along with Welsh bassist Taif (Dave) Ball, the band resumed live performances in late 1988, commencing a period of relentless gigging through to late summer 1989, when the band recorded a clutch of demo tracks, followed by Ball's departure and Raven's return.

Recorded in August and released in November 1990, *Extremities* is Killing Joke reborn, establishing the idiom that has, with minor variations, been the Joke's consistent core musical space ever since. Coleman returns to the vitriolic vocal-chord shredding of the early albums but mixes this with his pitch-clean but cavern-dark baritone. The Black Jester is in the ascendant. Geordie is better than he's ever been, incorporating elements from American alt-metal and industrial rock but without surrendering his unique style or succumbing to the lure of power-chord posturing or the rock-god guitar solo. Atkins adds dynamic syncopation to the Joke's bedrock pounding rhythms, and Raven holds everything together with familiar propulsive minimalism.

Lyrically the band are boiling over with rage, attacking consumerism, industrialisation and the willingly brainwashed masses. But there's also the Joke's tricksterish layer of occult knowledge with stitched-in suggestions for how seekers of wisdom can trigger their own enlightenment. The cover art features the eyes of Austrian actor Friedrich Feher from German expressionist masterpiece *The Cabinet of Dr Caligari*. There are two Latin epigrams on the back cover. '*Semper imitatum nunquam idem*', means 'Always copied, never cloned'; '*Hoc volo, sic iubeo sit pro ratione voluntas*' quoted from Juvenal's *Satires* No. 6, l. 223 translates as 'I will have this done, so I order it done; let my will replace reasoned judgement', an allusion to Crowley's concept of magickal 'will'. The album was released a few days before John major became Prime Minister of the UK, his government accelerating the lethal privatisation and profitisation that Thatcher's 'Age of Greed' had begun.

The Joke toured the new album in Europe and America until splitting halfway through 1991. Coleman finally emigrated to New Zealand further to develop the classical string of his eclectic musical bow, while the other members, along with Big Paul, launched Murder Inc. with Ministry and Pigface collaborator/member Chris Connelly, and future Ministry keyboard player John Bechdel. Yet again, it looked like the end of the band.

'Money is Not Our God' 5:16 (Coleman/Walker/Atkins)

This track slams down a marker that the ensuing album will sound nothing like the previous one. After a spoken intro, a vocalised incantation, some symbolic throat-clearing and an urgent root note from Raven, the opener hits you like an 18-wheeler smashing into a fruit stall as Atkins lays down an industrial-riveter rhythm and a distorted Geordie joins Raven for the song's main riff. This is a band reborn: their mood, their musicality and their message in perfect synchronisation. Coleman's voice is deeper here, with a gothic tone. The familiar layers of industrial noise have returned. The songwriting is stripped right back to riffs and rhythm with only a couple of key changes. The only sign of keyboards is a root-note synth drone, similar to those on the band's first two albums.

The lyrics are perfectly balanced between tricksterish provocation and an optimistic statement of 'painful truths' hard-won: that no amount of money can buy you ownership of the natural world, however much billionaires may want this to be so. In keeping with Killing Joke's rage against the consumerist machine, the song ends with pessimistic satire, correctly predicting 32 more years of dysfunctional materialism and ruinous consumerism taking our ecosystem and democracy to the brink of collapse: 'Ahhh… money!'

'Age of Greed' 7:22 (Coleman/Walker/Atkins)

This is where Coleman's eschewing of traditional pop/rock verse-chorus song structure, as evidenced on *Outside the Gate*, is folded back into Killing Joke's signature sonics and Geordie's self-regenerative riffing to create something entirely new for the band. There are eight distinct elements to this track, ordered in such a way that there appears to be no obvious logic, but everything nonetheless feels totally organic.

An American advertisement for a meat subscription, surely the zenith of blunt-force consumerism, is followed by an intricately syncopated Atkins drum break, and then we're straight into the main motif and a de facto first verse. This motif is then segmented, with only the first part used to introduce four lines of spoken-word lyrics that are more relevant at the time of writing than they've ever been.

A short melodic bridge leads to a headbanger-friendly cycling riff with Jaz declaiming the lyrics, followed by a second verse, including the beautifully concise satirical couplet: 'feather the nest and fuck the rest.' The song then resets with stick-clicks, taking us into a second bridge and a change of pace with a contemplative, phase-woozy sung middle eight and another humdinger line puncturing consumerist dystopia with 'the cash you've already spent'. A third bridge, featuring a descending riff with vocals, holds the meat of the song's theme: 'privatise the people's lives.'

The segmented motif returns, followed by a third verse, and then we're into that headbanging riff for a second time. A fourth, one-note bridge segues into a reprise of the first bridge, then the second. A final two-note motif underpins Coleman's raging exasperation at Thatcherite greed and neoliberal profit-seeking, with our resident trickster seriously contemplating some urban-guerrilla tactics. A single reverbed gunshot drumbeat stops the track dead. There are many reasons for Jimmy Page to love the Joke, of course, but one of them is surely their riffing brilliance. Few bands come close to Killing Joke's joyful profligacy and effortless consistency over such a ridiculously long timespan.

'The Beautiful Dead' 5:56 (Coleman/Walker/Atkins)
An early version of this track was released as a limited-edition 7" flexi-disc in 1990 for members of ODIC, the Order of the Distant Island Charter, the band's sometime club for Gatherers. It had originally been one of a handful of songs recorded as demos in West Germany in 1989 before Taif Ball was replaced by Raven. The demo version is on the 2007 reissue of *Extremities* as a bonus track under its original title, 'Jubilation'. The song's core is a funereal synth riff, a slow dance to an apocalyptic scaffold.

This album version is over a minute longer and features additional sections, most obviously the double-time syncopated middle eight and the unison spoken-word incantation that opens it. That aphorism distils the theme of the track: to find the correct path, take the one in direct opposition to that taken by the masses, the anaesthetised 'beautiful dead' of the title. 'The Beautiful Dead' is also notable for the foregrounding of Geordie's metal-style distorted staccato, soon to become a lynchpin of the band's sonic palette.

The second verse features yet another barnstorming couplet, with Jaz laughing at how everything falls 'apart at the seams' when we spend beyond our 'means'. Even going against the flow there is no hubris, as the lyrics ask us to consider if there will even still be a world should we awake. Twice Jaz asks whether he will inherit 'the good green earth'. Again, we're at peak prescience, as it increasingly looks like the asleep will destroy the world before the awake have a chance to enjoy it without the accelerating dysfunction and destruction wrought by the agents of greed.

'Extremities' 5:20 (Coleman/Walker/Atkins)
Nominally the title track, this is the epitome of a grower. Again, the structure is complex, with five distinct sections in asymmetric order. Once Geordie has tuned one of his strings up to a deliberately disorientating G-sharp, we're hit with a low-slung metal riff, played first on seasick synth, then joined by guitar. The chorus motif is a seventh-to-root vamp that lyrically holds the thematic kernel: apocalypse, dissent, 'horror-beauty', and ecstasy as a magickal gateway to wisdom, all in four short lines and another distillation of the KJ worldview. 'Extremities' is emphasised by the key change that happens over the final two syllables, suspending '-ties!' in an other-worldly void.

The track comes to a dead stop just after the two-minute mark, then resumes with a relaxed, prog-flavoured section that is in direct contrast to its lyrics, which relate the unconscious paranoia of 'watching for the signs' of the end times – our life clocks running down in silent dread. The second bridge in a new key relates an everything-but-the-kitchen-sink cataclysm. There's an earthquake, a tsunami, a drought, and a nuclear war all at once. It should be ridiculously overkill, but instead, it summons sheer terror. Our silent paranoia is restated, making the song's meaning incontrovertible, and then it's a race to the end with a tenterhooks octave from Geordie, the main riff restated, a short reprise of the 'Ex-trem-i-ties!' motif before the main riff through to a dead stop, punctuated by a Coleman scream. It shouldn't work but listen to it enough times and it totally does.

'Intravenous' 7:03 (Coleman/Walker/Atkins)
This is a mausoleum masterclass in destructive dissonance, ecological breakdown and the murder of our Earth mother, Gaia ('they... pump poison in your veins'). It showcases the full house of early 1990s Joke: Arabic influence, cataclysm-laden metal-guitar riffing, disturbing discord, jarring key changes, exposed vocal lines laying bare bitter irony, a single lyric intoned for maximum effect, contrasted personal and universal imagery, plus fury, despair and our inevitable annihilation captured in lyric-sonic synthesis. On top of all that, there's a subtly sophisticated use of ascending semitones across the intermittent moments of suspense before the next section kicks in, the whole thing culminating with a dissonant drop into oblivion. 'Everybody failed to heed the warning'.

'Inside the Termite Mound' 7:50 (Coleman/Walker/Atkins)
'Go! Go, go, go!' This is a crawling, swarming, chittering humdinger. Combining a malevolent Raven pop-slap with a rhythm that's an evil cousin to the one that drives Talk Talk's 'Life's What You Make It', this is Killing Joke having re-emerged from their dark chrysalis and unfurling their Luciferian wings with total dominion over their newborn idiom. A fiendish light/dark Lydian flattened-seventh synth sets the scene for Jaz to once again become a tricksterish ringmaster. 'Here we go, my dears!' he announces, revelling in

the Joke's resurrection as court jester to the anaesthetised consensus. There are industrial clangs and insectoid pattering. Geordie swoops and slices like a steampunk hawk. Coleman's intonation creeps inside the liminal cracks in music's diatonic surface.

Each of the three verses has a different mood. The first is about the outsider insects that hatch and live at night ('antennae tuned to inhuman vibrations'). The second is about the slave ants – educated and conditioned to behave: 'it's their purpose to serve'. The third is termite mound as both hedonistic escape and consumerist self-digestion: living for 'momentary pleasures'. All three relate to the album's titular themes (and to those of demo 'The Party'): extremes of human behaviour for good and ill – or both at once. Whatever your chosen meaning, there's no escape from the incessant activity and base delusion in which humans engage to stave off death and its spectre. Pairs well with XTC's acidic 'Across this Antheap'.

'Solitude' 4:57 (Coleman/Walker/Atkins)
This is the most obviously dichotomous song on the album, musically split between airy keyboards and chugging guitar, thematically about accepting the pain and misery of life as a path to embrace the nature of one's existence alone. Coleman is recounting a dark night of the soul, with self-knowledge finally gained as dawn breaks and all his troubles fall behind him 'like a shadow'. The track's structure echoes the journey, from contemplative solitude, through the chaos and turmoil of memories conjured by eldritch drum patterns and disorientating phased guitar, to a Rubicon where the adept 'surrenders to the will of god' and is thrown into chaotic darkness with discordant and ominous riffing, before a return to solitude but now with hard-won wisdom. Rather than end there, the dark chaos returns as this magus, now literally enlightened, chooses to launch himself back into the fray rather than remain alone.

'North of the Border' 5:52 (Coleman/Walker/Atkins)
Taking screeching dissonance to the next level, this track foregrounds the unmistakable scraping and sawing of a violin (most likely Coleman ironically incorporating his boyhood instrument into a KJ soundscape like John Lydon on 'The Flowers of Romance'). The teeth-jarring cacophony reproduces the track's core lyric, 'scrape my nails across a brick': a brutally direct summation of the existential anguish of being alive. Musically we're in the same beyond-the-minor-key territory as the rest of the album, here applying both Lydian and the ultra-rare Locrian to metal riffing and a segment that's the Joke's first foray into death metal's down-tuned doom-chug. Not a classic by any means, but a key part of the band's exploration of, and migration into, new forms.

'Slipstream' 7:07 (Coleman/Walker/Atkins)
This is another barnstormer and a throwback to early-1980s Joke, though here with Coleman's plaintive vocal pinned around *Night Time*. All the

classic KJ tropes are here. There are disorientating sci-fi synth effects: here, a swooping-jabbing rip in space-time. There are tribal drums, with Atkins amply demonstrating his manic-speed dexterity. There's Geordie's garrotte-wire guitar, ceaselessly circling its prey, dragging dissonant axe across harmony's buckling armour. And Raven holds it all down with root notes and adrenalised pulsing. Queasy guitar stands in for a ripple-dissolve as we flashback to the innocent joy of a children's playground and Jaz remembering that it was 'so beautiful to be young'. This is the song's theme: time is an illusion. The past and yesterday are 'all the same to me'. When we step outside time with music, ritual, magick or meditation 'time means nothing'. But there's danger here: we can easily get caught in the slipstream and never find our way back, hence Geordie's dread-inducing note-clash at the end.

'Kaliyuga – Struggle' 8:20 (Coleman/Walker/Atkins)

> It's a frightening time. It's a wonderful and terrible time. I figure this: all the members of Killing Joke are so different, they're such strong personalities, it truly is hard to reach any sort of consensus. But, if we can do it, there's hope for the world, because it's a microcosm of a wider society. And all the way through Killing Joke's music, there is a promise that after this time of darkness, we will reach the golden age. Speaking from a Hindu perspective, we are at the last stage of what is known as *Kali Yuga*, which is the age of iron and darkness.
>
> Jaz Coleman, interviewed by John Robb, *Louder than War*, 23 March 2022

Variously listed as either two distinct tracks or one track in two parts, this is a suitably epic album closer. In Hinduism, the *Kali Yuga*, is the fourth of the four *yugas* (or epochs) in a cycle. It's followed by the first epoch of the next cycle, the *Satya Yuga*, which is the superior of the four if you like nice things. Although by far the shortest of the four, the current *Kali Yuga* began in 3,100 BCE around the start of Early Dynastic Ancient Egypt and is set to run another 427,000-odd years. So probably best not to get your hopes up too much.

The first part is a two-minute keyboard instrumental that starts with an Arabic Double-Harmonic motif in the same mood as Coleman's 1990 album with Anne Dudley, *Songs from the Victorious City*. The piece then pulls in classical key changes and John Carpenter-style film-music discord to create an ominous, widescreen aural overture.

We then plunge straight into 'Struggle' with some frenetic and headbanger-friendly vamping. The song is built almost entirely from constant movement across semitone intervals. Musically this echoes the track's theme of struggle, as we constantly strive to climb and immediately fall back. Or fall back, get up and force ourselves onward, 'until you love getting up'. It's Sisyphus, forever cursed to push a boulder up a hill, only for it to roll back down again, but ultimately revelling in his work. A tale as old as human endeavour (and basic training for artists and seekers). This is the dark sister to Chumbawamba's classic 'Tubthumping'.

'Stop clinging on, let go, own nothing'. The subtext is magickal initiation: being reduced to nothing so you can rebuild yourself from the archetypal fool up. This is a process that will enable you to find everything 'on heaven and earth'. The band followed their own advice, focusing on their art and the Gatherers rather than on fame and fortune, and from here continued to create the seminal body of work of their 44-years-and-counting career. The ending is KJ's brand of optimism epitomised: ambiguous to a fault. A mantra is repeated five times: the struggle is 'long' and 'hard', but also 'beautiful'. Then a final, seemingly definitive step up is followed by peals of laughter from the band. It is, of course, the double-edged killing joke: just when you think you're making progress, the gods laugh in your face (but when you do finally make headway, you get to laugh in god's face for balance).

Bonus Tracks

The 2007 reissue features the four demo tracks recorded in West Germany in 1989, plus a live version of 'Age of Greed' and the music video for 'Money is Not Our God'. All four demo tracks are much closer in their sonics to *Brighter* than *Extremities*. Coleman's voice is cleaner than the album to come, his timbre more sonorous, less alt-rock growl. It's not a surprise that only one of the four made it to the heavier, more aggressive *Extremities*.

'The Party' revolves around an Arabic-adjacent Phrygian motif and has ominous guitar from Geordie and some proggy riffs. The party here has an end-of-the-world quality – reminiscent of Corman's *Masque of the Red Death*, with Coleman's invitation to 'join the masquerade', and observation that 'the party lasts as long as life'. It's masquerade as a metaphor for existence. Jaz reminds us that we can't take anything with us when we depart this Earthly plane, leaving the door open for interpretations running from the most hang-the-consequences indulgent to the most leave-no-trace ascetic. There's also a link back to 'Kings and Queens' in terms of subject matter and, for me, thematic doubling.

'The Fanatic' is also Arabic infused, this time using the Double Harmonic scale. The lyrics are suitably ambiguous: the bridge features the fanatic's internal dialogue of doubt and resolve, while the chorus ends with the provocatively prosaic: 'it's your opinions versus mine'.

Although it has the same title, 'Solitude' is an entirely different track to the song of the same name on the album proper. The demo 'Solitude' has the same woozily melancholic keyboards as 'Twilight of the Mortal' from *Brighter* and evinces the same exhaustion and exasperation with humanity as that album, though again, there is a glimmer of hope in an exhortation for us to 'go to any length for dreams to come true'. 'Jubilation' is discussed above with 'The Beautiful Dead'.

The 12-minute live version of 'Age of Greed' is from a concert in Lyon (either at the end of 1991 or the beginning of 1992). Following a two-minute intro mocking profligate consumption, there's an ultra-tight but much slower rendition than that on the album. Coleman adds the line 'just to teach you that everything has a price' after '…and pull the trigger', thus both metaphorising and deepening the implied threat.

In 2007, to complement the album's reissue, Candlelight also released *Inside Extremities: Mixes, Rehearsals and Live,* which features a set from Le Pied, Reims, France from June 1991.

Pandemonium (1994)

Personnel:
Jaz Coleman: vocals, keyboards
Geordie Walker: guitar
Youth: bass guitar
Geoff Dugmore, Tom Larkin, Larry de Zoete: drums
Hossam Ramzy, Said El Artist: percussion
Aboud Abdel Al: violin
Matt Austin, Paddy Free: programming
Produced at: Auckland, Cairo and London by Youth (see text below for studios)
Engineered by: Greg Hunter
Mixed by: Ron St. Germain (for remixes see individual tracks)
Label: Butterfly Recordings
Release date: August 1994
Running time (original CD release): 60:49
Highest chart places: UK: 16; US Billboard Heatseekers: 39
Current edition: 2005 expanded remastered reissue on Cooking Vinyl

> I had a house in Goa for ten years and started developing some of the DJs and artists [there and in London]. All these kids coming and going back and forth from India, techno DJs, lots of LSD, free Indian food for everyone every night. It was a big social experiment and a big creative experiment and what came out of that is what we call psychedelic trance. It was great to be on the frontline of that pioneering wave of how that began. I just really pushed and promoted it outside the Goa scene. One of the best times of my life.
> Youth, interviewed by *Vive Le Rock*, issue 87, 2021

The third of an informal trilogy of Killing Joke albums drawing on Arabic music, *Pandemonium* is a career high-watermark and a prime example of every collaborator contributing something essential to the whole. Yet again, the band adapted their sound and approach, never willing simply to repeat previous modes or stick to a prior template. The eclecticism on this record is truly ground-breaking, not surprising when you consider that Youth had recently been making house music as half of hit-makers Blue Pearl, while Coleman had been progressing his classical career.

The album is most famous due to the vocals for 'Pandemonium' and 'Exorcism' being recorded in the King's Chamber of the Great Pyramid of Giza (Nik Turner had recorded there in 1976 immediately after leaving Hawkwind the first time) and Jaz and Youth's experiences there are now the stuff of legend. For the full story on the bizarre goings-on in the King's Chamber during the recording sessions, watch Shaun Pettigrew's extraordinary Killing Joke documentary film *The Death and Resurrection Show*.

Pandemonium is the sound of a group of artists who are all in a relatively good place, not easily achieved in context of the financial, legal, business and personal conflicts of the previous six years. Yet again, you have to love how the Joke embrace everything from alt-metal to ambient trance yet still create a totally coherent whole, this partly because the album was almost entirely composed in the studio, meaning all the tracks developed with input from the whole group.

The album's journey took it across four continents (Egypt spanning two continents itself), from Coleman's York Street Studio in Auckland to Townhouse Studios, Metropolis and Youth's own Butterfly Studios in London, to EMI and Hani Mehana Studios in Cairo. The only significant change during recording was the replacement of Tom Larkin (of Wellington band Shihad) and Larry de Zoete (of Melbourne's High Pass Filter), who had both recorded drums in Auckland, by Geoff Dugmore (who recorded new drum tracks at Townhouse Studios).

The album was mixed at Metropolis by Ron St. Germain, but the band felt some of these mixes had not done the music justice, so unusually, they commissioned a batch of remixes before the album was released – a perceptive decision.

Mike Coles created all the artwork for the album and its associated releases, drawing on sacred geometry, fractals, and the iconography of deities across multiple cultures (the album cover features Greek god Hermes). Coles's ongoing contribution to the band's mythology and creative evolution cannot be overstated and as with KJ's music, he hits a career high here. The original Latin motto, '*Coppula eam, se non posit acceptera jocularum!*' appears beside a jester figure in the booklet artwork. This translates appropriately enough as 'Fuck them if they can't take the joke!'.

'Pandemonium' 6:42 (Killing Joke)

> It's the nearest, I think, we could ever get to a folk song, to be honest. Very open. Lovely one-riffer. It has an optimistic outlook to it. A lovely release and a slow tempo.
> Geordie, interviewed by *Classic Rock Magazine*, 22 May 2013

Irrespective of the version, this is the sound of a band yet again reborn. Here the Joke have found the perfect balance between coiled aggression, industrial power, ritualistic trance-induction, and the Arabic music that had been a growing influence on their sound since *Outside the Gate*. Killing Joke's openness to collaboration (over 20 creatives worked on this album in various capacities; over 30 if you count the remixes) is immediately apparent on title track and opener 'Pandemonium', which is a remix by Cybersank aka Ulf Karl Sanken Sandqvist. The original, longer mix by Ron St. Germain only appears on the single, the third from the album, which hit 28 in the UK Singles Chart, the band's highest position since 'Love Like Blood' almost ten years earlier.

After a dawn-over-Giza evocation, we plunge into a glorious wall of sound, anchored by progressive-metal guitar staccato and distorted bass. There are layers of violin, percussion and synthesiser. The vocal is clean, which suits a more reflective, wise and wry Jaz (our raging Mr Punch has again become a quick-witted court jester with a sharp line in provoking higher understanding and a magickal mindset, in addition to ripping our globalised dysfunction a new one).

The song's title (and the album's) is derived from Milton's *Paradise Lost*, in which 'Pandaemonium' is the capital city of Hell. The lyrics are beautifully ambiguous, invoking the carnival of demons that is both the apocalypse of St. John and a New Age delineated by our higher selves – our 'daemons'. The first verse introduces the song's interlocutor, a High Priestess or embodied goddess, who talks of 'supernatural aeons', of a future 'taking shape'. The chorus embodies the track's ambiguity, with a vision of 'tomorrow' accompanied by the sound of 'pandemonium'.

'Exorcism' 7:27 (Killing Joke)

'Exorcism' is a magickal purification ritual set to music. It's a track that above all (and so below) needs to be experienced. Against a hypnotic rhythm, Jaz summons up all the roiling darkness from his – and, if we'll open ourselves up to the possibility, our – unconscious, confronts it head-on, and washes it away. The added layer of numinous mystery and spiritual frisson is provided by the vocals having been recorded inside the King's Chamber. This is also a track on which Coleman's signature coughing finally reaches its apotheosis. Here he sounds like he's expectorating a fully-grown incubus. This was the first single from the album (almost five months before the album's release) but did not make the UK Singles Chart.

'Millennium' 5:35 (Killing Joke)

As with 'Pandemonium', the album version of this track is a remix by Cybersank, again leaning heavily on the low-slung metal guitar. The song is structured around an elegant verse-bridge-chorus spine, with the Arabic-centred ascending bridge providing a contemplative pivot for the chugging verse and potent chorus. Lyrically, there are some optimistic glimmers in the apocalyptic darkness. Like anyone reading this book who was around in the 1990s, Coleman proclaims he has the privilege of being around to see the effects on the planet of two millennia. Although that number of years is entirely arbitrary, it carries genuine weight in terms of the irreversible progression from pre-climate-change Holocene to pre-climate-catastrophe Anthropocene: 'extinction seems to be a plausible risk'.

There are some lovely double meanings in the end-times flames and floods, echoing the cleansing ritual of the previous track. Despite the signs and wonders, Jaz still believes we can save ourselves. The chorus is sublimely multi-layered, evoking resonances of nostalgia, regret, acceptance and the frisson of New Year's Eve companionship. It's the heart of the set: perfectly poised between terror and hope. This was the second single from the album and reached 34 in the UK Singles Chart.

'Communion' 6:57 (Killing Joke)
This is another throbbing, undulating, trance-inducing sonic rite, with the album's most effective use of violin and percussion – the ascending three-note motif (introduced 38 seconds in) perfectly describing our yearning for wisdom and connection. The chorus holds the song's subject matter: that moment generated by observance either solitary or communal, when the boundary between the living and the dead becomes porous and all souls can share in ceremony, wisdom, the pain of grief and the joy of being. That moment when 'everything's alive'. To be fully in this moment, one must forgo one's rational left-brained self and surrender to the primal forces of nature. But as we've already learnt multiple times across the Joke's oeuvre, these are also the moments when we risk madness, especially if we have no container or system within which to comprehend these forces. This madness can overwhelm, with all control lost and all focus on 'each stain upon my soul'.

But communion can lead to understanding. The track's final verse line is a succinct description of a critical step towards Jungian individuation and magickal Gnosis, with 'all my need for explanation' abandoned. This idea is echoed musically by the rising sequence, which follows the next chorus. A Geordie holding pattern and violin showcase follow (please wait patiently in the lobby of Chapel Perilous while we approve your exit) before a final chorus reprise takes us into 30 seconds of meditative calm – hard-earned through us surviving the eye of this sacramental storm.

'Black Moon' 5:19 (Killing Joke)
Musically, this is something of a throwback, but it's a strong song and no worse for wearing its KJ heritage on its torn sleeve. A break from the Middle Eastern idioms that define the album, we start with a *Brighter*-era melodic synth hook and counterpoint guitar motif, then launch straight into a dissonant verse with a gothic drum pattern and horror-movie synth straight out of the *Night Time* era. The chorus reprises the intro hook with Jaz at full howl, appropriate given the lyrical subtext. Here, there are Jekyll & Hyde resonances as well as obvious indications of a dark lunar transformation. In many magickal systems, New Moon is when one turns the focus inwards to reflect and plan, but if one looks inside and finds only one's shadow self, then this can paradoxically also be a time of blood and violence. The song is also notable for its chorus, in which an unknown female vocalist provides the response ('another side of me') to Jaz's call, suggesting a Jungian *anima* counterpart to the shadow-self Black Jester. The last verse ends with another elegantly ambiguous instruction: break the 'endless cycle' if you can.

'Labyrinth' 5:55 (Killing Joke)
Back to the Arabic influence, again filtered through Zeppelin-style gargantuan heaviness. And this is a good point at which to mention Geoff Dugmore's unfussy drumming, which is the epitome of session work: all power and precision with zero fuss (and all the more miraculous when you know that the drums for the album were overdubbed in three days and Dugmore had not heard any of the tracks before the sessions started). Lumbering guitar and bass riffs in counterpoint with zigzagging violin and an apocalyptic synth vortex (which always makes me think of Hawkwind) underpin Coleman trying to rage his way out of a maze constructed from dogma, bad conditioning and consumerism. It's a hypnotic rant, the choicest element being Coleman's spitting of the lyric 'get it all back' in an ironic repetition of a 'born again idiot' pontificating about the hereafter.

Coleman clearly believes in some form of *Spiritus Mundi* ('world spirit'), but he doesn't believe in the Christian myth of pain now and rapture later. This life is all we get in this body, so we'd better make the best of it, with a focus on self-education and world-earned wisdom, not the miasma of 'business, lawsuits, market forces' and education as a transactional means to a consumerist end. There's a wonderful subtext in the first line of that verse, where Jaz sings about 'Mystery Schools for the fools'. To fools, all learning is a mystery, even at a 'great seat of learning', but in the mystery tradition, all students commence their studies as archetypal 'fools'. If you're arrogant enough to assume you already know everything, you won't learn anything at all. The chorus refers to the upcoming millennium, a 'transient phase', living in which feels like running through a maze. Some doom-impending clangs and a short Geordie end-of-track breakdown seal up the labyrinth with us all still trapped inside.

'Jana' 4:06 (Killing Joke)
'Jana' is something of an outlier for the band. It's an unambiguous narrative about a young woman, the titular Jana, who tests positive for HIV-AIDS and tragically dies. It's a poignant song with more heart-on-sleeve emotion than standard Joke, though there are precedents in 'Love Like Blood' and 'May Day'. The album version is a slab of melodic heaviness, with Coleman's clean vocal on the verses creating an affecting balance with a more impassioned cry in the lyrically direct chorus. 'Jana' was released as the fourth and final single from the album in a lighter 'Youth Mix' with guitar and violin foregrounded. This version, which reached 54 in the UK Singles Chart, creates a pointed juxtaposition between the life-affirming rhythms and the tragic subject matter – as though we're listening to all the club anthems that Jana will never dance to.

'Whiteout' 5:43 (Killing Joke)
A live favourite and for me one of the band's standout tracks, 'Whiteout' showcases the Joke's practised brilliance at less is more. Constructed

from an industrial-trance background, a bluntly asymmetric riff cycle and phasing guitar, the arrangement interweaves and layers these building blocks in different permutations with deceptive ease to hypnotic effect. A short breakdown features Geordie at his most jaggedly succinct as Youth's loose-sinewed bass growls in the undergrowth. The one-word chorus is absurdly effective, and Jaz throws in perhaps his finest collection of grunts, snarls, trickster chuckling and demonic throat-clearing. Thematically, it's a righteously indignant slice of fury about the state of the world as it approaches a Common Era millennium, with Jaz resolving to eat, drink and be merry before departing for somewhere less mad – to 'leave this hell'. Drinking oneself comatose to self-anaesthetise may be a blackout, but imbibing as a sacred rite before leaving one's body for the great beyond is a '...whiteout, whiteout, whiteout, whiteout'.

'Pleasures of the Flesh' 5:42 (Killing Joke)

Musically, we're back in Middle Eastern mode with another trance-inducing Gnostic psalm, this time an undulating paean to our primal nature, by now hopefully recognisable as one of the Joke's core thematic concerns. If we don't acknowledge and accept our primal nature, it takes us over. But if we let it take control, it's hard to force the shadow back into its cage. Millennia of mystics, occultists and psychologists have tried to find a way to deal with this duality, creating systems and processes through which we can attempt to balance our two sides. The Joke had spent 15 years researching these systems by this point and here they're yet again inviting us to share in their fieldwork.

The key lyric is 'half god and half beast', which is a compact summation of this innate duality. The base instincts of our most primitive forbears are in constant tension with an ability to create such complexity that we can only describe ourselves as either made by gods (divine or extra-terrestrial) or gods ourselves. As surely envisaged, the layered soundscape caresses your senses and worms its way around your nerve endings, causing a sympathetic response in body and mind. The track ends on a major resolution, which in the context of a combination of Phrygian and our old friend the sharpened fourth throughout, creates a fiendish disconnect.

'Mathematics of Chaos' 7:23 (Killing Joke)

The album closer, in a remix by Youth & Greg Hunter, is driven by a suitably frenetic and Arabic-infused Geordie riff and sums up what has gone before with a final slab of apocalyptic pessimism, tempered by a glimmer of hope sparked by our capacity for transformation. In the verses, Jaz intones a list of chaotic breakdowns – both personal and planetary – the first verse ending with an idea which could as easily describe a relationship gone bad as superpowers in conflict: whenever we attempt to impose order, 'we create chaos'. In the chorus, Jaz expresses his doubts that anything can ever be better, but the last line has familiar ambiguity, simultaneously evoking both Jungian acceptance and the darkest surrender: 'all is as it was always meant to be...'

'Chaos' here has multiple meanings and resonances. There's the chaos of runaway consumerism and constant war. There are the fractals, derived from the mathematics of chaos, used by Mike Coles as one of the core visual elements of the artwork. And there's the Chaos Magick that was connected to several occult conspiracies regarding the collapse of Western civilisation as the third millennium approached. This is all encapsulated in the third and final verse, which starts with a reference to the ongoing conflict in the former Yugoslavia and ends with a nod to the crop circles, some with fractal geometry, which were at their peak at this time and seen by many as portents of civilisational collapse.

The last two-and-a-half minutes are a cacophony of sampled sounds and white-noise squelching, which ends with Uhura reciting the number '875020079' – the false coordinates to which Kirk has been beamed (you can also hear Spock stating the stardate '5423.8' for an entry in the ship's log). These are, as you have probably guessed, lifted from the original *Star Trek*, specifically 'The Mark of Gideon' (S3, E16), in which Odona (Sharon Acker), the daughter of Gideon's ambassador, enlists an initially unwitting Kirk into being the vector for a viral cull of her overpopulated planet. The quote is suggestive: there are too many of us (5.5 billion in 1994; more than 8 billion by the time you read this). Or, at least, there are too many of us relative to how much we each insist on consuming in the Global North. And too many of us for the billionaires and oligarchs who want to hoard the planet's remaining resources.

Bonus Tracks

The 2005 Cooking Vinyl reissue features two bonus tracks. First up is 'Pandemonium (A Thread of Steel in the Suspension Bridge of Time and Space Mix)' by Greg Hunter, a beautifully architectured extended trance take on the album's title track with swaying drum patterns and intermittent washes of distorted guitar providing sonic stanchions for cycles of effects-heavy violin. The second bonus track, 'Another Cult Goes Down (Portobello Mix)' originally appeared on the 'Exorcism' and 'Pandemonium' singles. It's an ominous slice of industrial dub (Portobello Road, famous for its market, is a narrow thoroughfare that runs parallel to Ladbroke Grove in London, through the area where the band originated).

Democracy (1996)

Personnel:
Jaz Coleman: vocals, keyboards
Geordie Walker: guitar
Youth: bass guitar
Geoff Dugmore: drums
Nick Holywell-Walker: additional keyboards and programming
Produced at: Henley-on-Thames, Oxfordshire by Youth (studio not credited)
Engineered by: Andy Scarfe (except 'Savage Freedom' engineered by Ott)
Mixed by: Paul Wright and Youth (except 'Savage Freedom' mixed by Ott and Killing Joke)
Label: Butterfly Recordings
Release date: April 1996
Running time (original CD release): 54:17
Highest chart places: UK: 71
Current edition: 2005 expanded remastered reissue on Cooking Vinyl

> The music business and art, you often put in little boxes: this is what you do and that's where you do a rock thing, you're a rock producer, you're a rock artist, stay there. A lot of what I do, which makes it hard to explain, is out of those boxes.
> Youth, interviewed in *Sketch, Drugs & Rock n Roll*, Dir. Paul Elliott & Sean Lamberth, 2016

Less than two years elapsed between *Pandemonium* and its follow-up, the shortest time since the 19-month gap between *Brighter* and *Outside the Gate*. It's as though the band underwent the deep catharsis of millennial apocalypse on *Pandemonium*, and even though on *Democracy* the millennium is still more than three years away (or more than four if you want to be pedantic), they're already on the other side and talking to us from there.

Mostly written in Cornwall, which aligns with *Democracy*'s strong pagan elements, the album was recorded in Henley-on-Thames. The subject matter ranges from the intimately personal to the spiritual and political, with a through-line of optimism regarding our potential for embracing both self-development and social progress, without sacrificing one for the other. Musically, *Pandemonium*'s eclecticism is left behind for a fundamentals-first approach, though there are still a myriad of remixes across all associated releases, which continues the previous album's fractal multiplicity, though now limited to a couple of tracks ('Intellect' is something of an outlier, with its psychedelic trance stylings). The Mike Coles cover shows a democratic multitude of faces, a *demos* of colours, shapes and influences. The band's daemon – here playful rather than baleful – is represented by an out-of-proportion *Pulcinella* with Coleman's face (*Pulcinella*, or the Anglicised 'Punchinello', is Mr Punch's seventeenth-century Italian antecedent).

In contrast to *Pandemonium*'s widescreen sonic panoramas, *Democracy* is undoubtedly more contained and perhaps sometimes *too* contained, though you could argue that the production's raw intimacy is exactly what Youth was aiming at. This is a slow-burner that reveals its thematic mysteries and emotional provocations over time, rather than with the immediacy of earlier albums. Plus, it's another necessary milestone in the band's development as the uncompromising aural assault, thrashing anguish and pummelling fury of its seven-year-itch successor are only enhanced by the hope and optimism that glimmer briefly within *Democracy*'s lantern. Although the band are down on this album and the tracks are never played live, there are many, including me, who spin it regularly. Dave Grohl has named it one of his favourite Joke albums.

There are four non-album tracks from the same era that provide thematic deepening and counterpoint: 'Four Stations of the Sun', 'Hollywood Babylon' and 'Drug' (these tracks are discussed in the Non-Album Tracks chapter) and 'Mass' which is discussed below as a Related Track.

'Savage Freedom' 4:50 (Coleman/Glover/Walker)
Immediately it's clear that, again, the Joke have refused to stand still. Gone are the world-music idioms and alt-metal grooves of *Pandemonium*, replaced by elegantly simple driving rock, though the band's riff-based, dissonance-layered DNA is still at the core of everything. Dugmore's pounding drums are the perfect foil for weight-of-the-world guitars and Coleman's anguished, throttled vocal. The lyrics outline the band's ethos: the savage freedom that exists outside the hell of regular employment, but which has its own downsides. The risks of existing outside the system are always the same: reinventing the system by default. The first half of verse two is the Joke's version of Townshend's New Boss/Old Boss: 'personality cults all over again'. The verses are underpinned by Geordie's sharpened fourth and seventh (particularly blunt as Youth is playing a flattened fourth in the bass riff). This dissonance suggests the doom we'll bring on ourselves if we repeat old destructive patterns.

But at least with 'savage freedom' we're not clock-watching 'the hours that we kill' or hiding our dreams from others – or, worse, from ourselves. The rest of the second verse and the last verse signal a more optimistic outlook for this album. There's a combination of the love of primal fire and the pagan ritual of *Fire Dances* with the idea that we can perhaps move forward without annihilating ourselves. 'I can see a way out' intones Jaz. That 'way out' is to see the world and its inhabitants as one.

'Democracy' 3:40 (Coleman/Glover/Walker)
A summer's day strummed-guitar intro is an ironic entrée to this bitterly satirical song about the deep flaws in so-called Western democracies – flaws that have only become more apparent between 1996 and 27 years later.

The melodic hook and non-dissonant arrangement provide a deliberate counterpoint to the commentary of the lyrics. Somewhat bizarrely, 'Democracy' reached 39 in the UK Singles Chart in March 1996, though maybe this fact simply underlines that the British electorate were ready for the false dawn that happened only 16 months later with the election of Tony Blair. Our supposed 'choice' is no choice at all as 'red, blue or yellow' all 'ridicule the Green'. Deeply ironic is the mention of not getting a referendum when the two the UK subsequently had set back democratic reform and then democracy itself by at least 20 years. The line about 'industrial psychologists' planning 'a campaign that is financed by big business' could be about Cambridge Analytica's role in the Brexit referendum.

The second verse is an exasperated turn away from the pantomimic farce of 'democracy', as reminiscent of Number Six (Patrick McGoohan) in nonconformist TV classic *The Prisoner*, Jaz declares that he is not a slogan, badge, or cross on a ballot. Mainstream politicians do not represent his 'deepest thoughts and wishes'. Again, as time goes on and meaningful reform seems less and less likely, stepping outside the dysfunctional system seems to be the only viable option for retaining one's sanity. Sorry, democracy didn't change.

'Prozac People' 6:55 (Coleman/Glover/Walker)

Awaking in an echo chamber of solitary confinement with only our crushing depression for company, we hear a lone melancholic guitar, marking out time till our jailer visits with more news of the world outside – which makes it sound even worse than our tiny, windowless cell. But help is at hand! Help to make us feel that it's not sane to be depressed, even though the world we've made is slowly killing us. So much for the first verse. A short bridge lists the aims of this pharmaceutical assistance: to 'level me out' and 'keep me up'.

In the second verse, Coleman puts an equinoctial spin on the term 'bipolar' by punningly relating the experience to his own geographic dichotomy, as he travels 'down the longitude of opposite emotions'. He relates how in the Northern Hemisphere, they saw 'my excitable and optimistic spirit', while in the South, they saw 'my anger and my tears'. And, of course, this also includes the exact opposite, with Coleman's own writings providing plenty of examples of serenity in the Southern Hemisphere and Vesuvian explosions of rage in the North. The chorus brims with the bitter irony of someone who knows their optimism is evanescent: 'I was one of the Prozac people'. Finally, we're deposited back in our echo-chamber cell to start the cycle again.

'Lanterns' 4:53 (Coleman/Glover/Walker)

Turning on the 'equinox sun', the mood brightens as the band's new-minted optimism takes over from the dark depression of the previous track. There's an anthemic vibe to this elegant and affecting song, with short verses counterpointed by a longer chorus/bridge extolling the simple pleasures of leaving civilisation behind and returning to nature where 'lanterns of hope shine on'. A short middle eight reminds us that nothing the Joke do comes without some level of ambiguity as a minor rising-falling riff takes over, but this soon gives way to a chorus-bridge reprise. A final short chorus has a new lyric, which again references the purifying and transformative nature of fire, leaving us in an unmistakably upbeat mood. All the fences being 'torn down' speaks to the dream of green collectivists, eco-anarchists and 'lunatic' idealists: humans in harmony with nature and an end to all borders (a dream pricked by the minor chord that ends the song). The track is named 'Lanterns of Hope' in the booklet, but simply 'Lanterns' on the cover.

'Aeon' 8:04 (Coleman/Glover/Walker)
The thematic and musical centrepiece of the album, this is also something of an unofficial epilogue to *Pandemonium*, re-contextualising and re-shaping that album's apocalyptic doom and millennial angst into a manifesto for how to survive the mess we've made. As a measure of epochs, the catastrophic millennium is replaced by the idea of the 'aeon', resonating with those calendrical systems that predicted a positive sea-change in human behaviour, such as the Mayan, and the idea of the Aquarian Age (which apparently starts somewhere between 1447 and 3597, though between 1844 and 2597 seems to be preferred, with 2012 being a firm favourite; in any event you'll be pleased to hear that it starts much earlier than *Kali Yuga* ends).

A marching rhythm, an optimistic Mixolydian riff from Geordie and some driving bass from Youth underpin the verses, while a chorus lightly shaded with Zeppelin and Arabic resonances brings tension to the narrative. The lyrics echo the idea that all religions are essentially one, with 'denominations of a thousand different deities' as 'endless carnivals of gaiety'. This is an idea at the core of occultism: that all exoteric religions hide a single esoteric truth, whatever system one uses to access that truth. There is 'crying', 'turmoil' and a perpetual 'arms race', but then Coleman notices 'a change' coming over him: 'tapping into the Aeon.'

The final verse recalls 'Lanterns', with 'balance of the eco-system' and 'self-reliance'. Tellingly, this verse isn't followed by the prophecy-fuelled awakening-from-darkness of the entire chorus, but only by its last line, as though hope has finally won out. This is the New Age as envisaged by Killing Joke: a combination of visceral paganism, cerebral occultism, democratic localism, community permaculture and global ecology. It's an aeon we can perhaps still claim, though the clock is ticking ever faster ...

'Pilgrimage' 6:30 (Coleman/Glover/Walker)
A long-standing personal favourite, this can hold its own against the standout tracks on any Joke album. 'Pilgrimage' looks both over its shoulder and ahead: with musical nods to *Pandemonium* and thematic progression away from it. Folk-style acoustic guitar, violin and ocarina momentarily lull before a

strident, storm-lashed riff launches us into a searching rhythm, reflecting the song's subject matter of a spiritual quest. Our seeker realises that his values are out of alignment with the consumerist masses (Coleman has written about the dual aspects of his search for occult wisdom: the 'Ocarina Player', who we follow here, and 'The Black Jester', who penetrates the mysteries through provocation and extremities). The Ocarina Player wants peace and realises that the West cannot provide it. He engages in some map dowsing (letting the unconscious mind or geomantic forces determine your destination, depending on your viewpoint) and takes off for places yet unknown.

The chorus, thrumming with Middle Eastern violin and cantering drums, captures the essence of the spiritual idea of pilgrimage, whether your 'god' is entirely beyond matter, transcendent, nature-based, or fully human. Perhaps we all need something or someone onto which we can project the divine so that we can be in awe of something other than ourselves. The track's narrative draws on elements of the band's spiritual and occult travels across multiple continents, though it especially resonates with a pilgrimage Coleman undertook as a nine-year-old to the Black Madonna at Montserrat in Barcelona. Since then, Jaz has been intrigued by and dedicated to the feminine mysteries of these icons, making Prague a Northern Hemisphere home partly due to that city's many examples. Following a spine-tingling breakdown, the bare bones final verse resonates with the idea that when you are open to the divine, synchronicities proliferate: 'so wonderful.'

'Intellect' 4:01 (Coleman/Glover/Walker)

An elegantly compact and beautifully structured track, from Geordie's opening note clash to Jaz's spoken-word final line, 'Intellect' hat-tips towards its Hawkwind-style sonics with audio generator-adjacent synth layers and a Phrygian-mode riff. The offbeat hits resonate back to 'Tabazan': another song about submitting to the primal. Lyrically, Coleman interrogates our obsession with left-brain thinking over right-brain instinct, especially as the intellect is so often used to disparage and mock. The first verse suggests how deconstructing everything – 'acts of love', 'rites of passage' – through the intellect can mean that 'reason then gives birth to lies'.

Coleman, who left school without formal academic qualifications, has often talked about his views on education: how everyone should have the time, space and resources to self-educate. In the Joke, Coleman is clearly an exceptional mind among exceptional minds, but sometimes you need to kiss your intellect goodbye and live purely from instinct: in the moment, from the body, without the analysis and rationalisation of the left hemisphere. This can allow us to access a primal state: 'to feel and cry, to move and run'. Again, it's impossible not to relate this to Zen: the combination of being in the moment and of laughter being truth. 'A dog doesn't question why he barks', and dogs, when treated kindly, certainly seem to be happier than most humans.

'Medicine Wheel' 5:18 (Coleman/Glover/Walker)

> I was a pretty strange child. My relationship with music is like an arranged marriage: by the time my brother and I were six and four it was decided that he would be the scientist, and I would be the musician, mainly because my grandmother saw me wriggling to music in my cradle.
> Jaz Coleman, interviewed by James Gill, *Metal Hammer*, 19 August 2020

And so, the wheel turns into a cauldron of spiritual ideas and personal experience. 'Medicine Wheel' is named after the configurations of stones in the Americas laid down by multiple First Nation tribes as symbols for various key facets of life's circular journey, so the idea of building a medicine wheel is both physical and metaphorical. An ocarina introduction leads into music that's as close to the psychedelic trance to which the band had become drawn in the 1990s as any non-remixed track. In the first verse, Jaz recounts the story of a woman building a medicine wheel in Sedona, Arizona, an area known for its striking red sandstone rock formations.

The following two verses compare, contrast then synthesise Jaz and his brother Piers, and their seemingly different but ultimately converging paths. Piers studied theoretical physics but as Jaz recounts, he often talks in ways that sound decidedly non-scientific: 'he talks of Gaia's love'. In contrast, Jaz 'wields a band of fire'. The idea of Killing Joke as a 'band of fire' should by now seem apt, considering the number of times flames are referenced. The baying wolves relate directly to 'Pssyche' and the band as a pack. All three: the woman, Piers and Jaz are each in their own way turning life's medicine wheel. As are we all, whether we are conscious of the fact or not. But being conscious of our own unique spiritual journey can lead to profound gratitude: 'I...am so grateful'.

The chorus uses a couple of familiar-by-now components to hypnotic effect. First, there's Coleman's knack for constantly shifting, seemingly randomised POVs as the person building the medicine wheel cycles through 'we', 'she' and 'he'. Second is a glorious use of call-and-response, as these lines are counterpointed with Coleman singing 'turning round, round and round'. And just when you think everything is resolved at the track's end as Geordie hits a rare major chord, the wheel turns again and we drop down a semitone to the unresolved seventh, suggesting the beginning of the next cycle.

'Absent Friends' 5:40 (Coleman/Glover/Walker)

On the surface, this track plays as if the band are so down on the idea of a song about love – even platonic love – that they insist not only on running straight down a full minor scale to provide the dourest counterpoint to the word 'love', but also to create a foreboding verse motif and a dark middle eight that sounds more like a fight-or-flight trigger than an inducement to love, whether erotic or platonic. But dig beneath and there is a sonic metaphor for going deep into either memory or metaphorical underworld to retrieve the joy or the soul of the person we have lost so we can be with them again, however fleetingly. 'The dead shall live again... by love'. And because the Joke can never have enough musical tension, Geordie contradicts the final minor-scale descent with a hanging major sixth for maximal frisson.

'Another Bloody Election' 4:26 (Coleman/Glover/Walker)
A satisfying wordplay on the (some might say, deliberately) exhausting nature of modern democracy and the spin and corruption that plague contemporary elections, especially in the Murdoch countries, this is a much more sophisticated and transgressive song than its outward appearance may portray. After some incoherently yammering voices, the main verse riff seems like a deliberate nod to Nirvana, especially as this track is ostensibly about US political culture.

The lyrics could have been written this week about the UK, as I sit here writing this chapter during yet another Tory Leadership contest to determine who becomes the fourth Conservative Party PM since 2010. Here is deceit ('false gestures'), the dysfunctional relationship between money and power ('How did you make your fortune?'), backhanders ('planning permission granted'), conspiracy ('cover-ups, official statements'), capitalist greenwashing ('McDonald's goes eco-friendly') and a lovely jab at the octogenarian disinformation merchant, which harks all the way back to the bitter irony of 'Pssyche' ('Mr Murdoch cares for orphans'). A simple climbing riff from Youth heralds the chorus as Jaz goes off script (this line isn't in the lyric booklet) and follows 'another bloody election' with 'another bloody erection', nailing the narcissistic priapism of electoral politics in the age of 24-hour infotainment and the oligarch press (the chorus ends with a falling motif that cheekily balances the rising one).

But there's still satire to spare, with some heavy Dugmore drumfire announcing one of Geordie's career-handful of guitar 'solos' coming across in context like a pointed attack on our obsession with fame, status and money served in easily digestible spoonfuls. And how glorious it is: three notes and some signature distortion saying more than many guitarists say with a slew of shredding and myriad digital effects. Another chorus featuring that wicked rewrite and we're out. It's a witty and nuanced way to end both a track and an album that have far more of both than sometimes given credit for.

Related Tracks
'Democracy (The Russian Tundra Mix)'
This is an almost 18-minute remix by The Orb (as Le Petite Orb) and Sheldon Isaac, which weaves together audio clips, found sound, synth, industrial/tribal rhythms, and minimal elements of the KJ track to create a multi-layered

soundscape that somehow still feels directly connected to its source. It's trippy, uncanny and not a little dystopian. This is the sole bonus track on the 2005 remastered reissue and is well worth seeking out.

'Mass' 6:03 (Coleman/Glover/Walker)
From the 'Democracy' CD single, this track comes across as both deeply personal and emotionally vulnerable. An insistent programmed backing propels a nerve-jangling Geordie riff as Coleman's protagonist suffers an existential crisis: 'Which holy book for guidance?' The answer appears to be 'eternity' on his own 'block of land', but there's implicit doubt about whether his significant other will find the 'security' she needs there. The melodic chorus is reminiscent of the *Brighter* era, but the vocals switch back and forth at syllable level between *Democracy*'s growl and *Brighter*'s clean timbre to haunting effect. The bridge is a classic one-word refrain – the song's title 'Mass' – over a jagged, dissonant early-1980s Joke riff. There's a short rave-style breakdown with some Geordie string-shearing before the final verse ends with discord-counterpointed optimism: 'my heart shall be my guidance'. A final chorus/bridge and a chaotic, levitating ending suggest both Gnosis and anarchy.

Killing Joke (2003)

Personnel:
Jaz Coleman: vocals, keyboards
Geordie: guitar
Youth, Raven, Geordie (uncredited): bass guitar
Dave Grohl: drums
Produced at: The Beauchamp Building, London and Grand Master Studios, Los Angeles (drums only) by Andy Gill
Engineered by: Andy Gill and Jerry Kandiah; Nick Raskulinecz assisted by Andrew Alekel (drums only)
Mixed by: Clive Goddard
Label: Zuma Recordings
Release date: July 2003
Running time (original CD release): 55:43
Highest chart places: UK: 43; US (Billboard Independent Albums): 30
Current edition: 2022 expanded remastered reissue on Spinefarm Records

> Killing Joke music is everything that I love about music – relevant, melodic, energetic, powerful. Everyone's searching for an album that has meaning and that has melody and that has a power that is different from anything else you've heard, and everyone's looking in all the wrong places. The funny thing about meeting Jaz and then hearing the music and lyrics we're about to record – everything's so relevant, it almost seems prophetic.
> **Dave Grohl (with Jaz), interviewed by Daniel Lukes, *Kerrang!*, 28 March 2003**

The band hit another rough patch in the early 2000s, with no label support and further financial problems. Coleman was focused on his classical career, which led to Geordie and Chris Connelly joining Martin Atkins and Jah Wobble as The Damage Manual (their one EP and sole self-titled album are well worth checking out). That band dissolved after a single tour, leading eventually to another Joke reformation and sessions for a new album in the first half of 2003, though independent label Zuma Recordings offered no advance. The Iraq War, which began on 20 March 2003, looms large over this second self-titled disc. Although 'Axis of Evil' and 'The Death & Resurrection Show' were both considered as album titles, *Killing Joke* is entirely apt for a record born in the crucible of post-9/11 warmongering – with several tracks overtly criticising America's military-industrial complex.

The album is notable for several additional reasons. It's a fitting reboot for a band that sounds as original, furious and uncompromising as they did 23 years earlier on their debut. There are several direct call-backs to the 1980 album – and to the preceding 1979 EP *Turn to Red*. Both Youth and Raven took part in this rebirth – a fitting testament to how the band found a way to exist with two bass players as full members. It's also only the third time that a non-member has been credited with writing on KJ tracks: producer Andy Gill. And, of course, arguably the most notable fact of all: that Grohl – already a rock legend both for Nirvana and Foo Fighters – plays all the drums on this album (Grohl is also no stranger to the tricksterish qualities of Aleister Crowley, including him in the delicious Foo Fighters 2022 horror film *Studio 666*). Geordie is on record as being unhappy with the album's lack of spontaneity and the high number of overdubs, but *KJ 2003* is technically and sonically extraordinary and spawned several classic Joke tracks and live staples. It's also a stylistic fulcrum between the Joke's 1990s albums and the recordings from *Hosannas* onwards. The 2022 Spinefarm reissue features two bonus tracks.

'The Death & Resurrection Show' 6:56 (Coleman/Walker/Glover/Gill)
One of the greatest album openers by anyone and a live favourite from its first performance, this is Killing Joke at Year Zero reset, brimming with forge-hot rigour, rage and righteousness. It's the latest bead to be added to the primal-pagan-occult thread that stretches all the way back to the band's creation. And this new bead dazzles with studied sophistication, quest-deep wisdom and bitter life experience. Geordie's hypnotic riff and Grohl's intricate off-beat patterns create the trance state within which Coleman weaves his spell: by turns cerebral, visceral and spiritual.

First, we are invited to prepare for the illumination-giving ritual, by marking out 'the points', building a 'pyre', assembling 'different drummers' and donning 'masks' and 'animal skins'. These are the foundations of this 'illumination'. The sly wit in the idea of 'different drummers' is simply too cute, the Joke now being on their seventh 'different drummer' since Big Paul's fractious departure during the sessions for *Outside the Gate*. With the bonfire now burning brightly, generating the magnesium flare of spiritual transformation, we are ready to accept not just our physical mortality but our metaphysical immortality. We are offered two examples: the death and resurrection of the solar god manifest in Jesus Christ, and the death and resurrection of the solar god manifest in Osiris. 'Recurring themes, time again.'

The last verse reminds us that ego death is a prerequisite of illumination, while the chorus challenges us to confront the deceit that death is the end because 'souls are recycled in the death and resurrection show'. The mention of Ezekiel's chariot relates to the occult 'Merkaba', a vehicle for ecstatic gnosis. Christianity, though it offers 'life after death', breaks the great cycle of death and rebirth with the dogma of judgement, purgatory, heaven and hell (in *Letters from Cythera*, Coleman refers to this as the 'cruelty of the prevailing Judeo-Christian concept of death'). The 'beloved mother of liberty' is yet another appearance by the archetypal feminine: the Black Madonna, Jung's anima, Isis, Ishtar, Sophia, the Triple Goddess, the Great Mother, Gaia. Invoking this energy by summoning her to you is one of the most effective mechanisms for attaining enlightenment: the certain knowledge that death is not an end, but rather another beginning.

'Total Invasion' 5:28 (Coleman/Walker/Glover/Gill)

> As far as... trying to go up against the government? It's just... unless the whole country did it, I guess.
> Katie Summers, spoken intro to 'Total Invasion'

This is another live favourite – indeed, the band's 2019 US Tour was named for it. Although the illegal invasion did not commence till 20 March 2003, when the sessions for *KJ 2003* had almost been completed, Bush had already laid the groundwork in January 2002, when he began to sow the seeds of the 'weapons of mass destruction' conspiracy (a conspiracy now proven beyond doubt), infamously coining the term 'Axis of Evil'.

The maliciously chugging guitars and temple-pounding drums create a menacing backdrop for Coleman's Gollum-style whisper. The lyrics are eviscerating, taking to task America for its greed and imperialism. Water poverty in Mexico is contrasted with the West's insatiable demand for oil, even if this demand means taking the whole planet to the brink of extinction. Democracy – which seven years previously had been gently mocked on the album named after it, albeit in the context of positive reform still being possible – is here reduced to a sour pantomime with 'all votes invalid' and a proliferation of lies. Yet again, 'man is cattle'. In contrast to the positive archetypal feminine referenced in the previous track, here a line about changing the invaded's god to 'the bitch Goddess' sounds instead like a bitter swipe at the Statue of Liberty, whose proclamation 'Give me your tired, your poor, your huddled masses yearning to breathe free' reads as a tragic parody in light of America's post-2001 foreign policy. Even more bitterly satirical is the mention of 'United Nations' – with Jaz punning Bush's 'coalition of the willing' with the organisation that still offers the best route to peace (Jaz has often talked about the UN in the same terms as the EU: a positive force for debate and compromise).

'Asteroid' 3:24 (Coleman/Walker/Glover/Gill)

The third perennial live favourite from the album – and the last in a barnstorming triptych of an occult ritual, manufactured war and welcome apocalypse – is 'Asteroid', a short, blunt-force annihilation, though still suffused with the Joke's uniquely wry wit. After a short quote from John the Divine's *Revelation* (8:10) and the sound of fire whooshing towards us, Coleman takes the role of burning rock over a planet-killer riff: 'fire from heaven... you'll never shoot me down.' If the Abrahamic God exists at all, then now would probably be a good time for him to hurl some righteous justice our way: 'Nature renewed by fire made whole' (in Latin, '*Igne Natura Renovatur Integra*' or 'I.N.R.I') with a subtext of '*Iesvs Nazarenvs Rex Ivdaeorvm*' – a reminder that the resurrection show follows death for us all, not just the Son of God. It's no leap to infer that if God has ever been imagined doing exactly this, then it could be seen as nothing more meaningful than a mile-wide chunk of space rock falling to Earth. The final layer is a para-historical one: imagining an Atlantean civilisation vaporised. The Joke's tricksterish grin here takes the form of a countdown and the gloriously impish rhyming of 'asteroid' with 'void'. In the final verse, Coleman switches POV to a human watching the flaming asteroid streak towards the ground with the prophetically poetic 'a hole in your Ark'. This ark is our home, 'Spaceship Earth,' as Buckminster Fuller called it. With perfect ambiguity, the song at once wants to destroy this Ark and see it saved.

'Implant' 5:18 (Coleman/Walker/Glover/Gill)
A dystopian synth pulse presages the whispered first line, a reference to the notorious 'top secret' manual *Silent Weapons for Quiet Wars*, which was apparently found inside a second-hand photocopier in 1986. This tract contains detailed instructions for the manipulation and control of populations by governments, though its provenance has never been confirmed and the story of how it came to be found is more reminiscent of 1963's *Principia Discordia* (apparently first printed on Jim Garrison's Xerox) than 1971's Pentagon Papers.

The Joke then proceed to deliver their verdict on Big Brother's surveillance state, ID cards, DNA databases and microchip implants. Geordie's riff is prodding and urgent. The bass swoops and growls while Grohl is at his febrile best, constantly shifting rhythmic emphasis and throwing off breaks like a man possessed. The third verse veers from totalitarian paranoia to sci-fi horror, conjuring genetic experiments and ungodly mutations 'deep below the ground'. Coleman ends the track by telling the state to destroy their ID cards and stick their implants where the sun doesn't shine, again joyfully mixing non-conformist Anglo-Saxon derision with indignant fury.

'Blood on Your Hands' 6:00 (Coleman/Walker/Glover/Gill)
The bleeding-out heart of the album, this is perhaps the Joke's single most vituperative assault on human evil. And as with so many of their tracks, it could have been written last week, dealing as it does with climate catastrophe, ecosystem-degrading agribusiness, chaos capitalism, war for profit and state-sanctioned murder. Geordie's riff here rings like an alarm bell: desperately trying to wake us from our anaesthetised slumbers. The first verse sees the band's beloved Prague flooded and the waters poisoned so that 'only GM crops grow'. The second verse sounds like a thinly veiled accusation regarding Princess Diana's demise. Even if her death was a tragic accident, the archetypal quality of her passing as the ritual sacrifice of the lunar goddess still seems to resonate through the increasingly dysfunctional British state and its feudal electorate.

The final verse nails the grotesque inequality between oligarchs and serfs as rulers exploit fossil fuel while the poor 'eat their stools'. The poor must, both literally and figuratively, eat shit. The chorus couldn't be more overtly condemnatory, with an assertion that 'five corporations earn more than forty-six nations', so plunging us into a hellscape of corruption. But even in this damnation, it's still recognised that the devil is only human, which perhaps offers hope that he can ultimately be defeated, even though we appear to be further from that defeat now than at any point since the album's original release. The juxtaposition of Jacques de Molay and Cecil Rhodes is glorious: Molay, the Knights Templar Grand Master literally burnt for spiritual illumination while English colonialist Rhodes, the devil, rides out to plunder and raze to the ground.

'Loose Cannon' 4:12 (Coleman/Walker/Glover/Gill)
Swinging on an elastic, nu-metal groove, 'Loose Cannon' is something of a reprieve from the musical and lyrical assault of the first five tracks. There's even a rare backing-vocalised response to Coleman's chorus call. The uncanny crackling synth intro and 'out on the town' menace drag us back to *KJ 1980*'s 'Primitive' and 'Wardance'. The protagonist is both rebel and automaton, trapped between unloading his instincts and downloading an oppressive program. There's some lovely wordplay as beating a pagan drum is juxtaposed with downloading to a 'stick'. The sky turning 'green' is a direct call-back to 'Complications'. Geordie is apparently responsible for the growling, loose sewer-grate bass, meaning that three Joke members play bass on the album. Then, just when you think you have the track sussed, they throw the curveball of a melodic and thoughtfully restrained middle eight – a disconcerting counterpoint to the droogs-in-an-underpass chorus. This 'primitive man' is both an 'urban animal' and a struggling soul with hidden fears and 'tears trapped inside' – in other words, this human is a roiling mess of contradictions. He's 'one step from a cannibal'.

As the lyrics imagine an end to borders, we're reminded that the Joke have many times expressed both the appeal of a world without passport checks and gun emplacements and the importance of tribal identity – a both/and dream encapsulated in the European ideal if not always in its execution. The band have, by this time, spent almost 25 years confronting the fact that humans appear to be capable of only evolving so far before reverting to the worst elements of narcissistic nationalism. The Joke's answer to this has always been that we must not only acknowledge our primal instincts but find a way to embody them without doing harm – because otherwise, harm seems to be *all* that we do. The first of two singles from the album, 'Loose Cannon' reached 25 in the UK Singles Chart.

'You'll Never Get to Me' 6:19 (Coleman/Walker/Glover/Gill)
If 'Loose Cannon' is a midnight storm finally sweeping out to sea, 'You'll Never Get to Me' is dawn breaking over a hidden cove. Musically and lyrically, this feels like a first cousin to the *Democracy* era. It's at once a

welcome respite from the blood-soaked terror and a majestically optimistic composition. The lyrics have the classic misery-to-hope arc but rendered in unique Joke fashion. The chorus again relates the positive memories Jaz has of his childhood, while his various cries of 'Oh!' encapsulate the misery, the hope, and the journey from darkness to light. The raw emotion articulated in the chorus could be about sometime colleagues, fair-weather friends, lovers, managers or record-company execs – and this diffusion is exactly what allows the listener to read their own nemesis into the song and thus connect with it.

'Seeing Red' 5:27 (Coleman/Walker/Glover/Gill)

After the intimidating swagger of 'Loose Cannon' and the main-stage elation of 'You'll Never Get to Me', we're back to the horrors of war both at home and abroad (and within), and an overt cast-back to earlier times. In terms of global conflict and our reaction to it, 'Seeing Red' is in direct dialogue with 'Almost Red', as the 24 years between the band's first EP and this album concertina in horrific recognition that nothing has changed. In 'Almost Red', against a backdrop of Cold War paranoia, Jaz wakes up every day, puts on his stereo and hears 'chaos for breakfast'. Here, they're 'dropping bombs again' and 'doing it in your name'. Jaz reads the papers with his 'marmalade and buttered toast', but the stench of hypocrisy in Britain's illegal warmongering and dysfunctional relationship with the US is unmistakable. The call-back is emphasised when the line 'red sky in the morning' from 'Almost Red' is directly quoted in the 'Seeing Red' chorus.

Geordie's single-note guitar riff is the epitome of less being more: an apocalyptic warning needle jabbing incessantly into your prefrontal cortex. Grohl's frenzied fills into and throughout the chorus propel the track with bleak fatalism as Jaz recoils from a rising sea of red: a three-alarm fire of rapacious greed and insatiable bloodlust. There's zero excess in either arrangement or form here. There's no middle eight or breakdown, simply three verses, three refrains, a tight two-chord bridge and a hard out, as though any more would be too painful. The third verse sums up the feelings of someone ashamed of the country of their birth as it bombs civilians for oil, creating refugees that it will treat abysmally. Coleman is again confronting the gut-wrenching paradox of being a nonconformist Englishman in exile: a deep love of homeland mixed with utter contempt, a mixture so alienating that it can lead to a feeling of total despondency. This was the second and final single from the album and did not chart in the UK.

'Dark Forces' 6:26 (Coleman/Walker/Glover/Gill)

> There are 200,000 species dying every day. We are living in the Sixth Extinction period.
> Jaz Coleman, on stage, Huxleys Neue Welt, Berlin, 19 October 2018

The welcome return of Coleman's evocative keyboards sets the scene for a take-down of The Powers That Be and a call to action aimed at those who would resist these 'dark forces'. The intro is apt, as the track calls to mind movie classics like *The Devil Rides Out* and *Night of the Demon* with the return of Coleman's Gollum-voiced mage. In the first two verses, he asks us to prepare for an occult battle with dogmatic monotheists and old-money conspiracies – the cabal of democracy-haters, far-right psychopaths and Rapturists who are currently destroying the world for profit and their own perverted pleasure. The entire distorted worldview of this death-cult cabal is punctured thus: 'Justification of desecration; who wrote this madness?'

In the third verse, there's some tricksterish ambiguity, with Coleman apparently taking the role of 'an inside man of the serpent clan'. He's a malevolent 33-degree Freemason, using his dark-power connections and perverted esoteric teachings as 'power for power's sake'. Like the bankers, politicians, fundamentalist ideologues and CEOs who get up to shady rituals to protect and increase their 'personal treasure trove' in the privacy of 'Bohemian Grove'. But Jaz could also be portraying a Rosicrucian magus, willing and able to combat these same dark forces with equally formidable magick. The minor-key verses are counterpointed with an uplifting Mixolydian chorus, a perfect musical fit for the tentative hope that it's not too late for us to do something about our perilous situation, if only we can arm ourselves with knowledge and take responsibility for our future.

'The House that Pain Built' 6:13 (Coleman/Walker/Glover/Gill)
The sound of a psychic door swinging open segues into a bludgeoning riff and Jaz incants the elements that anchor him through the howling pain and wild insanity: my faith, my love, my people and my freedom. He resolves never to 'let it go again'. In seeming contradiction, the bridge is about knowing when to let go – especially when the only other option is being 'manic'. In the chorus, Coleman reaches a Jungian acceptance, recognising that the lows define and create the highs. That 'catharsis' comes from suffering. And that the lows and the highs create both the internal and external worlds of Killing Joke: the house that pain built. Pain which leads to art and wisdom.

Bonus Tracks

'Inferno' 3:35 (Coleman/Walker/Glover/Gill)
A short, sharp, clinical excoriation of the catastrophically long-drawn-out disasters of imperialist adventurism by the West, 'Inferno' features a truly magnificent Coleman performance. Based on a simple, descending riff – falling like the 'shell bomb' of the chorus – it would have made a great single. The middle eight breakdown to bass and drums is properly terror-inducing, with Jaz whispering the alliterative 'leaders that bleed us' before abhorring the poisonous currency of war: American drones and the one-dollar bill –

death for dollars for oil. The last verse includes the nihilistic 'everything is wrong, and my mind turns black': a perfectly sane response to yet another pointless war.

'Zennon' 5:39 (Coleman/Walker/Glover/Gill)
This is a funereal quick-march with a mournful, Nirvana-ish motif and a simple but brutally fatalistic drum pattern. Another call-back to previous tracks – 'Requiem' and 'Tomorrow's World' – the lyrics centre on the innocent lives lost in war, encapsulated by the devastating lines that culminate in a nervous child soldier raising his gun for the first (and most likely the last) time. The final two repeats of the chorus are separated by a guitar emulating a falling bomb, but even here, the Joke offer the faintest glimmer of hope: 'and in the end, all we have is each other'.

Hosannas from the Basements of Hell (2006)

Personnel:
Jaz (The Black Jester) Coleman: vocals, keyboards
Geordie Walker: guitar
Paul Raven: bass guitar
Benny Calvert: drums
Strings written and recorded by: The Black Jester (aka Jaz Coleman)
Percussion: Ronnie Barak ('Invocation')
Effects: Reza Udhin (uncredited)
Produced at: Studio Faust Records (aka Faust Studios), Prague by Killing Joke
Recording Engineer: Jerry Kandiah
Mixing Engineer: Mark Lusardi
Label: Cooking Vinyl
Release date: April 2006
Running time (original CD release): 62:00
Highest chart places: UK: Did not enter Top 100
Current edition: 2022 expanded reissue on Cooking Vinyl

> When we started making records, playing gigs wasn't that much different. You'd rehearse, you wrote the songs, you mic'd it up and you played it! And now, if you're not careful, you might not even see the fucking drummer and the maker of the fucking record. It's all bits of this, cut-and-paste. It can sound impressive on first listen, but after subsequent listens, it's lacking human imperfection.
> Geordie, interviewed by Andrew Bansal, *Metal Assault*, 4 July 2013

After the intricate serial assembly of *KJ 2003*, which was antithetical to Geordie's preferred production methods, *Hosannas* saw the Joke recording together in the same space at the same time, and that raw spontaneity is evident everywhere on the band's twelfth studio album (you can imagine Geordie hurling *KJ 2003* out of a window because it sounded too 'produced', as Hawkwind's Dave Brock did with *Astounding Sounds, Amazing Music*). As with *Brighter*, *Extremities* and *KJ 2003* (though that album's closing song is darker than those of the other two), *Hosannas* begins and ends with upbeat tracks, creating another journey from light into darkness and back into the light again – a purifying, ritual-shaped journey. Coleman's working title for the project was 'War Zones', but the eventual composition and inclusion of more optimistic songs meant that this title would have proved unrepresentative. The chosen title – named for the second track – is a perfect paradox for a record which presents the two sides of the band's worldview: *Hosannas* (literal meaning: praise, adoration, or joy) *from the Basements of Hell* (the literal lowest level of the metaphorical lowest place). For all the splenetic rage and idealism-rupturing disappointment that defined *KJ 2003*, *Hosannas* yet again has the band refusing to stay still, combining the adept-level pagan positivity of *Fire Dances* with the experience, insight, and wisdom of a mage who's been engaged in decades of intense study.

Everyone is firing on all cylinders here, despite the challenging circumstances of the sessions (it would be easy to tar all of the Joke's output with this brush, but in truth, only six of their fifteen studio albums were forged against a backdrop of extreme personal and/or professional chaos). Coleman has found the perfect blend of rage and hope. Raven has never sounded better, transmuting his years of an on-off relationship with the band into dense, rumbling, low-end gold. Benny Calvert has the ideal blend of power and panache, winding himself seamlessly into the Joke's identity. Musically, Geordie is, as ever, the still eye of the battering hurricane: chiselling riffs that seem already to exist from the living rock of (mostly) just 12 notes. Engineering, production, and mixing by Mark Lusardi, who engineered and mixed the *Turning Red* EP, all strike the perfect balance between metal heft, progressive complexity, and post-punk spikiness: since *Extremities,* the band's three strands of intertwining DNA. The album's cover and booklet art reproduce paintings by Russian surrealist Victor Safonkin, whose imagination is ideally suited to the Joke's paradoxical nature. The booklet features the second version of the triple-headed serpent logo, this time designed by Raven. As Jaz instructs in his liner notes: 'play at welding volume'.

'This Tribal Antidote' 4:14 (Coleman/Raven/Walker)

This is the band's most effective distillation to date of their nonconformist philosophy and another album opener that focuses on the positive, with the first line urging us to lift up our spirits. The production, engineering and mixing are immediately noticeable as more immediate than *KJ 2003*, with Geordie's guitar, in particular, sounding far closer to a live performance (much of the album is assembled from single takes).

The first verse encapsulates the song, the album and perhaps KJ's entire oeuvre, as suffering becomes 'merriment' through cleansing with fire and music. Bad things at the personal and global level (the second line is tragically prescient of Raven's death) are made tolerable through ritual purification and celebration of life with one's tribe. The chorus emphasises this with an invitation to assemble and 'rejoice'.

In verse two, an idea to which the band have continually returned is again given voice. What the Joke create is not a 'show' or 'entertainment', but rather it is a 'ritual', a 'festival of dissent'. The third and final verse melds outsider positions on religion, economics and consumerism. After some subtle counterpoint from Geordie – the only variance from an elegantly simple verse-chorus structure – the song ends with an irrepressibly upbeat Jaz whoop. However dark the time of recording – and several accounts paint it as sometimes *very* dark – the Joke's creative furnace has again transformed pain and rage into strength and joy. A rousing hymn to the Gathering.

'Hosannas from the Basements of Hell' 5:52 (Coleman/Raven/Walker)
Layered from a four-horseman gallop rhythm section, doom-foreshadowing strings and demon-dirty guitar, this is a headlong plummet into the abyss, with lyrics to match. Here, Jaz's opening salvo is to 'Go psycho!' – an invitation to let loose one's worst angels. The strings – over which there were apparently heated arguments – add a deeply resonant layer, especially in the context of Prague's rich musical history. Even Coleman's alter ego The Black Jester, who is credited with writing the string parts and is at his most anarchic on this album, resonates with Prague's Black Madonnas.

Someone harbours 'thoughts of killing' someone else. But there's an alternate path: to surrender oneself to music. When the Joke are 'lost in the noise' they are 'free'. Playing together is a release valve that means they are neither individually nor collectively 'a murderer yet'.

The chorus is a personal favourite, harking back to the more melodic era of *Night Time* and *Brighter* but still retaining rhythmic consistency with the much heavier post-*Pandemonium* verses, it summons altercations both verbal and physical that are ultimately rendered inconsequential by the dead. We must 'face ourselves' and find hope at our lowest ebb: 'hosannas rising from the basements of hell.' The only single from the album, it reached 72 in the UK Singles Chart.

'Invocation' 7:54 (Coleman/Raven/Walker)

> I conducted the string orchestration myself. That was actually taken from my opera *The Marriage at Cana*, which I conducted at the Royal Opera House in Covent Garden in December 2001. I wanted to do an extraordinary rendition, so I went to Kazakhstan and used the orchestra there. I thought it would be fun!
> Jaz Coleman, interviewed by Justin Donnelly, *Sydney Unleashed*, 2006

This is an epic outpouring of the Joke's collective visceral energy: Geordie's sonic attack, Raven's minimalist momentum and Coleman's evolving symphonic and Arabic idioms. The band, Ronnie Barak's percussion, TBJ's strings and classical harp are locked into a hypnotically rising-and-falling motif like a musical iteration of the famous snake eating its own tail: a writhing, spiralling, hell-burrowing *ouroboros*. The deity being summoned is the Whore of Babylon, 'destroyer of worlds' – another reference to John the Divine's apocalyptic *Book of Revelation* (in the booklet, the song's subtitle is 'Of the Whore Bitch Goddess Babylon'). Humankind is a lost cause. All is darkness and hate. 'My enemy's enemy is my friend' (one of the most catastrophically destructive ideas in society and geopolitics). The temples are empty. False religions rise. The final hold and ecstatic release starting at 6:40 is gut-wrenchingly awe-inspiring and one of my favourite moments across all 15 albums. For the full orchestral/choral effect, 'Invocation' is one of the Joke tracks that provide the basis for Coleman's Gnostic Mass, *Magna Invocatio*.

'Implosion' 6:41 (Coleman/Raven/Walker)

A paranoid zigzagging fugitive of a Geordie riff – arguably one of the pinnacles of his six-string art – kicks off another song of extremities. Calvert is extraordinary here: battering the kit with the wild abandon of a force-ten gale and the precision of a covert meteorological weapon. Lyrically, verses and chorus contain contradictions within them. Musically, dark, minor-key verses (subliminal root-note synth adding preternatural texture) balance a dawn-breaking Mixolydian chorus. To emphasise the song's title, the second chorus is interrupted by a fist-clenching, loin-girding middle eight, which sets up the 'implosion' and the ensuing sound of eruption.

This is a seeker's take on not running away from life but embracing it in all its chaos, beauty and anguish – allowing life to implode into you, to burrow marrow-deep, to affect you to your core. This is Jaz conjuring Jungian ideas as only he can, with the Joke providing a unique aural platform for this wisdom. The final verse confirms the song's meaning as the truth arrives with 'a smile' and a 'state of grace': that the only sane response to the 'great game of life and death' is acceptance. The outro is a doozy, with a new tenterhooks motif on single violin played over the main riff as we await the final 'implosion' – our own. Joy and sorrow, illumination and damnation, praise and abasement – let it all burst into you.

'Majestic' 5:40 (Coleman/Raven/Walker)

'Majestic' has a delicious ambiguity at the heart of its core message: that one can step outside the dysfunctional global masochism of 'accelerated eco-meltdown', 'debt', and 'psychological operations' and still feel 'fantastic'. The ambiguity is in that part of the feeling (or for some people all of it, through *schadenfreude*) that comes from the pleasure of knowing something that others do not – and watching those others suffer for their idiocy and delusion. As Jaz sings: you can't simply tell people to become wise – each of us has to become wise on our own terms. This is part of the trickster's position: perversely enjoying the stupidity, sadistic greed, and lethal vanity of those whom you mock. But the Joke transcend this position in that, along with the mockery, they provide all the information and impetus that someone needs to commence a journey towards wisdom – to move from ignorance to illumination. This 'Joker dialectic', if you will, is encapsulated in the laugh that Jaz emits at the end of the short breakdown before the final verse.

Raven is the star of this track, musically. One note for the intro/breakdown/outro, one for the verses, and one for the chorus (three notes total), but has anyone ever propelled a song so brilliantly with such precision minimalism? The rhythm and tone are so energetic and dense that they provide all the deep-end ballast and forward momentum that's required. The track is bookended by lyrics that underscore the occult provenance of outsider wisdom and how to attain it. The first line is at once an exhortation to 'initiate' (verb) and to become an 'initiate' (noun) – to 'wakey, wakey' as various occultists, including Kate Bush's 'heavy people' have it. If we were in any doubt, the final chorus ends with an additional line: 'Just like magick – yes, I feel fantastic'.

'Walking With Gods' 8:36 (Coleman/Raven/Walker)
With a ritualistic riff rhythm and synth synchrony over which the song's elements ebb and flow, the Joke create an ode to initiation – the same initiation referenced in 'Majestic', the initiation that ultimately allows the adept to walk with gods (whether you believe them to be actual gods or symbolically-embodied archetypes is up to you).

The bridge tells us that 'salvation' is not found in a 'pill' but in 'your skill', a pointed differentiation between escapism and acceptance, between self-anaesthesia and living through one's genius (in the original Latin sense). Only armed with true illumination can salvation occur – and salvation is what enables us to move forward 'till death intervenes' (which, as we know from 'The Death & Resurrection Show' is not the end). The breakdown highlights lyrics that only appear once but are critical: we must push ourselves 'beyond the limits of human endurance'. The route to wisdom is not for the lazy or the faint-hearted, but as the chorus proclaims: enough courage, enough wisdom and we can 'enter Eden'.

Once the individual is on the seeker's path, their strength is only enhanced by being around like-minded people: in Joke mythology, this is the band as inner family and the Gatherers as extended family. The track ends with a similar sound effect to that which occurs during 'Implosion': perhaps another instance of enlightenment bursting through one's rational and muscular defences (what Wilhelm Reich described as breaking through one's armouring) to reveal the soul, or Jungian 'Self' or higher consciousness – or whatever you want to call it. Or maybe it's the uncoiling of our physical mortality and ascent to a higher plane.

'The Lightbringer' 9:38 (Coleman/Raven/Walker)
A song that can be interpreted literally, metaphorically, or symbolically, 'The Lightbringer' assumes we are now at least adept in the Joke's miracle-mirth mystery school and are ready to receive secret wisdom regarding the hidden history of our species. And this lesson is for neither the prosaic nor the unfocused, clocking in at almost ten glorious complacency-obliterating, perception-twisting, mind-bending minutes. The great works, buildings, and achievements of humans – as well as most of the stories monotheistic religion tells us about them – are lies.

Whether your counter-intuition to these lies is the intervention of Lightbringer as a literal fallen angel, Lightbringer as a metaphor for alien intelligence, or Lightbringer as the daemonic divine spark inside each of us, is left up to you – though the song's introduction and chorus might be a clue to what the band think (my italics): 'the rebellious spirit *in you and me*.' But then, as though Jaz has already revealed too much, the closing lines again thread ambiguity, casting this intelligence as perhaps existing outside us after all. Pretty much all esoteric systems deliberately manifest inner worlds and voices as outer realms and beings: this is, after all, how one attains Knowledge and Conversation with the Holy Guardian Angel. As Robert Anton Wilson has it, the best perspective is the agnostic one of both/and. Or as Timothy Leary famously says in *How to Operate Your Brain* (again, the italics are mine): 'To think for yourself you must question authority and learn how to put yourself in a state of vulnerable open-mindedness, chaotic, confused vulnerability *to inform yourself*.'

'Judas Goat' 6:21 (Coleman/Raven/Walker)
Being a massive prog-head, as well as a Cardiacs fan for only a couple of years less than I've been a Gatherer, this track really hits the sweet spot. It opens with deeply uncanny synth. The verses, bridge and breakdown are in the irregular time signature of 5/4 (extremely rare for the Joke). In fact, we have *multiple* time signatures, with the chorus in a rolling 6/12 that sits inside alternating 11/12 and 13/12 cycles, with different elements emphasising alternating down-beats. It's got an asymmetric stop-start guitar riff. Add to these elements that it's one of the band's darkest tracks with some of Coleman's most poetic and devastating lyrics and you'll understand why it's a personal favourite. The irregular rhythms are entirely in service of the song's mood and subject matter: everything thrown out of alignment, the world turned upside down, the triumph of the horned one. Even the title is multifaceted, conjuring betrayal, ritual scapegoats, and the cloven-footed Beast itself. It's the direct opposite of the joyful pagan processions to the Beltane pyre of *Fire Dances*, as we 'follow behind the Judas goat'. This is the Joke at the absolute peak of their powers.

'Gratitude' 7:04 (Coleman/Raven/Walker)
The album ends as it begins: with a paean to the Killing Joke family and Gatherers. But where 'This Tribal Antidote' sets the tribe as a response to the insanity of the world, 'Gratitude' starts from a position of the tribe as a solution, reminisces about the tribe's power and meaning, and gives thanks for its existence and continuance. Verse one conjures the intent as years of watching each other's backs eventually lead to the clouds parting and a 'golden dawn'. This golden dawn is both the literal new day and the Hermetic Order, whose teachings influenced Aleister Crowley and from which Coleman has drawn inspiration towards his own mystery school as laid out in *Letters from Cythera*.

Again, lyrically this is in the vein of *Fire Dances*, with emphasis on the honouring of life, its touchstones and mysteries through rite, food, drink and laughter. Musically, the song is built *Pandemonium*-style on a heavy descending riff from Geordie, with a layered guitar taking the violin part. This is apt, as *Pandemonium* was a stable, fruitful, and positive moment in the band's history and this track taps back into that feeling as the dark night of the album's spiritual journey comes to an end. The chorus centres on an uplifting chiming guitar motif, heralding the breaking dawn, the last word, 'gratitude', running into the return of the descending riff. The final chorus is extended by two additional lines as Jaz toasts the man who 'loves every hour of every day' and summons a feast for 'the friends and faces met along the way'.

It's a fitting way to end an album that during the exigencies of its extended recording sessions in Prague, must sometimes have felt would never be completed or released. And it adds deep poignancy to the imminent tragic event in the band's history – to have come this far, survived so much but to face such pain and grief. And for that pain and grief to transmute into forgiveness, reconciliation, and a band, yet again, reborn. This is even foretold in the song's third verse, in which no one is exempt from 'total redemption'. And so ends what I would argue is the first of the band's two late-career masterpieces.

Bonus Tracks

'Afterburner' 3:29 (Coleman/Raven/Walker)

This is a wonderfully – and deliberately – bizarre track. A combination of faux metal-anthem chorus and the Joke's perennial disgust at self and world, 'Afterburner' worms its way into your affections and demands attention: like a three-legged feral cat. It cleverly commences with the chorus, creating maximum disorientation as Jaz tells us to go 'faster, faster' and to 'speed it up'. At this point – especially if you didn't know any better – you could be forgiven for imagining that Jaz is singing about amphetamines or Formula 1 over the speeded-up back-to-front rhythm from 'The Death & Resurrection Show'. But as soon as the verses arrive, it's clear that this song is about dysfunctional consumer culture in *Extremities* vein. The track hinges on a creepy synth-centred breakdown punctuated by guitar stabs, which accompany the gloriously provocative lyrics. Our brains are being manipulated by subliminals: 'beautiful, violent images' of 'fucking and killing'. This is the killing joke and Jaz can't help but laugh. It's a perfect summation of the hours of blunt-force advertising, consent-manufacturing news and mind-numbing entertainment to which most of us are subjected every day.

An alt version of 'Afterburner' is dread-inducing paranoia fuel with the three-note synth motif foregrounded and Geordie's Proterozoic riff cycling under a single line of chorus from Jaz, repeated for maximum mesmerism. The vocal ultimately breaks down and the track comes to a dead stop. Perfect for a 3 am terror trip.

'Universe B' 6:13 (Coleman/Raven/Walker)

Starting with a masonry-blasting aural assault, this is another existential joke with an exquisite return to sophisticated dissonance and counterpoint. With a minor-key melody in tension against an Altered scale riff, the first verse lambasts the 'bleak future world' that we've made, punctuated by 'unholy pylons' across 'black deserts' – this dystopian war-for-oil chaos a natural result of our greed (and again foreshadowing the band's 2015 masterpiece). The musical and metaphorical bridge in pure Phrygian takes us from these 'atrocities and wickedness and strife' to 'a meaning and a goodness in this life', elucidated in an ambiguously melodic chorus in which love transcends death and time is 'a lie'. After two bars of isolated guitar, a short middle eight has Geordie and Raven play the Altered scale riff in unison with Jaz intoning the root note, 'for eternity'. It's a truly cortex-tingling moment.

The next verse imagines a place outside of this violence and destruction, a 'Universe B' which we can dream into being – as Jaz did with his island retreat in Aotearoa, as the band do when they record, as Gatherers do wherever they assemble. A place outside fiat currency and indentured employment, where dissenters can party 'through the night' while 'the last battle' rages. But this being the Joke, there is some perennial dissonance troubling the uplifting chorus: the return of that rumbling Altered scale bass riff against the esoteric optimism (Jaz singing an ethereal minor motif: seventh to octave to fourth). And if that isn't complex enough, Geordie hits the minor fourth for the first time in the last few bars of a verse-motif reprise, creating uncanny sonic magick.

Absolute Dissent (2010)

Personnel:
Jaz Coleman: vocals, keyboards
Big Paul: drums
Youth: bass guitar
Geordie Walker: guitar
Additional keyboards by: Reza Udhin
Produced at: Britannia Row Studios, London by Killing Joke
Additional recording at: Space Mountain, Spain and The Dreaming Cave, London
Engineered and mixed by: Clive Goddard
Mixed by: Richard Nutting and Clive Goddard ('The Raven King' only)
Additional engineering, keys and programming by: Michael Rendall
Assistant engineering by: Joel Cormack, John Cox, Davide Venco
Vocals engineered at Faust Studios, Prague by: Thomas Stiehler and Derek Saxenmeyer ('Absolute Dissent', 'In Excelsis', 'European Super State', 'The Raven King', 'Honour the Fire', 'Here Comes the Singularity' only)
Label: Spinefarm Records
Release date: September 2010
Running time (original CD release): 62:47
Highest chart places: UK: 71
Current edition: 2018 2 x LP expanded remastered reissue on Spinefarm

> Things need to be said that aren't. And Killing Joke's a vehicle for us to do that.
> Big Paul Ferguson, interviewed by *Classic Rock Magazine*, 22 May 2013

In a perfect blend of life and art in synchronous imitation, shared grief at Raven's untimely death led to the reformation of the original line-up when Jaz and Big Paul reconciled after Raven's funeral, which was held on 31 October 2007 (the mythically apt All Hallows' Eve). After a tour – captured as *Live at the Forum* aka *The Gathering 2008* – the band pulled focus to new material and, in late 2009, began to craft their first album together since *Revelations*. An EP entitled *In Excelsis* previewed three tracks in June 2010, before the album was finally released in September (it was plagued by bad luck and extended delays).

The writing and recording sessions for *Absolute Dissent* were obviously an intensely collaborative effort and this is most overt in the eclectic blend of Geordie's rejuvenated riffing, Coleman's classical and prog sensibilities, Youth's dub/dance threads and Big Paul's metronomic hammer-falls. Lyrically it's demonstrated by an increase in the band's rage quotient (listen to Big Paul's solo work for a sense of how magnificently furious he is with the state of humanity). The contributions of all four members to the album's themes also come through in the extraordinary breadth of social, philosophical and spiritual ideas which have been poured into the 12 songs.

The album was to be originally titled 'Feast of Fools', another blissfully sophisticated ambiguity, with the fools in question being both the rich and powerful who are destroying the planet and us for letting them do so with impunity. Echoing the title of the previous album, *Absolute Dissent* is a glorious pun on 'absolute descent': converging the band's radical nonconformity and occult interests. This album also has the writing credits listed as 'Killing Joke' for the first time since 1994's *Pandemonium*. The cover, by the KLF's Jimmy Cauty (in a long-delayed but inevitable meeting of the two acts), is a deliberately incendiary image of a Christian cross to which microwave towers have been affixed – a stringent comment on both (or one of, depending on your prejudices) the crushing of the spiritual by technology, and the inextricable link between the Evangelical/Pentecostal right and consumerism's technological control. This cross is also a call-back to the one inside the original *KJ 1980* gatefold.

'Absolute Dissent' 6:16 (Killing Joke)

The new era fittingly commences with a melodic, anthemic chorus: 'absolute dissent, I won't relent', signalling that the Joke are still adhering to the paradox of incandescent fury and ritualised optimism, though now with the addition of wry acknowledgement and wise acceptance. Big Paul's return is immediately apparent, with that tom-tom-centred drum sound at the heart of the mix. The verses, anchored by Youth's questing, octave-jumping bass, expose and confront the harms we're doing to the planet and ourselves – harms that the rich and powerful are often doing to everyone else: 'poison water', 'poison air', 'poison bodies' (and this song was written well before the horrendous impact of so-called 'forever chemicals' was widely known or understood). The subject of 'genocidal plans' reappears here, with Jaz abhorring 'space weaponisation' and 'unelected control' – and calling out chemtrails and the Jeckle Island conspiracy (the US Federal Reserve was allegedly formed by a secret cabal of sadistic, avaricious mass murderers on an island off the State of Georgia in 1910). The Joke's desire to share heretical ideas and outsider perspectives appears to be stronger than ever.

Many journalists (and some fans) are squeamish at the band's embracing of so-called 'conspiracy theories', but there is a serious point to the Joke's interest and intent: the truth of the world is not what we think it is, either overtly in the physical world of corporations, politics and society – or covertly in the hidden spiritual world. Even if the existence of chemtrails is unproven, there are enough evidenced instances of corporations and governments poisoning our soil, air, and water (not least the recent ongoing scandal of privatised water in the UK) for chemtrails to be metaphorically true, if not scientifically so. It has become something of a trope to say that in a time of accelerating uncertainty, 'conspiracy theories' can provide certainty where the reality is often more labyrinthine and complex. But Killing Joke use what many would call 'conspiracy theories' to do the exact opposite: to create the metaphorical uncertainty and intellectual doubt from which enlightenment and wisdom can flow. Simply put: The Powers That Be *are* lying to you and they *are* trying to kill you.

'The Great Cull' 5:57 (Killing Joke)
This track skewers the idea that an 'elite' (self-determined by 'usefulness', but in reality determined by money and power) should thrive while the rest of us must perish. The new right-wing politics has this idea at its hardened heart. As with Jeckle Island, the 'conspiracy theories' are often horribly close to the truth. The third verse of 'Absolute Dissent' describes the 'brainwashed masses' from the POV of these 'elites', they are nothing but 'fodder', 'useless eaters' and 'worthless breeders' to be eradicated with runaway climate breakdown, out-of-control pandemics, economic crises and social meltdown, along with the knock-on effects of all these. Here, the subject receives an entire song: a primal, thundering, unstoppable order of death.

Beginning with a namecheck for Thomas Malthus, whose ideas inform the contemporary right-wing politics of population control, the track takes in global food standards and GMO, big pharma, war and ecosystem collapse. Again, the mention of immunisation here will repel some, but as with chemtrails, there is a hidden truth: pharmaceutical companies profit from illness and disease, and have sold drugs that have harmed millions (not to mention that the destruction of entire ecosystems by corporations leads to zoonotic contagions that big pharma then profit from). This being the case, why would anyone in their right mind trust anything they say? Again, the band are horribly prescient, with the SARS-CoV-2 pandemic giving multiple governments worldwide the chance to thin the herd with maximum plausible deniability (e.g. countries such as the UK that pursued unethical and lethal 'herd immunity' strategies). And the deeper irony is that most of us must trust them when it comes to vaccination or risk death from the diseases they refuse to control or mitigate except when it suits them. As Jaz sings in the ominous middle eight: 'most of us must die.'

'Fresh Fever from the Skies' 3:24 (Killing Joke)
Geordie's spot-rooted, panic-inducing guitar motif and Big Paul's reptilian-brain rhythms are in adrenalised synchrony on this frenetically fervid track, recreating the experience of Coleman and others when they saw seven unidentified glowing objects in the sky over Ladbroke Grove. An ominous synth swell before the verses adds to the uncanny mood, reminding us of the band in their early 1980s heyday. Jaz creates a storybook feel with the opening lines, asking his mother about a light 'shining in the night'. He can't sleep. He's afraid. But then we swerve into familiar apocalyptic territory with 'markets crashing down' and 'Judgement Day at hand'. The track's title and urgent paranoia suggest the quintessential British alien-invasion sci-fi of John Wyndham and H. G. Wells. There's no suggestion that these are benevolent

aliens come to save us from ourselves. The best-case scenario is 'a firework', which as sung by Jaz, sounds more like a phosphorous bomb than a benign bonfire-night spectacle.

'In Excelsis' 4:04 (Killing Joke)

Another anthem that could easily rock an entire stadium, this is a hymn to freedom 'in excelsis', literally 'in the highest degree' – psychological, spiritual, political and philosophical. It's worth reminding ourselves that before the neoliberal consumerist consensus, 'freedom' was an idea in direct opposition to the prevailing reactionary social and political norms. The idea of 'freedom' has, since 2016, become annexed by the far right, who use the term to mean freedom from facts, truth and the consequences of their ideas and actions. The Joke stand resolutely outside this recent social history, having always espoused the perennial freedom of the self-determining outsider who mostly wants to be left in peace rather than tell everyone else how to live, but will fight back against coercive control when necessary. The key lines are in the second verse, with 'liberty our common goal' and an edict to 'smash the cabals that control'. 'This world is ours, we won't be sold'.

'European Super State' 4:42 (Killing Joke)

> It's the cause of a controversy. We wish to stir up the debate. Myself, I see a place where Mr Blair, Mr Rumsfeld and Mr Cheney can all be tried in the European Super State.
> Jaz Coleman, on stage, London Apollo, 16 October 2010

Following 'Europe', this is the second KJ track about the European project, though the *Night Time* track is more ambiguous. This is a hymn to the EU as a peace bringer and bulwark against war. Jaz has many times over the years spoken about how the band see the EU as a positive force – a union of like-minded nations, whose citizens can retain their tribal and national identities even as they add a layer of European identity (identity not being a zero-sum game as the far right would have you believe).

Against a Central-European synth backdrop that resonates with Kraftwerk and Tangerine Dream, Jaz sings the first verse from the POV of deep European cultural heritage, combining 'Judeo-Christian morality' with 'Greco-Roman intellect'. The 'civilising force' of Europe 'demands respect'. The EU flag is referenced, heralding a 'brand new empire', which is 'ours to build' and 'ours the choice'. It's our choice because the EU reflects the politics and culture of its member states: a higher number of democratic governments and the union becomes more democratic; fewer democratic governments and the union becomes less so. The chorus declares that every citizen is 'required to debate' as if being expected to debate could ever be construed as a bad thing. It's deeply ironic that rather than be an active part of the EU's democracy, the

UK ignored both this 'choice' and this 'requirement' till leaving was offered – and then decided to engage in reactionary cynicism rather than constructive debate. Released in May 2011 as the sole single from the album, the song did not chart (surely a re-release in 2016 would have been suitably tricksterish?).

'This World Hell' 5:27 (Killing Joke)
Just when you think the album has gone soft – anthemically uplifting, optimistically cajoling, unashamedly cerebral – along comes 'This World Hell' with a skull-splitting death rattle. It's a piledriving, lumbering chunk of ear-shearing metal with Jaz, a howling apostle of doom and shades of Swedish metal gods Meshuggah in its rhythmic axe swing. The whole band are in nihilistic lockstep, with Geordie and Youth riffing in unison and Big Paul executing machine-gun bass drum and math-metal quadruplet breaks like a progressive-metal magus. At the risk of being repetitive, the prescience from the first line is astounding as the anaesthetised masses keep quiet while food is used 'as a weapon', though 'rage in the streets' is surely imminent. The chorus hides that kernel of Joker tricksterishness in cannibalistic death-metal sentiment: 'Die, long pig!' (For those not au fait with cannibal lingo, 'long pig' is human flesh.)

The bone-crunching breakdown is followed by the sucker punch of verse three, with the Joke resolving to attract us with 'words of honey' like bees to nectar, to free us from the 'pain of debts' as we all 'return to nature' and share 'the spoils'. There is another way: eco-anarchism. But before we've had time to digest this strong medicine, along comes the outro with an even stronger final message. You'll never 'see heaven'; rather, you will live in a 'permanent hell'. It's aversion therapy for the weak of spirit: act now or lose everything.

'Endgame' 4:41 (Killing Joke)
This is a Giza pyramid slab of syncopated conspiracy theory, worst-case scenario wargaming and unvarnished truth. Let's address the 9/11 conspiracy first: as stated above, in art 'conspiracy theories' are metaphors for hidden webs of deceit and occult truth rather than rabbit holes for the deluded and confused. The intent of art should be to challenge both our perceptions and our preconceptions, not provide simplistic black-and-white answers. And, lest we forget, KJ are the jesters at the court of human greed and stupidity: cocking a snook at norms and conventions since 1979. As has been the case since their inception, the Joke are way ahead of their time. The chorus begins with 'Baxter's caught out sending spores', a reference to the American pharmaceutical company that in 2009 sent samples of H3N2 seasonal flu virus contaminated with lethal H5N1 from its Austrian laboratory to European sub-contractors, who unwittingly used it to make a vaccine that subsequently killed the animals it was tested on: a sequence of events that sounds suspiciously like a possible origin for SARS-CoV-2. Thirteen years later, one can't help but feel that the time lag between dark prophecy and

even-darker reality is shrinking apace. Ever the realists, the Joke advocate expecting the worst ('be prepared for martial law') while hoping for the best ('shock by shock, we're all starting to wake up'). This final glimmer of hope appears to be the only part that Killing Joke have been consistently over-optimistic about: that we'd finally wake up. At the time of writing, there's no significant sign of this whatsoever – indeed, you could reasonably argue that the opposite is true, and we are but a syncopated beat from the 'endgame'.

'The Raven King' 6:33 (Killing Joke)

Against a Bach-style bass motif and Geordie's chiming guitar, the lyrics open with the legend about the ravens leaving the Tower of London and the Kingdom falling, with echoes of King Arthur without Excalibur at the mention of 'Albion'. This is a symbolic kingdom, 'guarded by warriors we knew' and 'guided by our ancestral voices'. But it's also a newly forged kingdom of outsiders, with 'flags of black and red' (the livery of anarcho-communism, but also now the unofficial heraldry of Killing Joke: red for wine and blood, black for ego-death and dissent; see *XXV Gathering: Let Us Prey* in Live and Compilations for more on this). The chorus is plangently poetic, conjuring 'the spectre of the Raven King', as though in leaving the Tower, the raven has revealed his true nature as an alchemical sovereign: a once and future king for dissenting Englishmen.

The soaring middle eight is one of the highlights of the whole album, if not the band's entire career, hymning the transformation that connects 'all as one'. Although Coleman has stated that the song is not directly about Paul Raven, but rather about Raven's deep sense of attachment to a mythic sense of Englishness and liberty, the last verse conjures a 'spirit of resistance' and a 'restless call for this defiance', with sorrow turning to 'anger in your name', ending with '*carpe nocturna*, seize the night now' which were the last words spoken by Raven to Coleman in Prague. It's a fitting tribute to the national identity lost and the passing of a bandmate and brother. This is another of the tracks arranged for orchestra as part of Coleman's *Magna Invocatio*, and that version is hauntingly beautiful.

'Honour the Fire' 5:50 (Killing Joke)

> If us four alpha males can find consensus on anything, that offers hope for the wider world. I don't think there are many other bands whose members still go on holiday together four decades into their career. Rock music at its best is unadulterated liberty, and Killing Joke still stand for freedom. Which is why I'll keep this band going as long as I'm alive.
> Jaz Coleman, interviewed by Paul Brannigan, *Louder*, 28 October 2015

Musically a call-back to the *Democracy* era, this song – a march into meaning – is built on processional bass, chopped guitar and ostinato synth, with lyrics that capture a sense of moving out of middle age and consequently thinking about mortality and legacy (and the band's members have been closer to death than many). This is a plea for 'just one more sunset', 'one perfect gig... before I die'.

The chorus is another uplifting pagan psalm, focused on those perennial Joke themes of fire and the eternal feminine. The middle eight, as is so often the case, holds a distillation of the song's truth, as the 'spark of life' endures through both loss and gain. Through the most challenging times, the band has survived, coming together every few years to 'honour the fire'. And that 'honouring' includes the memory of those lost, remembrance that keeps that flame alive.

'Depthcharge' 4:17 (Killing Joke)

This is a barnstorming four minutes of compelling industrial ska with allusive, mythic lyrics about our alienation from the Earth and its old gods – and how that alienation has led us to the brink of catastrophe. This disconnect between humans and nature is condensed in the verses. First, a contrast between entertainment-anaesthetised automata and living, sacred nature drowned by rising sea levels ('lying in front of the box' is a direct call-back to 'man watching video' from 'Requiem'). Then a lament for the loss of direct communion with earth, sea and sky. The chorus intones Kali, who is creator and destroyer: the 'depthcharge' will create chaos, but from that chaos, new life will grow and new civilisations will rise (though we probably won't be around to see them). It's also pleasing to hear the return of Big Paul's elemental breaks – there's an absolute humdinger out of the second verse into the chorus. There's also some glorious vocalising from Jaz, like a skanking catastrophe-brink jester. The outro features the devastating lyrics 'none more beautiful, none more terrible'. Although ostensibly about Kali, these words foreshadow the collapse of our ecosystem – a collapse that will be *an* end to the beauty and terror of nature (and *the* end of the beauty and terror of humankind). This track forms a thematic triptych with 'Kaliyuga-Struggle' from *Extremities* and 'Kali Yuga' (see below).

'Here Comes the Singularity' 5:04 (Killing Joke)

As with *Pandemonium*, on which the Joke address the millennium and the various eschatological predictions surrounding it, the prophecies regarding 2012 are foreshadowed here (and in 'Timewave', see below) before they're placed centre stage on the band's next album, *MMXII*. 'Here Comes the Singularity' is reminiscent of earlier Joke, with a bouncy Geordie riff, Youth's unison bass, and melodic Jaz vocal offset by uncanny synth effects. The mood of the song is distilled in the short, ominously industrial bridge, paranoia-inducing middle eight and apocalyptic outro. Jaz asks: 'Who is the architect and who the hidden hand?' To which the best answer is probably the Zen one: *I am*. Verse two revisits the Iraq War, still rolling on at the time *Absolute*

Dissent was released, more than seven years after its commencement. The last couplet refers directly to the protest against that war on 15 February 2003 in London when one million marched 'against a traitor's war' but still no one in power 'heard the call'. The third and final verse is an anarchist's wish-fulfilment, as those who starve, poison and kill for profit finally receive their comeuppance.

'Ghosts of Ladbroke Grove' 6:32 (Killing Joke)

> Well, it's our tribal area, apart from we hate the way it's been developed. We miss all our old friends. That's where we started this, where generations of my family have lived, it was the first cosmopolitan experiment in this country. It's sacred land. It was an area of dissenters and thinkers, and now it's just full of bankers and wankers.
> Jaz Coleman, interviewed by Rob Haynes, *The Quietus*, 12 August 2010

This is a beautifully-sketched portrait – at once a lament for the multiple changes that have affected the area over the intervening 30 years and a celebration of 'all my brothers and soulmates' and 'this hallowed ground'. The track starts and ends with a haunting spirit-conjuring synth wash. The verses alternate between Coleman's anguished throat singing and Youth's uncanny whisper, Jaz providing a travelogue while Youth loiters with malicious intent. A dub version (or more accurately a 'dubbier' version) with headphone-friendly isolated growling bass, chamber-echoing drum hits and an extra-haunted outro is on the *In Excelsis* EP, the 'European Super State' CD single, and disc two of *The Singles Collection* (an 'edit' version).

Related Tracks
'Kali Yuga' 3:53 (Killing Joke)
The third track on the *In Excelsis* EP (it also appears on the 'European Super State' CD single), this is not a new version of the 'Struggle'-paired synth track from *Extremities*, but an entirely new song harnessing the melodic qualities of *Brighter* with the plutonium-heavy riffing of the post-*Pandemonium* era to brilliant, urgent effect. It's depressing to think of the ever-increasing global problems between 1990 and 2010, including accelerating climate change (and what we're now beginning to realise was already an irreversible tipping point), the so-called 'Global Financial Crisis' (though it was in truth a crisis of greed – as was the world's response to it), the ongoing Afghanistan War, the beginnings of so-called 'austerity' (aka cruelty) and the ascent of the far right. If we appeared to be living in the *Kali Yuga* in 1990, then by 2010, this was undeniable (see 'Kaliyuga-Struggle' in *Extremities* for an explanation of *yugas*). Here Coleman sings of 'mass migration or starvation', the spraying of toxic substances, mutilation, and 'children screaming' while Youth's rollercoaster bassline bounces us over bomb-cratered warzones. As with

'In Excelsis', there are harmonic backing vocals on the chorus reprise, but here they are plangent rather than jubilant, and the whole thing ends with Geordie ominously striking strings that are already oscillating with dying reverberations. Properly chilling.

'Sixth Sun' 7:08 (Killing Joke)
The 'Sixth Sun' hypothesis is that humanity can move into a more harmonious relationship with the Earth. Akin to the Aquarian Age, it is based on the creation myths of Mesoamerica, where it was believed that the present aeon has been preceded by four previous ages, meaning that we are currently living through the fifth aeon. Each previous aeon has been destroyed by the gods. This 'sun' too will end ('the cleansing of the world, a fiery shower') and a new aeon, the 'Sixth Sun', will replace it. Ironically, the Aztecs believed that the fifth sun needs to be sustained with offerings of human blood – which seems to be exactly what we are doing in the third millennium. The verses have Jaz using a dissonant chant-style vocal over a unison guitar/bass riff, while the bridge sees him switch to melody, with some soaring vocal-and-bass optimism in the chorus. Big Paul adds some motivating drum breaks at the end of the second chorus as we march in ecstasy towards our destruction and renewal. Recorded during the *Absolute Dissent* sessions, this track appears in rough mix form on *The Singles Collection*, disc three.

'Timewave' 3:29 (Killing Joke)
A calculated shock to the system, this is a short, sharp, metal-infused warning about 'Timewave Zero' as formulated by the late anthropologist, ethnobotanist and psychedelic mage Terence McKenna. The track summons accelerating novelty, fractal chaos and rabbit-in-the-headlights human inaction as we 'dance the dance of karma faster'. Coleman's vocal echoes this fractal quality by repeating lines in different places across the three verses, while the chorus propels us ineluctably towards our endpoint destination. The breakdown is full-metal terror, while the track's hard-out emulates history's imminent collapse to a fixed point. Pairs well with Time Zone's ground-breaking 'World Destruction' from 1984. A demo of 'Timewave' appears on the third disc of *The Singles Collection*, while a live version features on Night Two of live set *The Gathering 2008*.

'Feast of Fools' 5:53 (Killing Joke)
The final unused track from the *Absolute Dissent* sessions to be released (it's on disc three of *The Singles Collection*), this is a perfect balance of bright melodic verses and dark funereal chorus, anchored by a majestic, yet harmonically ambiguous Geordie riff and a gorgeous 1960s-style string arrangement played on synth. The verses spin around unison guitars as a clean-voiced Jaz effortlessly deconstructs the endemic deceit of The Powers That Be: 'I don't believe in the stories you are weaving'. (And even if The

Powers That Be sometimes tell the truth when it's in their interest, how are we supposed to know the difference?) The penultimate line of the first verse is immediately resonant with the last episode of *The Prisoner*, in which Number Six (Patrick McGoohan) pulls successive masks from the face of Number One: 'I pull your mask off, find that there's another'.

The third verse describes how the rich and powerful control the fools: telling you 'one thing' as they 'propagate another'. It also features a magnificently tricksterish pair of couplets in which Jaz makes it clear that he has 'no trouble' turning everything 'to rubble', but that annihilating it 'completely' must be done 'discretely'. In contrast, the chorus features Coleman's throaty disgust in full flow as he berates the 'feast of fools'. So, who are the fools – we who believe the lies, or the liars who will one day be brought to account for their lethal deceit? There's a prog breakdown, an ironically serene middle eight and some lovely Geordie flourishes on the outro. The chorus was repurposed for 'Penny Drops', B-Side of *MMXII* track 'In Cythera'.

MMXII (2012)

Personnel:
Jaz Coleman: vocals, keyboards
Big Paul: drums
Youth: bass guitar
Geordie Walker: guitar
Produced at: The Doghouse Studio, Oxfordshire and Faust Studios, Prague by Killing Joke
Recorded by: Clive Goddard, Michael Rendall and Tom Dalgety
Programmed by: Michael Rendall and Tom Dalgety
Mixed by: Clive Goddard and Tom Dalgety
Additional engineering and programming at Faust Studios by: Reza Udhin
Label: Spinefarm Records
Release date: April 2012
Running time (original CD release): 50:53
Highest chart places: UK: 44; Finland: 9
Current edition: None

The year of the London Olympics and lethal austerity in the UK (alongside various global prophecies revolving around both apocalyptic catastrophe and a golden New Age of peace and harmony) was the ideal year for the magicians of paradox to release their second album with the reconstituted original line-up. The Joke's fourteenth studio album follows the template of *Absolute Dissent*, with a combination of political and personal songs, though here the distillation goes further, with seven of the ten tracks around or under the five-minute mark and only one epic. Big Paul is even more strongly felt in the lyrics than on the previous album, with songs about the malign power of the state ('FEMA Camp'), technology ('Colony Collapse'), and unaccountable corporations ('Corporate Elect'), plus two dissenting anthems released as B-Sides: 'Penny Drops' and 'New Uprising'. The album is rounded out by two tracks about natural apocalypse ('Glitch' and the aforementioned epic, 'Pole Shift'), two about relationships inside and outside the band ('Primobile' and 'In Cythera') and two about spiritual regeneration ('Trance' and 'On All Hallow's Eve'). It's arguably the Joke's most perfectly balanced and succinct studio set of the third millennium.

MMXII (or, as I now call it, *MMXXII*, 2022, bringing the chaos that *MMXII* foretold) reached 44 in the UK Albums Chart and rendered two singles: 'In Cythera' and 'Corporate Elect.' After a three-album absence, this is a welcome return for Mike Coles. It's one of his most brutally dark covers, showing a bone-white human skull in profile against parched earth and an industrial horizon. Chimneys pump poison into the sky while what looks like a meat grinder hangs ominously in mid-air like part of a sentient abattoir. The juxtaposition again recalls the line from *Requiem*: 'He's just cattle for slaughter.'

'Pole Shift' 8:57 (Killing Joke)

This is an epic, colours-nailing opening track combining everything the band do musically and lyrically – from soaring sonic purity to crunching riff distortion, from ecological tumult to occult transcendence. Immediately we have a superb fusion of the Joke's prog tendencies (the synth opening would sound at home on an IQ album), an evocative Geordie motif, and an elegiac throat-edged vocal from Jaz. In a gut-wrenching take on the cataclysmic pole-shift hypothesis, the metaphorical truth of that idea is laid bare in the first four lines as Jaz suggests that it 'doesn't really matter' if the poles switch or the stars come to a stop or a tsunami kills millions, we're all still screwed. We have destroyed our only viable ecosystem and the disaster will be all too real – no hypothesis or conspiracy theory required.

The bridge flips the aural poles like a geomagnetic reversal, replacing haunting synth and plangent Dorian melody with a tectonic-plate splintering Altered scale riff and lyrics that subsume apocalypse, Timewave Zero, Sixth Sun and quantum singularity, leading up to the Phrygian chorus, in which the pole shift hits. But this shift has now become a metaphor for something positive, captured in the second verse. The pendulum has 'swung the other way', awakening us from our torpor 'towards a partnership of co-creation'. These ideas are endarkened in the occult sense by the subsequent bridge, in which today's taboos are 'tomorrow's delights'. The final bridge goes further, heralding 'communion with the stars' and 'quantum immortality' before we come full circle and end with that haunting synth.

'FEMA Camp' 5:02 (Killing Joke)

Through Presidents Democratic and Republican, there has been a slew of conspiracies against communities (usually poor and/or black) by corporations and Federal and State governments – the water in Jackson, Mississippi, as just one recent example, still unresolved at the time of writing. The 'natural' disaster of Hurricane Katrina was followed by an inarguably human-made catastrophe of incompetence, corruption, and class/race warfare, in which the poor and black inhabitants of New Orleans were subjected to something approaching ethnic cleansing. This fed into a network of conspiracies surrounding FEMA (the Federal Emergency Management Agency of the US), the most disturbing of which supposed that the US government was planning to detain its own citizens in camps. Combined with an attempt in 2011 by two US Senators to expand the definition of the military battlefield so that it would cover the entire US, these FEMA conspiracies led to some believing that the Federal government was planning, not only to arrest but perhaps to murder its own citizens.

These ideas form the basis for the lyrics of this track, which draws specific inspiration from a video of a supposed FEMA camp (weblink in the CD's booklet) which appears to have the worst possible associations in terms of barbed-wire fences, train tracks and incinerators. This obviously sparked something in the Joke, who have a long-standing connection to the idea of humans being transported and killed like cattle. Some uncanny synth leads to another of the band's funeral marches – by turns solemn and furious – with musical associations to both *Pandemonium* and *KJ 1980*. The last line of the second verse demands a fightback: 'so, I'm going to join up with the renegades.' Eleven years later, we know that accelerating climate collapse will eventually lead to tens of millions dead or displaced worldwide and that these camps might finally be used for their covert purposes – whatever they may be.

'Rapture' 4:16 (Killing Joke)
After a song blending the earthly and the spiritual ('Pole Shift') and a song focused only on the earthly ('FEMA Camp') comes a song that entirely concerns the spiritual. 'Rapture' (both title and single-word chorus) is an occult prayer-ritual that moves through knowledge, purification and ecstasy to a final journey into wisdom, a leap 'with certainty into the abyss'. The track begins with a phased synth similar in mood to the 'Whiteout' intro then settles into a Phrygian space-rock jaunt replete with reverb on Coleman's vocals. There are sonar-style clangs before the second verse, pagan whoops and cries in the middle eight and a glorious root/flattened-second clash from Geordie to end. It's late-era Joke compressed to its quintessence.

'Colony Collapse' 5:05 (Killing Joke)
A Geordie warning signal gives way to a subtly dissonant post-prog chord progression and a root-note verse backing before that uncanny chord sequence returns to cycle under the two-word chorus with elongated syllables (again, the chorus is the title). There's even a bedevilled violin in the short bridge. A swaggering guitar motif heralds the middle eight, preceding the warning signal's return. That's followed by some thundering Big Paul fills and repeats of the chorus with all the song's elements now in play. The track ends with a third warning and a hard out – this time, a single chopped root chord. The colony collapsing is the human one on planet Earth: assaulted by 'nano-computer technology' and 'self-assembling nanobots'. It's a pointed attack on cybernetics and AI (plus a reference to 'conspiracy theory' favourite 'grey goo' for good measure). It's true that 'the future doesn't need us' if the machines that we've created take over – and that future looks increasingly bleak. Jaz appeals to 'Beloved Mother' – the eternal feminine of Gaia, Kali, Isis and the Black Madonna – to 'intervene!'. Sadly, you could argue that climate collapse is her doing exactly this – erasing humans before our hubris renders the planet uninhabitable for millennia.

'Corporate Elect' 4:00 (Killing Joke)
A succinct, vitriolic proclamation in the vein of 'Money is Not Our God', this track encapsulates the Joke worldview in 2012 and provides the central pivot of the album. The first verse pulls no punches in calling out

the 'Grand Masters' who are 'pulling strings' to create a 'New World Order' based on 'neo-feudal blueprints'. 'We all got fooled again' – the pointed last line of each verse – is a nod to The Who's classic affirmation and must have particular frisson for Geordie, an avowed fan of that band. The chorus – heralded by a rising vocal portamento from Jaz – condemns the 'ADD generation' who appear permanently distracted by empty consumerism and propagandised media. The term 'corporate elect' perfectly describes the corporatocracy of 'immoral psychopaths' who are at once unelected and have 'elected' themselves unopposed (see companion track 'New Uprising' below in Related Tracks for what the Joke think we should do about this situation). The outro has Geordie on top form with some glorious tremolo picking, effects wrangling and feedback. A limited-edition single, the second from the album after 'In Cythera', was released in December 2012 and did not chart.

'In Cythera' 4:30 (Killing Joke)
The Joke surprise us by again showing they can write a perfect pop song if they so desire (and there's a nice resonance to the slightly New Order feel, as KJ toured with Joy Division in 1980, while Jaz and Geordie have collaborated with Peter Hook as K/93). This is a supremely elegant four-and-a-half-minutes, with verses in the simple minor key and a chorus in Mixolydian, but the melodies are truly gorgeous: a plaintive verse and a yearning chorus combining to deliver Coleman's message of regret, thanks and reverence for a significant other who helped him through some of the most challenging periods of his life. Jaz associates this other with 'Cythera', his island home in Aotearoa. The liner notes feature links to Watteau and his 1717 painting 'The Embarkation for Cythera', after which Coleman named his Southern Hemisphere redoubt (the painting is in the Louvre). The track was released in March 2012 as the first limited-edition single from *MMXII*. It did not chart.

'Primobile' 4:44 (Killing Joke)

> Four people with different destinations, but all going up the same flight of stairs.
> Big Paul (with Jaz, Geordie and Youth), interviewed by Phil Sutcliffe, *Sounds*, August 1980

This is a song specifically about the band – here focused on their interpersonal relationships. But as with all great songwriting, the personal is also the universal, meaning anyone should be able to find something to which they can relate in the sentiments and ideas shared. People can be 'separated from each other' but still 'bonded by time as one'. The past can be 'forgiven'. There's also a strong sense of the band – both individually and together – evaluating their legacy. Jaz asks whether their deeds will be 'remembered with loving praise'. Did they 'fight with courage' and 'make a better place'? The imagery of tilling the soil and planting a forest 'for the human race' is particularly effective. The chorus, with Jaz roaring at full tilt, is an apt summation of the Killing Joke itself: 'Holy is the laughter that overcomes all your fears.' Plus, there's another humdinger signature ending from Geordie – full of passion and dissonance. The title appears to be a portmanteau of two words to mean 'prime mover' – something that Killing Joke continues to be in the life of its four founding members.

'Glitch' 4:48 (Killing Joke)

If there's a Hollywood disaster movie for every apocalypse then the film that pairs with this number is *Knowing* (2009), the utterly bonkers Nic Cage one about the solar flares. These are a type of solar storm that can affect the Earth's magnetosphere and act like a natural EMP weapon, knocking out all electronic systems and devices. All the cars are 'crashing', and all the planes are 'grounded'. This Armageddon, as with 'Asteroid', is entirely outside our control, so there is no glimmer of hope on the horizon, only 'chaos' and societal breakdown. Everyone's reached 'boiling point', but there's no ice to hand (the Joke finding perennially English dark humour amid the end times).

Musically 'Glitch' is a perfect blend of Coleman's soaring symphonic opera (here the bridge's prog-adjacent ascending motif) and Geordie's gargantuan industrial metal (here a crunching descending riff that punctuates the verses), together creating a feverish and impishly witty warning about the dangers of our over-reliance on computers and electricity. The lyrics deliberately veer from the loss of genuine essentials to luxuries, making us question what we regard as the status quo. The arrangement is so lean that there's room for three extended verses (though the final verse is a reprise of verse one to push the message home), multiple repeats of the bridge, and yet another of KJ's minimalist choruses. There's even enough time for a pulverising mini-breakdown before the final bridge-chorus pair and some end-of-the-world SFX.

'Trance' 6:09 (Killing Joke)

> Till death do us part. We are here to tell you that in the future, the Earth will heal itself. Time is nothing. One day in the distant future, far ago, yesterday, tomorrow, the forest will stretch for eternity. And the dark gods shall be no more. The ancient mysteries shall be restored.
> Jaz Coleman, on stage, the Roundhouse, 17 November 2018

This is something of a companion piece to 'Primobile'. While the earlier track focuses on the personal and the professional, 'Trance' concerns the esoteric and spiritual ideas and experiences that bind together the band, their inner circle, their tribe, and the Gatherers 'through all the decades' (Youth quotes the 'Pssyche' bassline throughout, subtly to reinforce this theme). As with the occult, the song is a complex, multi-faceted, asymmetrically structured crystal that takes a while to enter into your mind and even longer to seep into your unconscious. The 'fields of light' in the chorus are specifically magnetic convergence points, while the verse lyrics are a succinct description of the KJ ethos. The line 'transmissions from the Vortex room' would make a brilliant title for a biography of the band (the 'Vortex room' is the occult space prepared by Big Paul and Jaz in a Battersea flat for their ritual on 26 February 1979).

The verses gradually pull these experiences and ideas from the band's gravitational orbit to that of all humanity, capturing our uniqueness as a species by referencing the alien genesis hypothesis. 'Pyramids and obelisks' unconsciously remind us that our civilisation was not the first and won't be the last – and yet every civilisation is miraculous. The final verse's last lines pull back even further to reveal the secret wisdom behind the multiverse, the geometry of creation 'hidden from the common view'. Geordie's bizarrely lopsided riff and derivations thereof combine with Youth's octave-jumping bass as a backdrop, while mid-verse instrumental sections create both disorientation and subliminal flow. A final guitar ostinato carries us from individual to universal consciousness, from perception to truth.

'On All Hallow's Eve' 3:22 (Killing Joke)

The latest in the Joke's unique line in pagan hymns, this track refers back to the Wheel of the Year nature worship of *Fire Dances*, as well as tracks like 'Communion' (*Pandemonium*) and 'Four Stations of the Sun' (*Democracy* sessions). The song is named for the Christian festival which precedes All Hallows' Day. Here this recalls pagan Samhain (which was integrated into the Christian festival) as well as the Mexican Day of the Dead. A simple devotional rhythm, crackling synth textures (like a broadcast from an Edenic 1950s) and Mellotron-style choir back the clean-voiced verses.

The second verse conjures 'endless drumming' and rituals to wake the dead (a good description of Killing Joke's performances), while Jaz requests that we 'bring gifts and spirits' (of both the distilled and incorporeal kind). The offerings listed – among them bread, cheese and cigars – are deeply personal to Coleman and the band, so carry powerful meaning. In *Letters from Cythera*, Jaz writes of the importance to him of a simple meal of 'cheese and bread', and of the simple joys of 'good wine' and a cigar (an earthly delight he shared with Raven). The band are famous for their backstage cheese boards, often supplied by Gatherers (see *A Prophecy Fulfilled* for more on this idiosyncratic tradition). The bridge and chorus – given an expansive quality by the addition of Geordie's exulting guitar and Jaz roaring with joy rather than rage – are a call to mark the day with not sadness but jubilation.

Related Tracks

'Penny Drops' 6:04 (Killing Joke)

> ...the whole idea of economic growth – it's a redundant concept. We should be looking at sustainability and the well-being of the human condition above anything. I'm absolutely not a capitalist; I'm not a Marxist, either. But I am a communist when it comes down to equal opportunities, divisions of the spoils. I believe that food and water is a human right. It's not just for the rich.
> Jaz Coleman, interviewed by *The Skinny*, 28 March 2012

This track from the *MMXII* sessions didn't make it to the album but appears on the 'In Cythera' CD single. Lyrically, it's a companion piece to 'New Uprising', the other track from these sessions that didn't reach the final cut but was subsequently released (see below). The title and chorus use the English phrase 'the penny dropped' which describes a moment of delayed revelation or insight (literally 'coined' in the 1930s when a penny would get stuck in early vending machines and only when the penny finally 'dropped' would the machine dispense its product and/or allow the next customer to insert their penny). Here the phrase applies to citizens of the world finally realising that The Powers That Be ('oligarchs protected by Official Secrets Act') do not have our best interests at heart and are planning to continue lifestyles of luxury without us in 'gated communities' as climate and other catastrophes hit. As the chorus suggests, this revelation may lead to chaos before it leads to a new dawn: 'when the penny drops.' The chorus, which has a beautifully constructed counterpoint between chords and vocal line, has been repurposed from *Absolute Dissent*'s unused track 'Feast of Fools'. Geordie's ending is a classic: the tension of Phrygian's flattened second against its flattened seventh before root resolution: penny dropped.

'New Uprising' 6:10 (Killing Joke)

It's anyone's guess why this absolute banger was left off the album proper and offered only as a bonus track online and as part of the 'Corporate Elect' single. It's a stone-cold aural assault with another deceit-blasting chorus and a breakdown that nods back to the band's first two albums. A driving, goth-infused synth motif leads into a lurching monster of a Geordie riff, thumping great Big Paul hits and tremolo picking from Geordie layered on top. The verses, sung by Jaz full-throated, reference a cauldron of possible revolution triggers: 'food riots', the breakdown of the 'social contract', 'hacking and WikiLeaks', 'industrial chemicals unleashed' (hugely prescient, as I'm editing this the week that the entirely human-made disaster in East Palestine, Ohio is unfolding). The bridge sees secrets 'exposed' before the chorus calls for 'insurrection' and a 'new uprising'. The middle eight is sublime, featuring dissonant treble guitar drones over tribal toms and a brutal sung-whispered Joke paradox: 'Where are the wars? We are the wars.' The main motif restarts only to come to an uncanny full stop, before again restarting to be followed by a double chorus and a hard out on that spectacular dissenting riff. And Jaz even throws in a shout of 'Go!' for good measure.

Pylon (2015)

Personnel:
Jaz Coleman: vocals, keyboards
Geordie Walker: guitar
Youth: bass guitar
Big Paul Ferguson: drums
Produced at: Vada Studios, Gloucestershire, The Lair, Bath, and The Hive, Prague by Killing Joke and Tom Dalgety
Mixed at: The Lair and The Doghouse Studio, Oxfordshire by Tom Dalgety
Recorded by: Tom Dalgety, Amak Golden, Michael Rendall and Bert Neven
Programmed by: Tom Dalgety and Amak Golden
Additional engineering and programming by: Joe Jones, Reza Udhin, Youth, Michael Rendall, Jamie Grashion and Edward Banda
Label: Spinefarm Records
Release date: October 2015
Running time (original CD release): 57:09
Highest chart places: UK: 16
Current edition: 2021 2-CD expanded remastered reissue on Spinefarm

The third of an unofficial triptych that began with *Absolute Dissent*, this is justly considered a late-career masterpiece and is one of my favourite Joke discs. The three albums with the reformed original line-up offer an eviscerating take-down of the world between the Global Financial Crisis and Trump/Brexit, reflecting the first three albums by the band, which deal with similarly urgent ideas. You can track the Joke's concerns from those early 1980s albums and see how the world's refusal to deal with the problems they explored led directly to the world as it stood in 2015, with no end to warmongering for profit, accelerating austerity, increased threat from zoonotic pandemics, Russia increasingly isolated, technology seemingly out of control, society utterly broken in much of the democratic West, and the populist Right on the rise. *Pylon* is as fresh, urgent, adrenalised and furious as the band have ever been, conclusively proving that the Joke is on anyone who ever doubted them – and underlining the words of Joke icon Alex Harvey: 'There is no complaints department, it's only up to you.'

Apart from that menacing pun ('pile on') and the word's meaning as an electricity-carrying tower or communications mast, a 'pylon' is also a gate, specifically of an Ancient Egyptian temple, rendering this *Pylon* a portal to a tech-dystopian hell, or an autonomous hinterland – or the Age of Horus. Depending on your perspective, we have already made our choice, or we are gathered 'outside the gate', pondering which path to take.

Tom Dalgety, who had recorded, programmed, and mixed *MMXII* alongside Clive Goddard and Michael Rendall, here becomes producer alongside the band, as well as sole mixing engineer: cranking the Joke's now signature sound another couple of notches. The balance between synth and guitars is again adjusted, with guitars prominent and synths fulfilling their original uncanny function. Geordie is an autonomous riff machine, firing sonic nails. Youth's bass twangs and snarls like a zombie wolf. Big Paul's drums are colliding anvils, while Jaz's voice is, remarkably, still intact, considering the flame-scorched technique he uses to produce his dirty vocals. Big Paul famously described Killing Joke as 'the sound of the Earth vomiting' – and with *Pylon* the band's furious purging provides their most bilious catharsis yet. The ten tracks of the original release are expertly balanced, creating a reality-weighted arc from the upbeat opener to the ambiguous last song. The Mike Coles artwork is superb, nodding back to *Pandemonium* but in antithesis: here, the cover-image mandala is that of an insidious New World Order of technological coercion and social control. *Pylon* reached 16 on the UK Albums Chart, the band's highest placing since *Pandemonium* in 1994.

'Autonomous Zone' 6:44 (Killing Joke)

> [It's] magick. I wouldn't swap it for 60 more years on the planet and a billion in cash. They are my arms and legs while I am theirs. We are one entity.
> Jaz Coleman, interviewed by Joseph Aprill, *Invisible Oranges*, 20 November 2019

The concept of the TAZ (Temporary Autonomous Zone) was conceived by the American writer, mystic and anarchist Peter Lamborn Wilson (aka Hakim Bey) and refers to a place outside the control of the state and beyond the dogmas of state-sanctioned ideology. You could easily argue that Killing Joke created their own 'autonomous zone' in 1979 and have stayed resolutely inside that zone ever since. Here the band coalesce previous themes about living beyond social norms into a manifesto for 'living outside of the grid'. The lyrics pinpoint the way that authoritarian regimes hold sway over their populations variously through coercion, by inflicting poverty and sickness, and by maintaining a near-continual state of political and spiritual anaesthesia.

Instead of that 'misery', the Joke advocate that we join them in their autonomous zone where 'lovers of freedom gather to laugh' 'under the flag of the black and the red'. Uncannily rhythmic synth creates an otherworldly atmosphere, while Geordie's chop-chops drive the track and Youth's irrepressible funk flourish propels us into the verses. The bridge and chorus play out against an Arabic-sounding two-note drone, apt in terms of Bey's deep connection to Sufism. In the breakdown, Big Paul's tribal toms act as a pivot between the zone's symbolic creation and the unleashing of primal energy that occurs once the zone's doors are thrown wide open: 'cacophony, lovely ear-splitting noise.'

'Dawn of the Hive' 6:29 (Killing Joke)
Pylon's de facto title track is where the band's long-term penchant for metaphorically sublime sci-fi dystopias combines with decades of festering

paranoia to create a quintessential late-career Joke track – foreshadowed five years earlier by the cover of *Absolute Dissent*. Coming across like the nightmare child of Nigel Kneale's *Quatermass and the Pit* and a YouTube 'conspiracy theory' rabbit hole, 'Dawn of the Hive' warns of an interconnected hive mind created by the tech which surrounds us – and of the long-term social and psychological consequences of which we are still blissfully unaware. An allusion to the Tarot card The Tower – which heralds catastrophe or massive change – is emphasised by a foreshadowing of the 'all-seeing eye', which is at once technologically terrifying and malevolently magickal. So potent is this marriage that its progeny are 'angels, holograms, visions and voices'. Everything is machine tooled to perfection: visceral synth pulses, Geordie's doom-panic riffing, Big Paul's piledriving pulse, Jaz's clean vocal (hauntingly sacred in the chorus), the speed-dub reverb, and the two brain-battering breakdowns enclosing a motif-modulated middle eight. Plus, it's a subtle thematic sibling to 'The Hum': command and control updated for the third millennium. Masterful.

'New Cold War' 6:51 (Killing Joke)

The prophets of civilisational collapse yet again predicted the world's direction of travel with this track, the thematic heart of the album, which seems even more apt now than it did in October 2015 when *Pylon* was originally released. The band's more melodic approach with mostly clean vocals reaches a zenith here, with dire warnings of global conflict presented in an elegant velvet glove rather than the gargantuan armoured fist of *KJ 2003*. Here the warnings are about a 'unicentric one world order', though not the flavour envisaged by utopians. This is the kind that appears to be spreading democracy through domestic uprisings (represented by the contentious 'colour-coded revolutions') but ends up with the entire political system being bought by corporations, with voters caught between the immovable object of authoritarianism and the unstoppable force of 'democracy', between an illusion of citizenship and the truth of vested interests having covert control. The kind of vested interests that would destroy our only viable ecosystem for profit, as 'corporate forces' look for 'mineral resources' in the 'Arctic wastes'.

In a doleful minor and with Jaz reverting to tightened throat, the chorus groups together several chaos/control ideas, including 'food prices soaring' due to sanctions, warmongering propaganda ('all the hawks cried more') and a reference to Minerva, the Roman goddess of wisdom and war, who relates directly to the Bavarian Illuminati and, through her companion animal the owl, to Bohemian Grove (see *KJ 2003*'s 'Dark Forces').

'Euphoria' 4:17 (Killing Joke)

This is a beautiful track, combining in one song the poles of gothic darkness and ecstatic fervour – another honest hosanna from the trickster's basement. The first verse sets an autumnal scene, with 'branches bare' and laughing magpies. Jaz 'can't shake this melancholy'. The magpie, associated in Joke lore with Raven, also signifies sorrow in 'Seeing Red'. The chorus stays in the same minor key – how's that for ambiguity – but the lyrics are unashamedly uplifting as the 'clouds break' and sunlight bursts through. The second verse asks us to forget the 'dark phantoms of the past' and 'like Orpheus' not to look back. Instead, we should focus on what's ahead of us. The Orpheus reference is double-tuned, as it refers both to the story of Eurydice, but also alludes to the band themselves, who can collectively lay a strong claim to the title of our age's Orpheus: musician, poet, prophet and visitor to the underworld. The middle eight plays this shift from melancholy to ecstasy in microcosm, with a short modulation from minor to major (the major key appearing like hens' teeth in late-era Joke) before reverting to the root minor key.

'New Jerusalem' 6:11 (Killing Joke)
Music has always been politically charged. In 1999 Hinewehi Mohi sang the New Zealand national anthem in *te reo Māori* at the Rugby World Cup final in Twickenham, a courageous choice that ultimately generated progressive change. In 2020 Golda Schultz sang a new arrangement of Parry's original setting of Blake's 'Jerusalem' by Errollyn Wallen, which was similarly divisive. These controversies are, of course, linked by Coleman: Jaz working with Hinewehi Mohi on the *Oceania* project, which led directly to history being made at Twickenham, and the Joke pointedly using the multifarious concept of a 'New Jerusalem' to inspire this track.

Ominous synth drone, Geordie's axe-falls and Youth's twanging bass set the scene for a syncopated motif from the end times dancehall. From a British perspective, the verses traverse entertainment addiction, the Iraq War, state surveillance, the asymmetric power of the banks, genocide in Gaza, selling out to corporations, and humankind's general lack of empathy. The line 'How do you feel about being misled?' has echoes of Lydon's 'Ever get the feeling you've been cheated?' and it's hard not to conclude seven long years after *Pylon*'s release that the answer is: absolutely fine, thanks. The chorus lyrics have the depth of ambiguity adored by KJ, with Blake's original verses having a strong radical, pacifist, spiritually non-dogmatic intent, in contrast with their post-Parry history of ethnonationalism (a legacy that has nothing to do with Blake or his words). 'Look what we've become: brainwashed Britain.'

It's brutally barbed and bitterly sarcastic: we could have followed Blake's radicalism and built an island utopia inspired by Celtic paganism and early Christianity. Instead, we subverted Blake's meaning and created a jingoistic Tory hellscape with 'another twat in the Number Ten flat' (and this was three years before British actor Danny Dyer's famous description of David Cameron).

'War on Freedom' 4:40 (Killing Joke)
Like an apocalyptic *Mad Max* 18-wheeler, this is an all-annihilating articulated death machine in march time, with a minor-key-root bass riff that drives the song all the way through to the end – without brakes, rest stops or breakdowns. Sophisticated dissonance comes from a flattened fourth in Youth's riff, in continual tension with the minor key's implied natural fourth. Verse, chorus and an unprecedently melodic bridge from Geordie all play out atop the low-end riff and merciless rhythm, musically echoing the brutal and unrelenting advance of authoritarianism. It's a ferociously funereal four-minutes-forty which flawlessly conjures the nihilistic onslaught of the corporate fascist coercion machine.

'Big Buzz' 5:03 (Killing Joke)

> Well, it's fantastic, it's a great celebration when we get together. I have a great laugh. It's intense and it's challenging emotionally. I mean, I'll be playing bass and Jaz will be going "Wanker!", you know? There's no holding back. It comes close to physical violence at times. It's not for the faint-hearted. But it's been my education. I love working in an environment where there are no rules. It's total honesty – brutal honesty. But if you've got the courage to do that, some amazing stuff can come out.
> Youth, interviewed in *Sketch, Drugs & Rock n Roll*, Dir. Paul Elliott & Sean Lamberth, 2016

The original single-disc album's shape heaves into view now, with pairs of end-times prophecies offset by single hymns to humankind's esoteric potential. This is the third of those occult psalms. It's one of the most uplifting tracks recorded by the band and is a return to the Mixolydian mode, often used by the Joke in the 1980s. The lyrics begin with simple lines of remembrance, which soon give way to a euphoric chorus describing a non-medicated high. The second verse ends with an almost quote from Aleister Crowley's *The Book of The Law*: 'Every man and woman is a star.' (The album returns to Crowley at its culmination.) The bridge lyrics have a gorgeous double meaning. The first time it appears as one line, 'still laughing after all these years', which could as easily refer to laughing at the insanity of Western civilisation as laughing with joy at finding an autonomous zone outside it. In its reprise, there's an extra line, 'tears of laughter, tears of pride', which starts with ambiguity but ends with only one possible interpretation: the justifiable pride Killing Joke have in their interpersonal relationships, their longevity and their body of work. But even here, there is subtle haunting dissonance at the last, as Geordie bends the final note down towards its flattened state. 'Big Buzz' has its origins in one of several instrumental demos by Geordie dating from 2007. These demos are much loved by Gatherers and worth searching out.

'Delete' 5:00 (Killing Joke)
A brilliant example of late-career sonic tension, this track is anchored in the minor key but uses a sharpened seventh to create a tightly wound dissent machine. The 'deletion' here is of a civilisation that is currently owned by 'eighty-five people', that uses 'doctrines of shock' to maintain control, that gets away with 'circumventing constitutions' and will 'never stop' – at least not till they *are* stopped. Geordie distils and enhances the track's unease after the first verse by adding a parallel sharpened fourth to the sharpened seventh, giving the riff a slightly Eastern feel. This provides a neat counterpoint to the next verse's focus on our dysfunction, with war as the West's 'All-Father of progress'. The chorus reprise adds a tricksterish rhyme: the 'self-elected elite' whom 'we must delete'. You can imagine them taking the rest of the day off after coining that couplet and well-deserved too. Geordie ends this one with a first/second/fifth clash that always makes me think of the CTRL-ALT-DELETE key-stroke combo. If only a democratic reset were that easy.

'I Am the Virus' 5:39 (Killing Joke)
The penultimate track of the original ten-track running order, this is a conspiracy cornucopia, a paranoid pummelling that wants you to question everything you read and hear – to ask whether the media deceit, power structures and state violence of which you're aware may be only the tip of a long-buried toxic landfill. Big Paul absolutely batters his kit under one of Geordie's most darkly urgent riffs. From the rear-view mirror of 2022, the lyrics seem absurdly prescient. Some have even suggested that the Joke are party to a kind of magickal crystal ball, but the sad truth is that the trajectory of the West has been towards total collapse since at least the Global Financial Crisis, probably since 9/11 and perhaps much earlier.

Adam Curtis's BBC documentaries make a brain-boggling companion oeuvre to the three albums from the reformed line-up, pulling the origin back as far as lethal American collusion in the Middle East over oil during FDR's presidency. In the first verse, the Joke nail this exact cause, observing 'a darkness in the West' based on 'oil swilling'. The second verse ends with another all-time great rhyming couplet: our 'deep denial' linked inexorably to 'contagion released from a phial'. This sets up the penultimate line of the third verse, 'the public's blank stare', a long call-back to the first two albums and their thematic focus on the anaesthetised masses. The verse's last line returns to one of Coleman's perennial topics of this millennium: the illegal Iraq War. Here he unleashes the killer line: 'Did you sleep okay last night, Mr Blair?'

The chorus is another anthem of dissenting rebellion. The 'spirit of outrage' is a 'Hydra-headed beast' 'that never sleeps'. The West is controlled by forces that have already planted the seeds of their own destruction, so whether that destruction occurs of its own accord or is hastened by revolt is ultimately academic. *We are the virus.* The virus that destroys everything. The virus that wipes the slate clean so everything can start again.

'Into the Unknown' 6:15 (Killing Joke)

> You see, in this band, we believe we were reincarnated so that we could ease the pain of a new dark age.
> Jaz Coleman, on stage, the Roundhouse, London, 17 November 2018

Geordie and Big Paul kick off the original album's last track with what sounds like a trumpet and drum heralding a night-time initiation. An appropriately dark and urgent Phrygian riff takes over as Jaz intones the first verse, which sets the apocalyptic scene: 'Is this the winter of humankind?' As the chorus begins, the final structure of the album reveals itself: three trilogies of songs, each trilogy comprising one hopeful flickering and two raging infernos, closed out with a single song that moves from darkness to light.

That chorus features a truly glorious key modulation, with the compositional sophistication of the band on full display. The first stanza of the chorus refers back to that Crowley quote in 'Big Buzz', as 'man takes his rightful place amongst the stars'. 'The celestial barge awaits' is a reference to the Egyptian Sun God Ra, whose daily transit across the sky in his barque was conceived as a microcosm for a life's journey through birth, ageing, death and, ultimately, resurrection. As we already know: 'souls are recycled in the death and resurrection show.'

The second stanza of the chorus calls back to the Joke's emblematic Tarot card, The Fool, as we step 'into the unknown'. As neophytes, we take a step off the cliff because nothing is known or understood; as mages, we take a step off the cliff because the unknown is all that remains. It's a magnificently resonant moment in the band's career, taking us all the way back to that ritual in February 1979 when, as novices, Jaz and Big Paul challenged the unknown and received pure paradox in reply: the killing joke.

The last two lines of verse two are *Pylon*'s second direct reference to Crowley's *The Book of The Law* 'one law to follow, do what you will'. These lines also convey the implicit 'love is the law, love under will' as understood by all students of the occult. The track – and the original album – ends with a sublime musical echo of the unknown from Geordie: a lingering fifth, to which the listener can add either a resolving octave or an unravelling sharpened fourth. It's a deeply ambiguous way to end this cycle of songs: hovering between annihilation and transcendence. (Note: The band recorded a track called 'Love is the Law' during the *Pylon* sessions, which was due finally to be released as part of the aborted 40th Anniversary limited-edition boxset.)

Bonus Tracks

'Apotheosis' 6:28 (Killing Joke)

The first two bonus tracks split from the ambiguity of 'Into the Unknown': 'Apotheosis' breaks hopeful while 'Plague' breaks bleak. The verses here have a classic-metal feel, heightened by dissonant sci-fi clangs and whooshes, but the chorus is in the vein of *Brighter*, with evocative synth counterpoint. The entire song is a wonderfully sophisticated mixture of Phrygian and Dorian modes creating an all-pervading sense of light breaking through darkness. The first verse sets the scene with unbridled optimism as we strive to become more than human: 'Prometheus is rising'. The idea of Prometheus freed is an eloquent metaphor for humankind reaching its full potential. Prometheus gave humans fire and was punished by Zeus for this transgression. The fifth century BCE Greek dramatist Aeschylus wrote *Prometheus Unbound* as the second part of a presumed trilogy, which in turn inspired Percy Bysshe Shelley's lyrical drama of the same name (Shelley compared his hero to Milton's Satan, aka Lucifer 'the light-bringer'; see 'The Lightbringer' on *Hosannas*).

West Coast philosopher and occultist Robert Anton Wilson followed both with a book named *Prometheus Rising*, in which, with his consummately tricksterish approach, he sets out ideas and techniques to unlock the hidden potential of individual human beings. The Joke have taken these ideas to craft a song that also takes inspiration from Timothy Leary and Terence McKenna (see 'Timewave' in *Absolute Dissent* Related Tracks) regarding the ascent of humans to the next stage of their existence using a combination of non-dogmatic spirituality, expanded consciousness and outlier science. As the chorus has it: 'Suddenly, I can see for eternity; suddenly, time just melts away'. The track ends with another implosion of illumination.

'Plague' 5:52 (Killing Joke)

'Comfort lovers of the good life acquiesce'. You could add #DontLookUp and it'd be a perfect tweet. Musically, the track is based on a possibly deliberate re-use of the first three notes of the main riff from 'Money is Not Our God' (a rare note combination on the Lydian Sharp-9 scale), which would link the destruction of our only viable ecosystem to our insatiable love of money and addiction to pointless stuff. Verse two nails it with Gaia dying of 'asphyxiation' as we chase 'wealth and power'. The plague is our insatiable greed.

'Star Spangled' 5:31 (Killing Joke)

A terrific widescreen synth riff and key-anchored guitars lay the foundations for a brutal assault on the Land of the Free and its pernicious global reach: 'Imperial agenda bleeding us'. We start with the acid sarcasm of 'this is paradise' before summoning a Romero-style post-apocalyptic scene in a country that's convinced it is pre-apocalypse while agitating and propagandising for the apocalypse itself. The War on Terror (not to mention its direct antecedent, the War on Drugs, both mocked by the title 'War on Freedom') and America's insistence that it is simply exporting democracy are given ironic short shrift here. Following on directly from 'Plague', this is also an attack on the military-industrial complex that appears intent on killing us all for – and with – dirty energy. Indeed, this monomania is so extreme that it appears to have occult provenance, as mud is devoured 'in ritual blood'. The chorus is bitterly anthemic as it mocks America's own sacred song, while the breakdown features Geordie at his most forbidding.

'Panopticon' 8:46 (Killing Joke)

A gargantuan progressive-metal epic, this is Orwell's *Big Brother* meets Wilson & Shea's *Illuminatus!* as a caustic comment on the surveillance state using the idea of the 'panopticon'. The 'panopticon' was theoretical architecture conceived by English social theorist Jeremy Bentham in 1786-87, which allows all the inhabitants of a prison to be surveilled by one control position, regardless of who is being watched at any one time, or whether the control position is even occupied. Taken to its logical extreme, it's a metaphor for us watching ourselves: the ultimate in 'self-censorship, self-policing' as the lyrics have it. The verses relate how our tech addiction has given the corporatocracy unprecedented access to our lives.

The reference to 'Great Work' in verses two and three is suggestive – the 'Great Work' is the magickal process of self-enlightenment, but here the idea is twisted to mean both a mass dumbing-down and the 'Great Work' of malicious mages to control the world. This is underscored in the chorus, which refers to Adam Weishaupt, founder of the Bavarian Illuminati in 1776 and, some believe, the power behind the foundation of America, as revealed on the one-dollar bill (Masonic/Illuminati iconography first appears in the KJ canon on the *Revelations* LP back cover and inner sleeve). It's an all-encompassing conspiracy to take us across almost 240 years, from control by occult ideas, to all ideas being so totally absorbed by technology and algorithms that it's impossible to tell what philosophy is driving the world other than profit. Disconcerting synth quadruplets are rhythmically apt but create uncanny dissonance, while the breakdown is sliced by razor-edged Geordie figures against synth washes and tom-tom breaks, leading into a glorious Zep-resonant middle eight. The track ends with a restated falling figure from Geordie, leaving little headroom for the idea of escape.

'Snakedance' 5:37 (Killing Joke)

This is a pagan psalm to the forbidden pleasures of the flesh. The undulating verses describe a 'dark playground', 'a serpent's lounge' where the guests 'couple in the shadows'. The chorus, which has a deliberately naïve quality, describes how the dancer has 'got me mesmerised'. It's the push-pull of bodies in heat. A dance as old as time. Or at least as old as the reptilian brain. The original studio version did not appear till the 2021 reissue. Heavy on the dancehall brass sample, Youth's 'Rattlesnake Dub Remix' appears on both the 2015 expanded special edition and the remaster.

There are also Radio Edits of 'Euphoria' and 'Big Buzz'.

Non-Album Tracks

Early Tracks

There is a cluster of early tracks that were only ever played live or recorded for John Peel. On 17 October 1979, the Joke's first Peel Session comprised 'Wardance' and 'Pssyche' (both sides of the Malicious Damage 'Wardance' single from February 1980) plus 'Nuclear Boy' and 'Malicious Boogie'. 'Nuclear Boy' is a three-minute slice of reggae-infused apocalyptic dread, with Jaz playing the titular character who doesn't need 'nature' or 'real music', 'just a blow-up doll for a blow-up Earth' (some lovely punning there). The breakdown is tight as a public bunker come the four-minute warning, with Geordie's tone as close to out-and-out rock as it ever comes. 'Malicious Boogie' clocks in at a lean 2:02, with disco keyboards, ultra-funky guitar (again, the only time you hear this from Geordie) and a motif – especially when played on Coleman's synth – that seems to presage John Carpenter's main title music for *Escape from New York* of 21 months later (it's even in the same key).

'Animal' and 'You're Being Followed' only appear officially on *The Unperverted Pantomime*, recorded in November 1979 (see Live – The 1970s below). 'Animal' has a satisfyingly syncopated groove across the verses with some effective keyboards from Jaz, but the bridge is a tad basic and was quickly superseded by increased compositional and sonic complexity. The cuttingly ironic lyric 'objective: money' still hits home, though. 'You're Being Followed' is easily the best of this group of tracks. It's much closer to the Joke of the first two albums with a malevolent bass line incorporating a sharpened fourth, and some properly dark lyrics, including the dystopia-dissenting 'you're being followed, so be a joker'. It would take till *Absolute Dissent*'s 'Depthcharge' before the Joke revisited the discordant industrial ska of this track.

Driven by the rhythm section – Youth with a Ruts-style minor-key bass riff and Big Paul in pulsing backbeat synchrony – 'What's the Matter?' is full-bore punk, with Honey Bane guesting on lead vocal and a head-splitting oscillating synth ostinato to end. It was captured on the officially sanctioned bootleg *Live at the Venue*, a gig from February 1980 (see Live – The 1980s below).

Turn to Red EP (aka *Nervous System* aka *Almost Red*)

The *Turn to Red* EP was initially released in October 1979 as a 3-track 10" on the Malicious Damage label that the band set up with Mike Coles. It was then re-released in December by Island Records as a four-track 12" and this is the version discussed here. The EP showcases the foundational elements of Killing Joke but is also a key stepping-stone to the fully-fledged identity established on the first album. The iconic cover art by Mike Coles features London's Centre Point building reflected in an unseen mirror against a blood-red background. In the foreground at left are a smiling mother and daughter cut from an advertisement but here conjuring government nuclear-safety propaganda. Their eyes are red, suggesting the petechiae of a violent death. At right, also with red eyes, though on him they look positively demonic, is the first appearance of the Mr Punch/Joker figure, revelling in and/or causing the chaos being unleashed by Armageddon.

Turn to Red 2020, originally due to be a UK Record Store Day release, but postponed due to the Covid pandemic, features remasters of the title track and 'Almost Red', plus two Youth remixes of 'Turn to Red': 'In Dub' and 'In Dub Extended'.

'Almost Red' 3:46 (Killing Joke)

The additional track on the Island release is a de facto disco mix of 'Turn to Red', though as it features full verses it's most likely closer to the original studio recording of the track before Lusardi and the band remixed it as 'Turn to Red'. We start with a bomb-falling fret slide from Geordie, then a cod Giorgio Moroder sixteenth-note riff on the synth establishes the groove, but with so much rubato that a disorientating feeling is immediate, further accentuated by random triplets. This is Boston Dynamics robots dancing at an AI revolution staging area: jerky, industrial, inhuman. Big Paul's four-to-the-floor is broken up by Youth's chorus-effect bass riff.

Verse one is sharply ironic as Jaz, enduring 'just another day' surrounded by automata, waits for 'the dream'. We're all already walking dead, oblivious to the imminent apocalyptic nightmare and still craving the consumerist dream. As true now as in 1979. The lyrics continue with paranoia and dread. A 'preacher man' is screaming. The preacher could as easily be summoning fire and brimstone from heaven as yelling while the flesh slides from his skeleton. Even Jesus can't save you from Armageddon.

A short bridge with some ominous guitar ostinato and a squelching synth effect that sounds like a foetal ultrasound leads into verse two, which features the pointed line 'chaos for breakfast' (later used as a compilation title). The lyrics showcase the Joke's mordant wit, playing with the English traditional saying 'red sky at night, shepherd's delight; red sky in the morning, shepherd's warning' (itself a colloquial version of Matthew 16:2-3), rhyming 'four-minute warning' with 'red sky in the morning'. There's a drop out to synth riff and kick-drum, after which the bass and squelch effect return, but the arrangement now feels increasingly unstable. The whole thing soon runs out of steam and comes to a dead stop. Intriguingly, the line 'metallic sound it peels my ears', half of which appears in 'Turn to Red', does not appear here.

'Nervous System' 4:18 (Killing Joke)

> I always say I retired at fifteen when I joined a band. I stopped work then, when I left school.
>
> Youth, interviewed in *Sketch, Drugs & Rock n Roll*, Dir. Paul Elliott & Sean Lamberth, 2016

The first track on Killing Joke's first studio release (though the Malicious Damage 10" label erroneously lists 'Turn to Red' first), 'Nervous System' includes many of the strands for which Killing Joke became known over the three years of Youth's first stint in the band: punk attitude, reggae and funk grooves, lyrics with pointedly political, social and cultural commentary, and harmonic dissonance (though at a much more subtle level than on the first three studio albums).

Youth's funky bass initiates a rolling reggae groove with a sharpened sixth (there's that dissonance, right out of the gate), while Big Paul taps out a cymbal pulse before a reggae break leads into a push-pull syncopation with Jaz's keys. Like a punk town crier, or a jester at the court of capitalism, Coleman issues a shout to gain our attention: 'Hey!' The lyrics outline the daily grind of social conformity and dog-eat-dog greed under consumerism with the deliberately understated comment: 'it's a bit of a joke'. The minimalist chorus, another KJ benchmark, juxtaposes nervous and social systems, alongside a stated intent to get out of both. After a typically bare-bones breakdown with jazzy keyboard fills, Coleman expels a sigh of ambiguous exasperation, which perfectly presages one aspect of the band's worldview (the other two main strands being roiling rage and flickering hope). Although the keyboards would all but disappear, the dissonance, especially from Geordie's guitar (at this point his Les Paul Cherry Sunburst), would be amplified till the band cemented their sound on *KJ 1980*.

'Are You Receiving' 4:59 (Killing Joke)

This is the first track that the Joke wrote, and its genesis is now a pillar of KJ folklore. In short, Jaz and Big Paul had left Geordie to inspire a last-chance Youth to demonstrate his four-string prowess. Coleman and Ferguson returned to find guitar and bass locked in a propulsive riff-chug tandem and immediately joined in. Thus both 'Are You Receiving' (the original-release title does not have a question mark) and Killing Joke were born. The song is written and arranged in a post-punk power-pop style that would partly re-emerge in the Joke's arsenal three years later. It was a vital part of the band's nascent identity before the dissonance, industrial elements and primal drumming came to the fore. As it is, musically, this song could be The Damned or The Ruts in their prime, though Jaz's vocal style and the Coleman-Ferguson lyrics are close to fully formed and already unique.

The track is in Dorian, a rare mode for KJ, but common at the more melodic end of post-punk. Geordie kicks off with a playful hint at 'The Stars and Stripes' while Big Paul initiates his fill-into-segment style. The middle eight features some rather un-Geordie-like rock guitar and un-Joke-like root-note unison but also introduces the band's trademark discord with Youth's insistent, tension-ratcheting root set against Geordie's second-to-fourth vamp while Jaz intones a pointedly witty faux news report. This section breaks down into some lovely stereo-panned phasing and is followed by a final chorus with call-and-response – yet another KJ signature established out of the gate – before a traditional root-note end. The lyrics are a prescient proposition: furiously prophetic ('no more motivation, total domination'), dystopian ('when you're watching TV, creating lunacy'), sci-fi/magickal ('we retreat to our heads with our ideas of space'), subversive ('because they're frightened of your soul'), satirical ('this is an order from the United Police Force of Great Britain'), allusive ('this is life in the fall'), nihilistic ('our destination is nowhere') yet with a sliver of hope ('we keep searching for the positive'). It's the whole poetically provocative package birthed all at once.

'Turn to Red' 3:58 (Killing Joke)
This de facto dub mix only uses six lines of lyrics, though a 'four-minute warning' gives a clear sense that the song is about nuclear apocalypse. A lolloping bass riff with a sharpened fourth (talk about setting out your stall early doors) provides the track's bedrock but Big Paul's drums are the star here, a simple kick-drum four-to-the-floor providing the foundation for bursts of reverb-drenched snare strikes and funky paradiddles courtesy of engineer Mark Lusardi. Geordie adds a bomb-falling fret slide, palm-muted machine-gun sixteenth notes and an ostinato air-raid siren root. Keyboards top off the sonic layers with syncopated chords, while an ominous synth adds squelching industrial distortion and metallic metronomy. The original Island Records pressing features a locked groove that repeats the word 'red' ad infinitum.

'Pssyche' 4:57 (Killing Joke)
The B-Side of 'Wardance', 'Pssyche' is the most overtly transgressive of Killing Joke's early compositions, with lyrics that pull no punches about the despair, alienation and hypocrisy of British society at the time of its original release in 1980 – aspects that feel no less contemporary today. Musically, it's one of the band's most complex early tracks, with multiple propulsive riffs from Youth and a cracking middle eight. 'Pssyche' led to John Lydon championing the Joke, as Youth, who had played with John's brother Jimmy in 4" Be 2", ensured that the song reached John's ears via a hand-delivered cassette.

The track starts with the cry of an outsider canine 'alone in the pack' and a shout from Jaz (later, when played live, the intro conjures a whole pack of lonely wolves as the singers in the band howl in unison). Over a full-on four-to-the-floor from Big Paul and incessant root notes and synth whooshes from Jaz, Geordie vamps as the band's members (minus Geordie) take turns to declaim the lyrics. Youth, epitomising the English, is ground down but struggles on nonetheless, with a gunshot effect after 'keep on going' to drive the point home (or perhaps it's a whip-crack from an unseen martinet to keep the dogs in line). A descending-then-ascending bass motif takes us into Jaz's first verse, which features the magnificently clever line 'you peel illusion and then you find it's a transfer', with another gunshot/whip-crack in tow.

A new octave-jumping bass riff acts as a bridge into that middle eight, which is built on the intro but now with a heavily pedalled guitar showpiece ('solo' never really feels apt for anything Geordie does) and yet another gunshot/whip-crack. A second new rising-falling bass riff takes us into a reprise of the intro and Jaz's second verse, which equates the street with a firing range on which we can choose only between avoiding the bullets or carrying a gun. The octave-jumping bass riff and another intro reprise take us into Big Paul's turn, the most deliberately shocking (Nazis, nuns, priests, masturbation and rapists all get a look in and I'm possibly not the only one who thinks of Jimmy Savile and the establishment cover-up of his crimes when listening to this verse). The final line conjures the abject hypocrisy of a certain section of British society – a section that has recently grown in power and influence. Indeed, this line is so penetrating it hurts, brilliantly encapsulating the 2022 Easter controversy in the UK over whether God would send refugees to Rwanda. A last appearance by the octave-jumping bass riff takes us into a final intro reprise, which speeds up and splinters before the song ends with a guitar chord. A rage-hot classic and an enduring live staple.

'Killer Dub (aka Bread & Jam)' 19:01 (Killing Joke)
Available in various versions on bootlegs, this track finally received an official release on the 2004 Malicious Damage compilation *Chaos for Breakfast*. It's an instrumental jam built on Youth's sinewy reggae bassline and Big Paul's industrial clangs, rim shots and cymbal rides. Layered on top are warped chord chops from Geordie, while Coleman's synth provides woozy washes and oscillating ostinato. This is a useful reminder of how central to the Joke's DNA is the limber physicality of dub rhythms. A trippy five-minute Youth remix appears on disc three of 2014's compilation *In Dub*.

'Take Take Take' (*Ha*, live) 4:56 (Killing Joke)
The change of bass player is immediately apparent on this slab of menacing discord, which would be at home on *Revelations*. Raven's rhythmically propulsive style is immediately established, though the multi-string dissonance soon vanished as the band moved into a more melodic period. Leading out a lumbering procession, Raven establishes an insistently malevolent root, as Geordie creates a teeth-jangling two-step motif. The bass shifts down for a bridge riff, which leads into a crunching chorus. The final line, 'Take, take, take, TAAAKE. JOKE!' is as brilliant a summation of the band's outlook as could exist: we must swallow both the joke of life and the band itself on their own terms or not at all.

Birds of a Feather Single

The final collaboration between the band and Conny Plank, 'Birds of a Feather' was released in October 1982 and reached 64 in the UK Singles Chart. It also marks Raven's first studio release and the initial appearance of a key part of KJ history. All three tracks from the 12" (including title-song remix 'Flock the B Side') appear on the 2005 expanded remastered reissue of live EP *Ha*.

'Birds of a Feather' 3:46 (Killing Joke)
'Birds of a Feather' itself kicks off with Ferguson taking the tribal beats further than previously, with the Burundi influence at its most overt. This drumming style had been popularised over the previous three years by Adam and The Ants drummers David Barbarossa and Chris Hughes aka Merrick. The title references the English expression 'birds of a feather flock together'.

The verses are driven by a simple bass riff in Lydian, with Geordie adding a descending motif without dissonance. The chorus is in a chant-friendly major, though here Raven drops to a flattened sixth, while Geordie provides dissonance with rising and falling semitones, suggesting the band aren't quite ready to cast off their discordant heritage. This dissonance also slyly reflects the gulf between the co-opted football-chant idiom and the Joke's occult intent. The chorus vocals are sung in unison with plenty of reverb. Geordie ratchets up the dissonance against a minor middle eight and the song fades out with a repeated chorus, which uses alternating first and second-person plurals.

The lyrics contain the first reference in a Killing Joke lyric to 'gathering', a term coined in Iceland by Jaz that came to mean a KJ gig, with the word 'Gatherer' used to describe someone who religiously attends live shows, though eventually, it came to mean any die-hard fan of the band. The idea that one needs to seek out both those who see the world as we do and those from whom we can learn is encapsulated in Timothy Leary's call to 'find the others'. In music, tribal identity is key. Countless bands have become nexus points for their fans to assemble with those of a like mind, exemplified in the creation or co-opting of other single-fan and fan-group nouns such as Pondies (Cardiacs), Freaks (Marillion), Juggalos (Insane Clown Posse) and Maggots (Slipknot). Few bands, however, have so rigorously applied the idea that their tribe should be a force not just for congregation, but for learning and evolution.

'Sun Goes Down' 4:19 (Killing Joke)
This is another song about conditioning and war, by now familiar Killing Joke subject matter, though this iteration is particularly nuanced and subtle, especially in the use of raga scales (in this case, the Double Harmonic) to relate the song to India and the Middle East. The verse lyrics feature counterpoints between London street scenes and the wars of Empire that are inextricably linked to them through history, culture and culpability: 'look out my windowsill, watch bloodshed'. A line about aimless people 'kicking a football' has thematic resonance to the tribal chants of 'Birds of a Feather'. The chorus relates back to 'Empire Song' and the interminably protracted sunset of the British Empire. It's little wonder that 'a man went mad'. And so

did an entire nation. The song ends on the intro-verse motif, suggesting the final seconds of sundown as the fiery disc dips below the horizon, perhaps never to return.

'Hollywood Babylon' 6:56 (Coleman/Glover/Walker)
Written for the infamous 1995 Paul Verhoeven film *Showgirls*, which is set in Las Vegas, 'Hollywood Babylon' foregrounds Youth's dance-music mastery to create an urgent slice of underbelly noir. The track opens with some dark, ominous synth and anguished backward vocal, then adds a four-to-the-floor techno beat, clanging industrial synth and distorted guitar before settling into a pulsing groove. Geordie and Youth add minimalist guitar figures to the short post-prog bridge, while the anguished backward vocal returns during the chorus, repeats of the bridge, and the middle-eight breakdown, with Geordie's ostinato creating visceral tension. The lyrics are notable for another brilliantly effective change of tense/subject, here from 'would' to 'do' as Jaz questions whether 'thoughts of sexual fantasy' or 'the things I've done' undermine his ability to be loved. There's even some trademark coughing in there if you listen closely. It appears on the third disc of the 3-CD deluxe edition of 2013's *The Singles Collection*.

'Drug' 4:33 (Coleman/Glover/Walker)
The video game adaptation *Mortal Kombat* (1995) spawned two albums. The *Original Motion Picture Soundtrack* was so successful – going platinum and reaching ten on the *Billboard* 200 – that a spin-off compilation album, *Mortal Kombat: More Kombat* was released in 1996. This second group of tracks features eight exclusive contributions, including Killing Joke's 'Drug'. Again, Youth's trance stylings are centred, though here Geordie's guitar is much more prominent, with some *Pandemonium*-style heavy riffing. The lyrics render the track an obvious companion piece to *Democracy*'s 'Prozac People', with the chorus counterpointing 'get out of my head' with a monotonous, lobotomised 'drug… drug… drug… drug…' refrain. This song is clearly not about mind-expanding psychoactives, but rather concerns itself with over-prescribed and over-marketed so-called 'mood-stabilisers' which can 'numb the mind' and 'gag our voices'.

Coleman is again spinning universal truth from his own fraught experiences with prescription pills, and this is no more apparent than in the darkly ambiguous middle eight, which is a bitter sister piece to *Pandemonium*'s 'Exorcism'. In the latter track, the act of 'washing it all away' is cleansing and cathartic; here, the same idea is rendered with ironic nihilism as the words gradually slide out of synch with the music like a mind slipping loose from its moorings. It's as though the titular drug is washing away personality, dreams and ultimately soul, with the song's protagonist having zero choice in the matter. 'Drug' is on the third disc of the 3-CD deluxe edition of 2013's *The Singles Collection*.

'Four Stations of the Sun' 5:24 (Coleman/Glover/Walker)
Casting back to *Fire Dances*, but here filtered through a further 13 years of the band's metaphysical journey, this track from the *Democracy* sessions calls for us to acknowledge the inextricable links between paganism and Christianity and recognise that 'every deity forms one', as the metaphorical stations of the cross are blended with the astronomical solar year. Musically the track is centred on dirty guitar, slithering bass and basic-man drums, with Coleman providing a simple synth ostinato and vocals in the benign version of his trademark growl. The keyboards-forward bridge has some nifty key changes that start off suggesting 'Kings and Queens' but then subvert that expectation before running into the anthemic chorus proper. The band are in a hopeful mood, emphasised in that chorus: 'I turn around to see four stations of the sun.' The studio version was finally released in 2013 on the third disc of the 3-CD deluxe edition of *The Singles Collection*, while a longer, Arabic-infused Hallucinogen (aka Simon Posford) trance remix is on 1998's *Wardance – The Remixes*.

'Our Last Goodbye' 5:18 (Coleman/Raven/Vrenna/Walker)
In 2000, between *Democracy* and *KJ 2003*, the Joke contributed the closing track to the compilation *Free the West Memphis 3*. The album was recorded to support the defence of three teenagers who in 1994, were controversially convicted of the murders of three boys in West Memphis, Arkansas. One of the teens, Damian Echols, was sentenced to death. It's a superb collection of tracks, including original songs by Steve Earle, Tom Waits and Mark Lanegan. The Joke's original track is credited to Coleman, Raven and Geordie, along with sometime NIN and Marilyn Manson member Chris Vrenna.

Vrenna's cantering drums and Raven's prowling bass underpin haunting synth, Geordie's menacing guitar and an emotive, clean vocal from Jaz. The title and lyrics clearly relate to the death penalty, as a condemned prisoner says goodbye to their loved ones. The track ends with the ominous sound of a prison door clanging shut. The Joke are on record as abhorring the death penalty in general and America's criminal justice system in particular. The spoken-word parts of the song pull no punches in their relating of America's grim history of incarceration and state-sanctioned murder to those of China, Saudi Arabia and Iran. After new forensic evidence cast further doubt on their convictions, the West Memphis three negotiated plea bargains and were finally released in 2011, vindicating both their protestations of innocence and the many people who had campaigned for their release (and giving that final sound of the prison door an entirely new meaning).

Lord of Chaos EP

> I've never known anything like the time we are living in now; not since the Cuban Missile Crisis, but now in comparison, we have multiple flashpoints.

'Lord of Chaos' is about complex systems failure, when technology overloads and AI misreads the enemy's intentions.
Jaz Coleman, Spinefarm Press Release, February 2022

Seven years inactive as a studio band and the Joke sound as furiously prophetic as ever on this EP. Undaunted by Coleman's brush with death in 2021, the following year saw a short UK tour and the release of the band's first fresh material since *Pylon* in 2015. Released in March 2022, this four-track EP features new songs 'Lord of Chaos' and 'Total' plus remixes of two *Pylon* tracks: 'Big Buzz – Motorcade Mix' by Tom Dalgety and Nick Evans, and 'Delete in Dub – Youth's Disco 45 Dystopian Dub'. Both new tracks clock in at under five minutes with compact lyrics and taut arrangements. The 'Motorcade Mix' of 'Big Buzz' is a four-to-the-floor dance anthem with layered synths and all of Jaz's vocal featured. Youth's 'Delete in Dub' is the polar opposite as its title suggests: desolate and disconsolate, with the frenetic drum-and-bass style rhythms conjuring unstoppable machines rather than tribal ceremonies. The cover is one of Mike Coles's finest, combining medieval apocalyptic Christian imagery with a gonzo cowboy warlord sporting a disturbingly dissonant boy's face.

'Lord of Chaos' 3:58 (Killing Joke)
Pretty much picking up where *Pylon* left off – in Phrygian mode and with a similar sound, again produced by the Joke and Tom Dalgety – 'Lord of Chaos' is about the symbolic entity we have created from a multiplicity of apocalypse triggers: nukes, AI, climate breakdown and geopolitical instability. And even worse, the unknown possible interactions *between* those triggers: consequences that it's impossible effectively to model or predict. Looking back to *Brighter* in terms of civilisational rise-and-fall subject matter and a melodic approach – noticeable here in the Mixolydian chorus – the verses observe the perversity of 'our hubris, poverty and greed'. The chorus warns of how quickly everything can collapse, even as we keep adding new ingredients to the risk stew. The key change from chorus to verse lands on the last word of the line 'and the Lord of Chaos is in', tipping us from the tension between doom-laden lyrics and melodic music into abject pessimism. The howling SFX and pointed slowdown of Geordie's last note feel like civilisation ending.

'Total' 4:24 (Killing Joke)
One of the Joke's most elegantly explicit chorus lyrics is again simply the title, but here it resonates with 'Total Invasion', and with the greed and warmongering behind 'regime change'. With the total despond of the manic personality and the total fear of a world on the brink of Armageddon. And most urgently with the ideological system that is on the rise around the world: totalitarianism. With a haunting melody, the verses lament the state of

our world, a state that Jaz can't avoid, even by 'blocking out the past'. He is 'spinning out again'. The third verse appears to be about the pandemic but is poetic enough to evoke whatever reading you desire – or the cognitive dissonance of many readings at once. 'Conflict within' is related to 'strife without' as we 'blindly follow' and 'merge into the One'. This 'One' relates both to the Lord of Chaos of the previous track (totalitarian ideologues use chaos to rise to power and the threat of chaos to cling to it) and to the all-seeing eye of the 'Panopticon'. The idea of 'all becoming one' is often used as a positive trope of non-dogmatic spirituality and Aquarian philosophy, but to the Joke, this is simplistic – we can only truly gather as self-aware individuals; otherwise, we are not congregating, we're simply complying.

'Full Spectrum Dominance' 6:10 (Killing Joke)

This streaming-only single was released in March 2023 and is in the same vein as the two new *Lord of Chaos* EP tracks: gargantuan riffs, sophisticated melodic tension, brutal rhythmic power, subtle syncopation and lyrics that again confront our rapidly accelerating dystopia. The Joke apply their advanced sonic weaponry to warn us about powers that already control us with a peacetime version of the US military's concept of 'full-spectrum dominance'. This is the idea that a conquering force must dominate the enemy across every element of the theatre – from psychological warfare to the denial of basic resources. But as the Joke have clocked: there is no 'peacetime' – our own governments are at war with us, their own citizens.

Jaz calls back to the first KJ albums by conjuring social alienation with the 'bars of my bedroom cell'. We are all infected – with pathogens, both biological and psychological – spreading our germs as 'the world turns'. There's a sublime juxtaposition of organic and inorganic matter, recalling subterranean strands in the Joke's thematic DNA: 'acacia leaves and microwave trees'. A sprig of acacia signifies immortality in Freemasonry, suggesting that the cabals that control – billionaires and their useful idiots – are aiming to live for a Pharaonic eternity while the rest of us are consumed by the effects of ecological breakdown if we haven't already been poisoned by toxic air, water and soil. Big Paul's annihilation express propels us towards a Geordie flourish and our impending doom, cut off before we can properly acknowledge or understand it. Youth's 'Pure Trance Dub Remix' dominates the full stylistic spectrum – from piston-pumping beats to quake-queasy reverb.

Live

Please note: the aim of this chapter is to give an overview, and to highlight some live sets and performances that are available officially. This chapter does not include coverage of collectables or unofficial bootlegs (or, more accurately, of bootlegs that have not later been sanctioned by the band).

Live – The 1970s

As there's only one year of Joke activity here, it's lucky that seminal set *The Unperverted Pantomime* is still one of the band's key works. Recorded on 1 November 1979 at a venue now unremembered (though probably somewhere in the North of England), it was first released in 1982 on limited-edition cassette with anguished-jester cover art. The 11-track set features the only cover ever recorded by Killing Joke, 'Bodies' by the Sex Pistols (with Alex Paterson on lead vocal). This release also includes the Peel Session recorded on 16 December 1981. In 2003, Geordie co-curated an Alchemy Records CD version (now with a question mark added to the title). This compilation omits the Peel Session and instead assembles several rarities plus a Capital Radio session from January 1980, along with remastered versions of eight of the eleven live tracks. KJ Records re-issued this version in 2006.

In 2008, Eastworld Recordings released a CD-DVD combo titled *The Original Unperverted Pantomime* featuring all 11 live tracks plus the Peel Session and video of a live performance at East Side Club, Philadelphia, from 1981. The striking red-and-black cover is of a Venetian-style jester. In 2019, Cadiz Music issued a remaster of the original 1982 version with full-colour cover art of the anguished-jester painting. This features the same tracks as the original, less encore 'Bodies'.

Live – The 1980s

The 1980s saw Killing Joke's commercial high watermark and this is the decade with the most choice when it comes to live sets. First up is *Ha*. Stylised *"HA"*, this EP was the band's first commercially available live recording and their first recording of any kind with new bass player Paul Raven. It was captured on 9 and 10 August 1982 at Larry's Hideaway in Toronto and produced by Conny Plank, who had produced *Revelations* earlier that same year. Released in November, it reached 66 in the UK Albums Chart.

No Way Out But Forward Go (Rockpalast, Loreley, West Germany, 17 August 1985) was first released by NMC Music in 2001 and then in 2006 by KJ Records. Some versions include an Enhanced CD of the filmed gig (see Video/DVD below). The release is rounded out by title-swapped versions of 'Chessboards' and 'Adorations' from West German TV (with video of both on the Enhanced CD).

In 1995 Windsong International released *Killing Joke: BBC in Concert,* which combined two live performances by the Joke: the 13-track Reading Festival headline performance from Friday 22 August 1986 (omitting

'Adorations', 'Eighties' and 'Rubicon') and a gig at the Paris Theatre, London on 6 March 1985 from which only three tracks were included: 'Tabazan', 'Tension' and 'Pssyche'.

The full Reading set was finally released by Virgin in January 2010 (I was there and still recall it as yesterday; three of my favourite bands were on the bill: Cardiacs, Hawkwind and the Joke). There are problems with the sound both on stage and as recorded, making this primarily a nostalgia release, though the driving power and hypnotic force of the band are undeniable and the sound improves as the set progresses. The full Paris Theatre set, released the same month (but dated 23 March, presumably the date of broadcast) is far superior: it's clear that the band can hear themselves throughout and the mix is more balanced. Also, the pre-*Brighter* eight-track set is a good balance of *Night Time* tracks and live favourites.

Volume one of Candlelight's *Bootleg Vinyl Archive* collects four 1980s bootlegs. *Live at the Venue*, 10 February 1980 is most notable for its encore, 'What's the Matter?' with Honey Bane from support act The Fatal Microbes on guest lead vocal, but the whole set is intriguing for its keyboard-heavy death-disco vibe. *Live in London*, the Lyceum, 26 July 1981, is a superb set from the *What's THIS For…!* tour, originally available as *The Original Killing Joke*. *Live at Odeon* is a 23 October 1981 set in Bologna, Italy. A Gatherer event, promoted as a 'Midwinter Party' (tickets were free for ODIC members, the Order of the Distant Island Charter being the band's fan club at the time) is captured on *Live at Porchester Hall* from 22 December 1988, with Martin Atkins on drums and Taif Ball on bass. The night featured additional performers, food and punch (the drink not the puppet).

Live – The 1990s

There are only two official live releases from this decade. First is a concert from Le Pied, Reims, France, on 7 June 1991, which is part of *Inside Extremities: Mixes, Rehearsals and Live* (released 2007). This set, which features excellent sound quality, leans heavily on *Extremities*, but there's a mesmerising performance of 'Frenzy'. 'Pssyche', with Atkins sharing the vocals, is especially dark. The same 2-CD release also features a performance of 'The Fanatic' from Le Truck, Lyon, 20 May 1989.

The second is the four-track *Jana – Live EP* from the Forum, London, 19 October 1994. There are another two tracks from this gig on the 'Jana' CD single, which means you can playlist a magnificent ad hoc 6-track set. Coleman is in great voice and the Manor Mobile recording and Chris Potter's sympathetic mix do the band maximum justice. The live version of 'Jana' is for me, the most potent of the song's available iterations. It's achingly poignant, starting with a stripped-back arrangement of acoustic-style strumming in the first verse, but with full anguished heaviness on the chorus and some effectively dissonant counterpoint from Youth in the later verses.

Available as an officially sanctioned bootleg, a fan-favourite gig at the London Astoria on 20 April 1994 combines tracks from the soon-to-be-released *Pandemonium* with classics from *KJ 1980, What's THIS For…!* and *Night Time.* It's a performance full of feral intensity and coiled aggression, Dugmore's drums and Geordie's guitar holding everything together while Jaz and a returning Youth provide constant adrenalised motion. The *Pandemonium* tracks are energetically raw and there's an especially cute moment in the 'Eighties' breakdown where Geordie switches to the 'Come as You Are' riff.

The Astoria concert is collected on the second volume of Candlelight's *Bootleg Vinyl Archive*, along with some early demos from 1980 (originally *The Bum's Rush*), another set from the *Night Time* tour (this time from West Germany and including 'Sun Goes Down'; originally available as *The Act is Done*) and *Live at Joker Place* (a set from Palais d'Hiver, Lyon, France, 13 March 1985).

Live – The 2000s

> That's right. We use these occasions to expel, to expel all our extraneous guilt, that we may be carrying inside us. Look, when you lie, you get a knot, like a ball, in your solar plexus. That's when you're lying to yourself. And guilt, and fear, must be cast out here. We will lift it up, in the boundaries of these walls, and expel all the nastiness.
>
> Jaz Coleman, on stage, the Forum, 4 October 2008

The first decade of the new millennium offers an embarrassment of riches when it comes to Killing Joke live. First up is *Malicious Damage*, recorded on 12 October 2003 but not released till 2019, on multiple formats (see Video/DVD section below). *XXV Gathering: Let Us Prey*, a set from 25 February 2005, was similarly released on multiple formats in 2005-2006 (see Video/DVD below). 'Whiteout' and 'Complications' do not appear on the CD or vinyl versions.

Recorded in summer 2008 at Youth's Space Mountain Studio in Spain, and released by Eastworld in November of that year, *Duende – The Spanish Sessions* is essentially a run-through of the setlists for an imminent tour and is most notable for being the first time that the original line-up had recorded together since 1982. Geordie, who adores nothing more than one-take sessions, is on fire and rightly foregrounded in the mix (if you're a guitarist who wants to learn a Joke song, you could do significantly worse than starting here). The acoustic and production are less kind on Big Paul's drums and Jaz's vocals, but the band are undeniably tight and it's fascinating to hear Ferguson's primal take on the *Pandemonium* tracks written after his departure ('Millennium' is the standout of the three). The highlights of the classic tracks are 'Tension', 'Are You Receiving' and KJ's signature song

'Pssyche' in perhaps its definitive studio recording – check-out Youth's frenetic yet pinpoint bass, Jaz's whoops, and the original verse allocation with Youth, Jaz and Big Paul all singing.

The 2008 tour was captured over two nights at the Forum in London on 3 and 4 October. These recordings were originally released on the nights of the gigs by Concert Live, titled *Live at the Forum Part 1* and *Part 2*; one part for each night, which had (mostly) different set lists. These recordings were reissued in 2009 by Eastworld as *The Gathering 2008*. Night One consists of the first two albums performed in their entirety – albeit not in their original running order – along with 'Eighties' and 'Love Like Blood' from *Night Time*, plus live stalwarts 'Pssyche' and 'Change', as well as a run out for the band's first piece, 'Are You Receiving'. The concert has a celebratory air: acknowledging the astounding synchronicity of the band's formation and extraordinary longevity, plus the Joke expressing their obvious joy at the reunion of the original line-up. A minute's silence in remembrance of Raven renders the festivities deeply poignant.

Night Two may not be quite as tight musically as Night One, but the raw power of the band is seismic, and Jaz tops his performance from the previous gig. As Coleman says from the stage before a currency-collapsing 'Money is Not Our God': 'Well, something always fucking happens when we get together. I tell you something: the banks have gone down. And then there'll be a war. It's called money because there isn't any.' Other standouts are a four-song run from *Pandemonium* on the first disc and the three encores at the end of the second: 'The Pandys are Coming', 'Empire Song' and 'Wardance'. As with Night One, there's an early track in 'Turn to Red', here introduced by Youth: 'I want to thank Nick Stewart from Island Records for giving us five grand for this in 1980. It really sorted us out'.

Live – The 2010s

> Thank you! Well, I would just like to thank my colleagues. I would like to thank, first of all, Geordie, who's the oldest surviving Gatherer. He's been present at every Killing Joke event since '79. He's the most loyal and tenacious man I know. It has been a great honour to spend my life with this man. I love him so much. And then, there's Youth, who's brought honour and glory to the Killing Joke family. You have Youth to thank for us doing a new album next year. And then, without Big Paul, there wouldn't be any Killing Joke at all. He's the man who made it happen. I'm so happy since he came back three years ago, my life has been richer and fuller. I'm overwhelmed.
>
> Jaz Coleman, on stage, Hammersmith Apollo, 16 October 2010

The 2010s kicked off with the reformed original line-up touring *Absolute Dissent* and that set is captured on *Live at the Hammersmith Apollo*

16.10.2010. This is a celebration of the original line-up's first studio album since 1982 and tracks range across *Absolute Dissent*, *KJ 2003*, *What's THIS For...!* and *KJ 1980*. Jaz's introductions are gloriously strident ('This World Hell': 'At the current rate of consumption, we need a new planet by 2030'; a blistering 'The Great Cull': 'Depopulation. They've started') while Geordie again impishly incorporates the 'Come as You Are' riff into an aeon-ending rendition of 'Eighties'. The final three encores ('Change', 'Complications', 'Pandemonium') are benchmark performances.

Down by the River, recorded at the Royal Festival Hall on 1 April, was part of the Ether Festival 2011 at London's Southbank Centre. The gig was also part of the *Absolute Dissent* tour and features the band playing five of that album's ten tracks plus a long list of classics. Geordie has stated that he didn't tell the band they were being recorded because he wanted to capture the Joke's spontaneity. This strategy appears to have reaped rewards, as this is probably my favourite official Joke live album. A highlight of the gig, which I attended, was a video back-projection by Mike Coles including elements of his Joke sleeve art combined with news, feature, and documentary clips. The black-and-white footage of a dancing Fred Astaire, which accompanied 'Wardance', was as cognitively dissonant as it gets. Youth was dressed in a white suit (throwback to his infamous rotting-in-situ white suits from the early days, one of which was apparently burnt in a hospital furnace) while Jaz sported a combat-style boilersuit. Big Paul's drums sounded suitably massive in the Festival Hall acoustic. Highlights of the set are a soul-searing 'Communion', a malevolently bouncy 'Bloodsport' ('What's it like to be bottom of the food chain? There'll be no more aeroplanes!'), 'The Fall of Because' and 'Depthcharge'. The cover art, conceived by Big Paul, is one of the band's most striking images, depicting a malicious, red-gloved jester on a riot-police line and a small boy holding a red balloon in the background.

Recorded on 4 November 2016 at the Brixton Academy, London and released by Live Here Now, *The Great Gathering* features a career retrospective from 'Requiem' to 'I Am the Virus', taking in tracks from eight of the band's fifteen albums. Jaz's fury is white hot, perhaps partly due to the end of the UK's membership of the EU and everything that this means. He introduces 'Eighties' – the decade when humans began their final descent into oblivion – by declaiming the imminent end of the Anthropocene: 'Well, it looks like the age of man is coming to an end. It's time to drink and fuck'. During 'Change', he announces: 'here we are, in fascism', predicting both Trump's win only four days later and the UK's headlong descent into authoritarianism. It's a superb set with visceral renditions of 'Change', 'The Wait' and 'Pssyche'.

There are two official live albums from the 2018 40th Anniversary Tour, which were titled *Laugh at Your Peril: Live at the Roundhouse* and *Live in Berlin*. The two sets are similar, with the London set (the Roundhouse, 17 November 2018) adding 'Unspeakable' and dropping 'Turn to Red', 'Change' and 'In Cythera'. The 20-track Roundhouse performance is a celebratory affair with further astute and inflammatory song introductions from Jaz and some valedictory banter at the end, but it's the 22-track Berlin set (Huxleys Neue Welt, 19 October 2018) that just edges it. The mid-set run of 'Asteroid', 'The Wait', 'Pssyche', 'S.O.36' and 'Change' – plus a sublimely trippy and massively dubtastic 'Turn to Red' – is breathtaking, with Youth introducing the last of these tracks thus: 'Allegedly, I first met Jaz at a blues sound system in Ladbroke Grove in 1979. And this was one of the first tracks we put together, a little while after that'.

Total Invasion: Live in the USA was recorded on 24 November 2019 at PNC Arena, Raleigh, North Carolina, when the Joke were on tour with Tool. There are five classic tracks plus 'Pandemonium' and three from *KJ 2003*. Jaz's voice isn't at its best, but as ever with KJ live sets, the energy is infectious and there's a strong rendition of 'Complications'. The Mike Coles cover is a redux of his classic image from early 1980s New York gigs, depicting a waving/drowning woman wearing a Lady Liberty crown (presumably in 2019 she's now submerged by climate-catastrophe floods, perhaps a sly nod to the ending of the original *Planet of the Apes* film).

Live – The 2020s

Honour the Fire, recorded on 9 April 2022 at Hammersmith Apollo on the last night of the eponymous tour, was released by Cadiz in May 2023. This is a career-retrospective set with tracks from nine of the fifteen studio albums, including rare live outings for 'We Have Joy' and 'Mathematics of Chaos'. It is also available on DVD and Blu-ray.

Video/DVD

The Original Unperverted Pantomime, East Side Club, Philadelphia, 17 August 1981 (released 2008)

Originally intended as raw footage for a Dadaist-Situationist artwork, this set shot in black-and-white by Michel Polizzi is a vital record of the band in their early days. Jaz is still mostly behind his keyboards, which hampers his movement, though there's something remarkable about the way his physicality is contained and caged by the Oberheim, giving his frenetic, jerky movements additional intensity. Geordie is still providing intermittent backing vocals. The sound, captured on a single mic stuck to the camera, is astoundingly well balanced, but Youth's bass is foregrounded: growly, punchy, loose, yet adamantine (plus, due to the optimum camera angle from stage right, there is also generous coverage of Youth's playing). Big Paul is a powerhouse, by turns tribal sinew and motorik flywheel. For the first three tracks, Youth sports a US firefighter's helmet for reasons unknown. 'Bloodsport' doesn't feature on the Eastworld DVD due to tape damage, but the entire set is available to watch online.

No Way Out But Forward Go, Live at Rockpalast, Loreley, West Germany, 17 August 1985 (released 2001)

This is something of a classic, from the 'Booids' intro tape to a formidable performance of 'Wardance'. The UNESCO World Heritage Site of the Loreley Amphitheatre is a suitable backdrop for the Classical-civilisation loving Joke and the German crowd is up for it, even though Jaz mockingly starts the gig by saying that 'it's good to be back in the USA', overtly a comment on the number of Stars and Stripes flags being waved, but also likely a jibe at the number of American military bases on West German soil ('and Uncle Sam says it's not long now'). Raven is resplendent in combats and marching boots, echoing the military theme, and here providing the band's driving pulse. The set mixes tracks from *Night Time*, *Revelations* and *KJ 1980* including stand-out performances of 'Complications', 'The Hum', 'Empire Song', 'Kings and Queens' and 'Night Time' (with Geordie creating a full-bore feedback drone). Coleman singing the first verse of 'Pssyche' direct to the flag-wavers at the front is solid gold, while the reverb on Big Paul's verse-four 'fuck' is sublime.

Requiem, Live at Lokerse Feesten, Belgium, 8 August 2003 (released 2009)

Running to just over the hour mark, this is a great festival set with a large stage, top-flight PA and mission-critical monitor speakers. The mix is slightly sterile with minimum crowd noise and there is way too much reverb on Jaz's vocals, but the whole band seem to be enjoying themselves. Ted Parsons, the band's drummer for the *KJ 2003* tour, is a powerhouse, equally at ease with the pounding rhythms of the early catalogue and the more intricate drumming performed by Grohl in the studio on tracks like 'Total Invasion' and 'Blood on Your Hands'. The multi-camera filming is excellent, especially if you want constant well-lit close-ups of Geordie's fluid fretwork, idiosyncratic chord shapes and extraordinary right hand. The final five tracks, in particular ('The Wait', 'Whiteout', 'Frenzy' and 'Pssyche', along with a truncated 'Pandemonium' as an encore) sound terrific.

Malicious Damage, Live at the London Astoria, 12 October 2003 (released 2019)

Two months later, in the same incarnation, the band recorded this full performance at the London Astoria. Again, there's not enough audience noise, especially as Jaz spends quite a bit of time in-between songs interacting with the crowd. Nonetheless, due to the comprehensive nature of the set, it's an essential record of the band in this incarnation and there are adrenalised renditions of 'Blood on Your Hands', 'Change', 'Follow the Leaders' and 'Kings and Queens'. There's a nice surprise when the by-now rarely performed 'Empire Song' is featured, plus 'Whiteout' is an absolute barnstormer. Jaz wears combat-style face paint for this gig, as does Raven (the Iraq War had started just a few months earlier in March 2003 with America's invasion). Violinist Karel Holas from Czech folk outfit Čechomor (with whom Jaz collaborated on 2002's *Proměny*) joins the band for the first and last numbers, 'Communion' and 'Pandemonium'.

XXV Gathering: Let Us Prey, Shepherd's Bush Empire, London, 25 February 2005 (released 2005)

This is a benchmark gig, with the band on truly blistering form. Scheduled for the almost-anniversary of Jaz and Big Paul's magickal ritual in 1979, the concert took place at the Shepherd's Bush Empire in London on 25 February 2005 (the actual ritual took place at 3 pm on 26 February, also Coleman's birthday). Young Benny Calvert attacks the drums with the ecstatic enjoyment and physiological abandon of someone for whom every dream has apparently come true at once and wants to drain every drop from the opportunity. Jaz, in full red-and-black face paint, is in superb voice and is particularly exercised with British State conspiracies, especially the death of Dr David Kelly over the 2003 Iraq War 'weapons of mass destruction' debacle, mentioning this in both the companion interview and on stage. There's a rare appearance from a *Fire Dances* track in 'Song and Dance'. Long-time associate and friend Alex Paterson of The Orb joins the band on stage for the final bow.

XXV Gathering is also the first release to feature the hammer-and-sickle style 'KJ' logo. Still in use today, this is an apt ident for a band whose non-party politics absorbs radical democracy, anarchism, and revolution (the red flag, the modern meaning of which originated with the 1871 Paris Commune, was used by anarchists before the black flag). As mentioned above regarding 'The Raven King' and 'Autonomous Zone', the black-and-red flag is also an anarchist insignia, specifically representing anarcho-syndicalism or anarcho-communism when flown red first (an example is the cover art for Black & Red, Coleman's 2020 collaboration with Czech didgeridoo player Ondřej Smeykal). When flipped on its diagonal axis (black first) this livery forms the background to the cover for Coleman's *Magna Invocatio*. As mentioned above regarding 'The Raven King', the Joke's love of these colours is also based on their alchemical and occult significance.

Compilation Albums

Laugh? I Nearly Bought One!, the first official KJ compilation was released by Virgin in 1992 and is infamous for its Mike Coles cover art, which is based on a photograph of Nazi abbot Alban Schachleiter. The tracks are from every album up to that date except *Fire Dances* and *Outside the Gate*, plus 'Turn to Red', 'Pssyche' and a Kimsey mix of 'Wintergardens' (though not the longer restored original Kimsey mix on the 2008 reissue of *Brighter*).

In 1995, Virgin released *Wilful Days*, a complementary selection of non-album tracks and remixes, this time spanning the band's career all the way from 'Are You Receiving' to 1992's 'Change' remixes (excluding *Extremities* but including 'America' from *Outside the Gate* in its 'Extended Mix'). Cover art is again by Mike Coles, based on the *Turn to Red* EP.

Malicious Damage released a 25th Anniversary five-CD box set in 2004 called *Chaos for Breakfast*. This comprises the *Turn to Red* EP plus the first three singles. The 'Follow the Leaders' disc includes a version in which the lyrics of the first two verses are entirely different. The fifth CD features demos plus a 19-minute version of 'Killer Dub (aka Bread & Jam)'.

In 2004, Virgin released *For Beginners*, a career retrospective spanning *KJ 1980* to *Outside the Gate* (and this time including *Fire Dances*). In another bid to appeal to Joke completists, there are four previously unreleased mixes: an alt version of 'We Have Joy' (also on the 2005 expanded remastered reissue of *Revelations*), unreleased single edits of 'Harlequin' and 'Victory', and the restored original Kimsey mix of 'Rubicon'.

A BBC Radio 1 sessions compilation, *The Peel Sessions 1979-1981*, was released by Virgin in 2008. Also included is a Richard Skinner session from May 1981 featuring three tracks from *What's THIS For…!*. (A fifth and final Peel Session from July 1983 is on the 2005 reissue of *Fire Dances* as bonus tracks).

Spinefarm released a lovingly put-together singles retrospective in 2013, *The Singles Collection 1979-2012*, for which Coles's cover art revisits *What's THIS For…!* and its single 'Follow the Leaders'.

Remix Albums

Rough Trade released *Alchemy – The Remixes* in 1996, a Butterfly Recordings compilation featuring remixes from 1992 to 1996 and centred on *Pandemonium* and *Democracy*. It also includes a previously unreleased 'Black Sun Mix' of 'Drug'.

In 1998, Dragonfly Records released *Wardance – The Remixes*, again focused on those same two albums, but also featuring a 'Hallucinogen Remix' by Simon Posford of the *Democracy*-sessions track 'Four Stations of the Sun' along with a previously unreleased 'Deedrah Remix' by Frederic Holyszewski of 'Love Like Blood'.

In 2008, along with the clutch of remastered studio albums released that year (and also dedicated to Raven), Virgin released a compilation of KJ remixes called *RMXD*, which compiles various B-Side remixes from between 1982 and 1988. The previously unreleased tracks are 'Eighties (Serious Dance Mix)', 'A New Day (Dub)', an 'Extended Mix' of 'Blue Feather' and a 'Dub' mix of 'America'. The cover is a motley collage of original single cover art.

In Dub, a comprehensive career-to-date collection of remixes curated by Youth, some previously unavailable, was released in 2014 on KJ's own label. In 2021, a 12-track highlights version titled *In Dub – Rewind (Vol One)* was released by Cadiz. This features two tracks not on the 2014 release: 'Turn to Red (Nuclear Dub Instrumental)' and 'Money is Not Our God (Isolator Dub)', which is subtly different to the 'Babylon Dub' on the original release.

In February (streaming) and March 2023 (physical formats), Cadiz released a second Youth-curated compilation titled *In Dub – Rewind (Vol Two)*. This is a stunning set – perhaps the crowning achievement to date of Youth's KJ remixing. It features multiple tracks not previously available, the standouts being remixes of 'Autonomous Zone' ('Berlin Hacker Dub'), 'Panopticon' ('The Lamb of the Perverse Dub') and two of 'The Death & Resurrection Show' ('Aggressive Attitude Dub'; 'Cup & Sword Ambient Dub'). Plus, finally, a remix of 'Bloodsport' ('Rinoserous vs Youth Dub'). Immediately essential.

Author's Lists

Author's Top 20 favourite album tracks

1. Darkness Before Dawn (*Night Time*)
2. Tension (*What's THIS For...!*)
3. The Wait (*Killing Joke 1980*)
4. Blood on Your Hands (*Killing Joke 2003*)
5. Rejuvenation (*Fire Dances*)
6. Judas Goat (*Hosannas from the Basements of Hell*)
7. I Am the Virus (*Pylon*)
8. Whiteout (*Pandemonium*)
9. The Gathering (*Fire Dances*)
10. Exit (*What's THIS For...!*)
11. Corporate Elect (*MMXII*)
12. Tomorrow's World (*Killing Joke 1980*)
13. Pilgrimage (*Democracy*)
14. Rubicon (*Brighter than a Thousand Suns*)
15. New Jerusalem (*Pylon*)
16. Invocation (*Hosannas from the Basements of Hell*)
17. We Have Joy (*Revelations*)
18. Kings and Queens (*Night Time*)
19. Money is Not Our God (*Extremities*)
20. This World Hell (*Absolute Dissent*)

Author's Top 5 favourite albums

1. *What's THIS For...!*
2. *Fire Dances*
3. *Pylon*
4. *Night Time*
5. *Hosannas from the Basements of Hell*

Author's ten hidden gems (tracks not on an original album release; excluding remixes)

1. 'May Day' (*Outside the Gate* bonus track)
2. 'Mass' ('Democracy' CD single track)
3. 'Universe B' ('Hosannas from the Basements of Hell' CD single track)
4. 'Feast of Fools' (*Absolute Dissent* sessions rough mix on *The Singles Collection*, disc 3)
5. 'New Uprising' ('Corporate Elect' CD single track)
6. 'Kali Yuga' (*In Excelsis* EP track)
7. 'Hollywood Babylon' (written for *Showgirls*; *The Singles Collection*, disc 3)
8. 'Wilful Days' ('Me or You?' single B-Side)
9. 'The Party' (*Extremities* bonus track)
10. 'We Have Joy' alt version (*Revelations* bonus track)

Author's ten favourite live albums (in chronological order)

1. *The Unperverted Pantomime*, unknown venue, 1 November 1979 (released 2019)
2. *Ha*, Larry's Hideaway, Toronto, 9-10 August 1982 (released 1982)
3. *Extremities Live*, Le Pied, Reims, France, 7 June 1991 (released 2007)
4. *Jana – Live EP* + 'Jana' CD single, the Forum, London, 19 October 1994 (released 1994)
5. *XXV Gathering: Let Us Prey*, Shepherd's Bush Empire, London, 25 February 2005 (released 2006)
6. *The Gathering 2008*, the Forum, London, 3-4 October 2008 (released 2009)
7. *Live at the Hammersmith Apollo 16.10.2010* (released 2010)
8. *Down by the River*, Royal Festival Hall, London, 1 April 2011 (released 2011)
9. *The Great Gathering*, Brixton Academy, London, 4 November 2016 (released 2016)
10. *Live in Berlin*, Huxleys Neue Welt, 19 October 2018 (released 2019)

Author's Top 10 favourite cover versions (with original release info; some of these also feature on 2010's KJ covers compilation *Absolute Respect*, marked *)

1. 'Pssyche' by Econoline Crush (*Purge* EP, 1994) *
2. 'Millennium' by Fear Factory (*Transgression*, 2005) *
3. 'The Death & Resurrection Show' by Jeff Beck & Johnny Depp (*18*, 2022)
4. 'Love Like Blood' by Sybreed (*The Pulse of Awakening*, 2009)
5. 'Europe' by Amen (Live from BBC session, 'Too Hard to Be Free' single, 2001) *
6. 'The Wait' by Metallica (*The $5.98 EP: Garage Days Re-Revisited*, 1987) *
7. 'Seeing Red' by Prong (*Songs from the Black Hole*, 2015)
8. 'Requiem' by Foo Fighters (Live at the BBC, *00979725*, 1997) *
9. 'Love Like Blood' by Icehouse (*The Berlin Tapes*, 1995)
10. 'Requiem' by Eagulls ('Nerve Endings' single, 2013)

Also available from Sonicbond

On Track series

Alan Parsons Project – Steve Swift 978-1-78952-154-2
Tori Amos – Lisa Torem 978-1-78952-142-9
Asia – Peter Braidis 978-1-78952-099-6
Badfinger – Robert Day-Webb 978-1-878952-176-4
Barclay James Harvest – Keith and Monica Domone 978-1-78952-067-5
The Beatles – Andrew Wild 978-1-78952-009-5
The Beatles Solo 1969-1980 – Andrew Wild 978-1-78952-030-9
Blue Oyster Cult – Jacob Holm-Lupo 978-1-78952-007-1
Blur – Matt Bishop – 978-178952-164-1
Marc Bolan and T.Rex – Peter Gallagher 978-1-78952-124-5
Kate Bush – Bill Thomas 978-1-78952-097-2
Camel – Hamish Kuzminski 978-1-78952-040-8
Caravan – Andy Boot 978-1-78952-127-6
Cardiacs – Eric Benac 978-1-78952-131-3
Eric Clapton Solo – Andrew Wild 978-1-78952-141-2
The Clash – Nick Assirati 978-1-78952-077-4
Crosby, Stills and Nash – Andrew Wild 978-1-78952-039-2
The Damned – Morgan Brown 978-1-78952-136-8
Deep Purple and Rainbow 1968-79 – Steve Pilkington 978-1-78952-002-6
Dire Straits – Andrew Wild 978-1-78952-044-6
The Doors – Tony Thompson 978-1-78952-137-5
Dream Theater – Jordan Blum 978-1-78952-050-7
Electric Light Orchestra – Barry Delve 978-1-78952-152-8
Elvis Costello and The Attractions – Georg Purvis 978-1-78952-129-0
Emerson Lake and Palmer – Mike Goode 978-1-78952-000-2
Fairport Convention – Kevan Furbank 978-1-78952-051-4
Peter Gabriel – Graeme Scarfe 978-1-78952-138-2
Genesis – Stuart MacFarlane 978-1-78952-005-7
Gentle Giant – Gary Steel 978-1-78952-058-3
Gong – Kevan Furbank 978-1-78952-082-8
Hall and Oates – Ian Abrahams 978-1-78952-167-2
Hawkwind – Duncan Harris 978-1-78952-052-1
Peter Hammill – Richard Rees Jones 978-1-78952-163-4
Roy Harper – Opher Goodwin 978-1-78952-130-6
Jimi Hendrix – Emma Stott 978-1-78952-175-7
The Hollies – Andrew Darlington 978-1-78952-159-7
Iron Maiden – Steve Pilkington 978-1-78952-061-3
Jefferson Airplane – Richard Butterworth 978-1-78952-143-6
Jethro Tull – Jordan Blum 978-1-78952-016-3
Elton John in the 1970s – Peter Kearns 978-1-78952-034-7
The Incredible String Band – Tim Moon 978-1-78952-107-8
Iron Maiden – Steve Pilkington 978-1-78952-061-3
Judas Priest – John Tucker 978-1-78952-018-7
Kansas – Kevin Cummings 978-1-78952-057-6
The Kinks – Martin Hutchinson 978-1-78952-172-6
Korn – Matt Karpe 978-1-78952-153-5
Led Zeppelin – Steve Pilkington 978-1-78952-151-1
Level 42 – Matt Philips 978-1-78952-102-3
Little Feat – 978-1-78952-168-9
Aimee Mann – Jez Rowden 978-1-78952-036-1
Joni Mitchell – Peter Kearns 978-1-78952-081-1
The Moody Blues – Geoffrey Feakes 978-1-78952-042-2
Motorhead – Duncan Harris 978-1-78952-173-3
Mike Oldfield – Ryan Yard 978-1-78952-060-6
Opeth – Jordan Blum 978-1-78-952-166-5
Tom Petty – Richard James 978-1-78952-128-3
Porcupine Tree – Nick Holmes 978-1-78952-144-3
Queen – Andrew Wild 978-1-78952-003-3
Radiohead – William Allen 978-1-78952-149-8
Renaissance – David Detmer 978-1-78952-062-0
The Rolling Stones 1963-80 – Steve Pilkington 978-1-78952-017-0
The Smiths and Morrissey – Tommy Gunnarsson 978-1-78952-140-5
Status Quo the Frantic Four Years – Richard James 978-1-78952-160-3
Steely Dan – Jez Rowden 978-1-78952-043-9
Steve Hackett – Geoffrey Feakes 978-1-78952-098-9
Thin Lizzy – Graeme Stroud 978-1-78952-064-4
Toto – Jacob Holm-Lupo 978-1-78952-019-4
U2 – Eoghan Lyng 978-1-78952-078-1
UFO – Richard James 978-1-78952-073-6
The Who – Geoffrey Feakes 978-1-78952-076-7

Roy Wood and the Move – James R Turner 978-1-78952-008-8
Van Der Graaf Generator – Dan Coffey 978-1-78952-031-6
Yes – Stephen Lambe 978-1-78952-001-9
Frank Zappa 1966 to 1979 – Eric Benac 978-1-78952-033-0
Warren Zevon – Peter Gallagher 978-1-78952-170-2
10CC – Peter Kearns 978-1-78952-054-5

Decades Series

The Bee Gees in the 1960s – Andrew Môn Hughes et al 978-1-78952-148-1
The Bee Gees in the 1970s – Andrew Môn Hughes et al 978-1-78952-179-5
Black Sabbath in the 1970s – Chris Sutton 978-1-78952-171-9
Britpop – Peter Richard Adams and Matt Pooler 978-1-78952-169-6
Alice Cooper in the 1970s – Chris Sutton 978-1-78952-104-7
Curved Air in the 1970s – Laura Shenton 978-1-78952-069-9
Bob Dylan in the 1980s – Don Klees 978-1-78952-157-3
Fleetwood Mac in the 1970s – Andrew Wild 978-1-78952-105-4
Focus in the 1970s – Stephen Lambe 978-1-78952-079-8
Free and Bad Company in the 1970s – John Van der Kiste 978-1-78952-178-8
Genesis in the 1970s – Bill Thomas 978178952-146-7
George Harrison in the 1970s – Eoghan Lyng 978-1-78952-174-0
Marillion in the 1980s – Nathaniel Webb 978-1-78952-065-1
Mott the Hoople and Ian Hunter in the 1970s – John Van der Kiste 978-1-78-952-162-7
Pink Floyd In The 1970s – Georg Purvis 978-1-78952-072-9
Tangerine Dream in the 1970s – Stephen Palmer 978-1-78952-161-0
The Sweet in the 1970s – Darren Johnson from Gary Cosby collection 978-1-78952-139-9
Uriah Heep in the 1970s – Steve Pilkington 978-1-78952-103-0
Yes in the 1980s – Stephen Lambe with David Watkinson 978-1-78952-125-2

On Screen series

Carry On... – Stephen Lambe 978-1-78952-004-0
David Cronenberg – Patrick Chapman 978-1-78952-071-2
Doctor Who: The David Tennant Years – Jamie Hailstone 978-1-78952-066-8
James Bond – Andrew Wild – 978-1-78952-010-1
Monty Python – Steve Pilkington 978-1-78952-047-7
Seinfeld Seasons 1 to 5 – Stephen Lambe 978-1-78952-012-5

Other Books

1967: A Year In Psychedelic Rock – Kevan Furbank 978-1-78952-155-9
1970: A Year In Rock – John Van der Kiste 978-1-78952-147-4
1973: The Golden Year of Progressive Rock 978-1-78952-165-8
Babysitting A Band On The Rocks – G.D. Praetorius 978-1-78952-106-1
Eric Clapton Sessions – Andrew Wild 978-1-78952-177-1
Derek Taylor: For Your Radioactive Children – Andrew Darlington 978-1-78952-038-5
The Golden Road: The Recording History of The Grateful Dead – John Kilbride 978-1-78952-156-6
Iggy and The Stooges On Stage 1967-1974 – Per Nilsen 978-1-78952-101-6
Jon Anderson and the Warriors – the road to Yes – David Watkinson 978-1-78952-059-0
Nu Metal: A Definitive Guide – Matt Karpe 978-1-78952-063-7
Tommy Bolin: In and Out of Deep Purple – Laura Shenton 978-1-78952-070-5
Maximum Darkness – Deke Leonard 978-1-78952-048-4
Maybe I Should've Stayed In Bed – Deke Leonard 978-1-78952-053-8
The Twang Dynasty – Deke Leonard 978-1-78952-049-1

and many more to come!